THE TREASURY OF THE GUN

BY HAROLD L. PETERSON

TECHNICAL CONSULTATION BY

HOWARD L. BLACKMORE
President of the Arms and Armour
Society of Great Britain

CLAUDE BLAIR
Victoria and Albert Museum, London

WILLIAM REID
H.M. Tower of London

A RIDGE PRESS BOOK

GOLDEN PRESS / NEW YORK

This Edition Prepared for Distribution by Crown Publishers, Inc.

THE TREASURY OF THE GUN
BY HAROLD L. PETERSON

Special Photography by
ARIE de ZANGER

❋

A RIDGE PRESS BOOK / GOLDEN PRESS
NEW YORK

*The Company of Military
Collectors & Historians, through its
Reviewing Board, takes pride
in sponsoring this book as an accurate
and useful reference work
in the field of arms literature.*

*Henry I. Shaw, Jr.
Editor in Chief, CMC&H*

REVIEWING BOARD
*Herschel C. Logan
James E. Serven
Samuel E. Smith*

Editor in Chief: JERRY MASON
Editor: ADOLPH SUEHSDORF
Art Director: ALBERT A. SQUILLACE
Art Research: PETER LACEY
Associate Editor: EVELYN HANNON
Associate Editor: FREYA CARNRITE
Associate Editor: EDWINA HAZARD GLEN
Art Associate: LEON BOLOGNESE

PREPARED AND PRODUCED BY
THE RIDGE PRESS, INC.
PRINTED IN THE U.S.A.
PUBLISHED BY GOLDEN PRESS,
850 THIRD AVENUE,
NEW YORK, NEW YORK 10022

CONTENTS

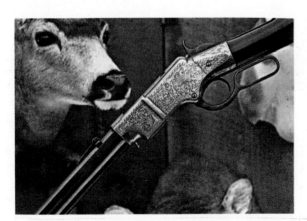

ACKNOWLEDGMENTS

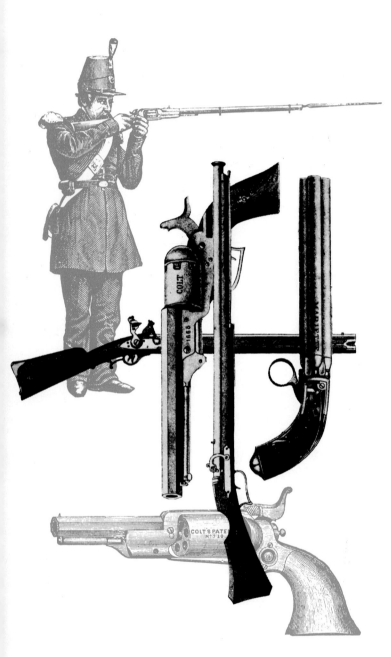

ALL COLOR PHOTOGRAPHS OF GUNS BY ARIE DE ZANGER EXCEPT PAGES 72, 78, TOP 163, BY ROBERT MOTTAR.

Cover: Against background of 16th century German and Italian armor are (from left to right) 18th century French flintlock pistol, Remington new model army revolver (percussion), German **jaeger** rifle, dating from 1730's, Plains Indian tomahawk 1860-1870.

GUN SOURCES

ABELS, ROBERT, New York City: **54-55, 104-105** (carriage in collection of Suffolk Museum, Stony Brook, L.I.), **107, 108, 212, 218-219** (3).

ANONYMOUS COLLECTION: **118** (4), **199** (4), **206** (middle and lower), **218-219** (1, 2, 4-6). BAVARIAN NATIONAL MUSEUM, Munich, Germany: **60** (top).

BELCHAMP HALL, Essex, England: **66-67** (4).

CARPENTER, AUSTIN C., Plymouth, England: **196** (1 & 2).

DU MONT, JOHN S., Greenfield, Mass.: **221.**

EDINBURGH CASTLE, Scotland. Photo by Ministry of Works, Edinburgh, Crown Copyright Reserved: **35** (4).

FOX, GERALD, Longmeadow, Mass.: **214** (right).

HENDRICKS, DR. CHARLES S., Altoona, Pa.: **186-187.**

H. M. TOWER OF LONDON, England. Photos Ministry of Works, London, Crown Copyright Reserved: **47, 63** (lower), **70** (3), **78** (top), **85** (courtesy of Countess of Seafield), **99** (right), **148-149, 162, 163** (2), **169, 171, 205.**

H.R.H. THE DUKE OF BRUNSWICK AND LUNEBURG, Hanover, Germany. Photos by Ministry of Works, London, Crown Copyright Reserved: **60** (lower), **165.**

HUBBELL, BENJAMIN F., Hartford, Conn.: **87.**

JACKSON, ARCHER, Evanston, Ill.: **157** (upper).

KINDIG, JOSEPH, JR., York, Pa.: **58-59** (1-4, 6, 7), **163** (3).

KUNGHEJN ARMÉMUSEUM, Stockholm, Sweden: **136-137.**

LEONARD, HERMAN M., Greensboro, N.C.: **168.**

LEXINGTON HISTORICAL SOCIETY, Lexington, Mass.: **84.**

LINCOLN MUSEUM, Washington, D.C.: **240** (1).

LOCKE, WILLIAM M., Cincinnati, Ohio: **11, 12-13, 213, 215, 232** (1 & 2). **238** (top).

METROPOLITAN MUSEUM OF ART, New York City: **20** (1), **24, 40-41, 44, 45, 62** (2 & 4), **63** (upper), **64** (1 & 2), **66-67** (1 & 5), **69** (3), **70-71** (1 & 4), **73** (bottom), **82, 89, 112, 132** (4), **144, 148** (center), **157** (lower).

MORRISTOWN NATIONAL HISTORICAL PARK, N.J.: **166-167.**

MUIR, BLUFORD, Washington, D.C.: **59** (5), **86, 90-91, 127** (5), **141, 153** (upper).

MUSÉE D'ARMES, Liége, Belgium: **196** (3).

MUSÉE DE L'ARMÉE, Paris, France: **72.**

NATIONAL HISTORICAL MUSEUM, Stockholm, Sweden: **33** (3), **34** (3).

PETERSON, HAROLD L., Arlington, Va.: jacket and title page (except revolver courtesy of Robert L. Miller, Arlington, Va.), **14-15, 22, 25, 28-29, 50-51** (except Indian and Japanese guns courtesy of National Rifle Association, Washington, D.C.), **74-75** (17th century American room setting courtesy of Smithsonian Institution, Washington, D.C.), **94-95** (except uniform courtesy of Donald W. Holst, of Smithsonian Institution), **127** (3), **128-129.**

PILGRIM HALL, Plymouth, Mass.: **88.**

RENWICK, WILLIAM G., Tucson, Ariz.: **96-97, 132** (2).

RILING, RAY, Philadelphia, Pa.: **127** (4).

REMINGTON ARMS COMPANY, Ilion, N.Y.: **184** (left), **196** (4).

SMITH, SAMUEL E., Markesan, Wis.: **126** (1), **194, 198** (3), **210** (except bottom), **225** (lower).

SMITHSONIAN INSTITUTION, Washington, D.C.: **106, 118** (1), **120** (1), **126** (2), **151** (top), **153** (lower), **170, 178** (two lower guns), **180-181, 183** (lower), **184** (top), **198** (2), **207, 214** (left), **233** (3), **240** (2).

SPRINGFIELD ARMORY MUSEUM, Springfield, Mass.: **175, 190** (1).

SWEET, WILLIAM, Attleboro, Mass.: **110-111, 114-115, 121** (3-5), **124** (1-4), **139, 193, 200-201, 222-223, 226-227, 241** (3).

THE ROTUNDA, Woolwich, England: **198** (1).

TØJHUSMUSEET, Copenhagen, Denmark: **230-231.**

U.S. FISH AND WILDLIFE SERVICE, Washington, D.C.: **191** (2).

VICTORIA AND ALBERT MUSEUM, London, England: **65** (3) Crown Copyright Reserved, **78** (bottom).

WADSWORTH ATHENEUM, Hartford, Conn.: **209.**

WEST POINT MUSEUM, N.Y.: **142-143, 158-159, 176-177, 178** (top).

WINCHESTER GUN MUSEUM, New Haven, Conn.: **69** (2), **79, 80-81, 102, 118** (2 & 3), **120** (2), **122** (left), **146** (right), **154-155, 178** (second from top), **183** (top), **196** (5), **206** (upper), **208, 210** (bottom), **225** (upper), **234-235, 236-237, 244-245** (both).

SOURCES OF PRINTS AND PAINTINGS

The following sources are repeated frequently and will, therefore, be referred to in the list below by the initials preceding their names.

BC—Anne S. K. Brown Collection
  Providence, R. I.
KG—Kennedy Galleries, N.Y.C.
ML—Pierpont Morgan Library, N.Y.C.

PC—Picture Collection, New York
  Public Library
PD—Prints Division, New York
  Public Library

CHAPTER ONE: **16**—St. Augustin, "La Cité de Dieu," Abbeville, 1486. **18**—French Old Testament, c. 1250, manuscript 801, ML. **19**—English 15th century "Ordnances of Chivalry," manuscript 775, ML. **20**—(2 & 3) Oscar Guttman, "Monumenta Pulveris Pyrii," London, 1906; (4) Manuscript Bodl. 181, Bodleian Library, Oxford. **23**—"Chronique de Jehan de Courcy," c. 1430, manuscript 805-806, ML. **27**—(top left) Guttman, opp. cit.; (top right) Roberto Valturio, "De l'Arte Militare," Verona, 1483; (center left) Manuscript Ee. 3.59, Cambridge University Library; (others) 15th century woodcuts from various sources.

CHAPTER TWO: **30**—Werner Rolevinck, "Fasciculus Temporum," Utrecht, 1480. **32**—(1) Christ Church College, Oxford; (2) Additional manuscript 47680, f. 44v., British Museum. **33**—(4) Manuscript 14, E. IV, Volume 3, British Museum. **34**—(1) Austrian National Library, Codex 3062; (2) Guttman, opp. cit. **36**—(top) J. J. Wallhausen, "Art Militaire au Cheval," Frankfurt, 1616; (bottom) Hand-painted additional illustration, Jacques de Gheyn, "Le Mainiement d'Armes," Amsterdam, 1608, Smithsonian Institution. **37**—Wallhausen, opp. cit. **39**—(left) Print by de Gheyn, PD; (right) "Theuerdank," Augsburg, 1537. **40-41**—(left) Hans Bol, "Venationis, Piscationis et Avicicupii Typii," Amsterdam, 1580-1588, PD. **41**—(right) Gillis Saeghman, "Verscheyde Oost-Indische Voyagien," Amsterdam, 1663-1670. **42**— (left) Benin bronze, Carlebach Gallery, New York City. **42-43**—Inatomi-ryn Teppo Densho, "The Secrets of Shooting with Guns of the Inatomi School," illustrated by Nagasawa Shigetsune, c. 1612, Spencer Collection of New York Public Library. **45**—(top) Johann Gottfried, "Newe Welt," 1631. **46**—Franz Hogenberg, "Engravings of Scenes from the History of the Netherlands, France and Germany, 1588-1622," Cologne, c. 1625, PD. **48**—Hans Sebald Beham, "Der Buchsenmeister," PD. **52-53**—Gottfried, opp. cit.

CHAPTER THREE: **56**—De Gheyn, "Riding School or Exercise of Cavalry," c. 1600, PD. **58-59**—(animals) Thomas Cockaine, "A Short Treatise of Hunting," London, 1591. **61**—Courtesy of the Earl of Leicester. **62**—(1) "Zeitschrift für Historische Waffenkunde," Volume 13; (3) Johannes

Bussenmacher, "Reutterbuchlein," 1601, PD. **65**—(4) "Duel Between Hauptman Christoph Ziegler and Major Heinrich im Thurn," Schweizerisches Museum, Zurich; (5) Engraving by Pauly Major, BC. **66**—(2) "Histoire Abregée des Provinces-Unies des Päis-Bas," Amsterdam, 1701; (3) De Gheyn, "Reiter Buch," 1640, BC. **68**—Johann Wilhelm Baur, "Don Paolo Giordano," 1636, PD. **70**—(2) "Histoire Abregée," opp. cit. **73**—(detail) Jacques Callot, "Siege of Breda," BC.

CHAPTER FOUR: **76**—Bussenmacher, "Spanish Rider," opp. cit. **80**—Victoria and Albert Museum, London. **83**—Louis Anquetil, "Compendio de la Historio de España," Madrid, 1806. **87**—Richard Blome, "The Gentleman's Recreation," London, 1686. **88**—Samuel Drake, "Tragedies of the Wilderness," Boston, 1844. **89**—Saeghman, opp. cit.

CHAPTER FIVE: **92**—Plate by Rowlandson for R. Ackermann, "Review of the Loyal Volunteer Corps," London, 1799. **99**—(left) William Woollett (after Stubbs), "Shooting," 1770, PD. **100**—(left) Amos Doolittle, colored engraving, BC; (right) Paul Revere, colored engraving, BC. **103 & 107**—Charles Johnson, "A General History of the Lives and Adventures of the Most Famous Highwaymen, etc.," London, 1736. **108**—PC.

CHAPTER SIX: **116**—J. H. Green, "An Exposure of Gambling," Philadelphia, 1847. **121**—PC. **122**—(right) "The Sportsman's Portfolio of American Field Sports," Boston, 1855, PD. **123**—"Leslie's Weekly," March 12, 1859. **124**—PC. **127**—(6) Orlando Norie, "Encounter by Lt. Hills and Sepoy Cavalry," BC.

CHAPTER SEVEN: **130**—Ezekiel Baker, "Twenty-three Years Practice and Observations with Rifle Guns," London, 1804. **132**—(2) Guttman, opp. cit.; (3) "Zeitschrift," opp. cit., Volume 2. **134-135**—(left) Johann Will, "American Rifleman," Augsburg, 1777, BC; (center) "Battle of New Orleans," contemporary American print, BC; (right) Water color of soldier of Rifle Brigade (95th Regiment) at time of founding (1812), BC. **138**—William Carey, "Conference in the Stockade," KG. **144**—W. Milnor, "Memoirs," Philadelphia, 1830. **146**—(left) William Duane, "A Handbook for Infantry," Philadelphia, 1814. **148** (left) & **149**—Baker, opp. cit. **151**—(lower) "Harper's Weekly," 1862. **155**—Julian Scott, "Behind the Earthworks," KG. **156**—John W. Ehninger, "The Turkey Shoot," 1879, M. and M. Karolik Collection, Museum of Fine Arts, Boston.

CHAPTER EIGHT: **160**—"Outing," April, 1888. **172**—(top) Carl Nebel, "The War Between the U.S. and Mexico," New York, 1851, BC; (bottom) Samuel Chamberlain, "My Confession," West Point Museum. **174**—PC. **179**—Capt. C. A. Stevens, "Berdan's U.S. Sharpshooters," St. Paul, 1892. **180**—"Century," October, 1891. **183**—(bottom) BC. **184**—"Century," November, 1890.

CHAPTER NINE: **18d**—Valturio, opp. cit. **192**—Reinagle and Gilpin, "Col. Thornton and His Famous Gun," courtesy of Alan P. Kirby (photo by Newhouse Gallery). **195**—William Burney, "The British Neptune," London, 1807.

CHAPTER TEN: **202**—"Leslie's Weekly," August 16, 1856. **204**—(top) Orlando Norie, "78th Highlanders at the Taking of Sucunderbagh, Siege of Lucknow," 1857, BC; (bottom) George Catlin, "Shooting Buffaloes," KG. **209**—"Death of Capt. Walker at Huamantla in Mexico," lithographed and published by Baillie, 1847, New-York Historical Society. **216**—"Century," October, 1888. **219**—PC. **224**—Courtesy of Richard E. Allender (photo by Library of Congress).

CHAPTER ELEVEN: **228**—PC. **238**—Frederic Remington, "Fight for the Water Hole," Museum of Fine Arts, Houston.

247, 248—Rolf G. Haebler, "Wie unsere Waffen Worden," Leipzig, 1940.

*I*n the vast array of things man has invented to better his condition, few have fascinated him more than the gun. Its function is simple; as Oliver Winchester said, with Nineteenth Century complacency, "A gun is a machine for throwing balls." But its ever-increasing efficiency in performing this task, and its awesome ability to strike home from long range, have given it tremendous psychological appeal.

For possession of a gun and the skill to use it enormously augments the gunner's personal power, and extends the radius of his influence and effect a thousand times beyond his arm's length. And since strength resides in the gun, the man who wields it may be less than strong without being disadvantaged. The flashing sword, the couched lance, the bent longbow performed to the limit of the man who held it. The gun's power is inherent and needs only to be released. A steady eye and an accurate aim are enough. Wherever the muzzle points the bullet goes, bearing the gunner's wish or intention swiftly to the target.

These remarkable capabilities were evident even in the first crude guns, and for more than six hundred years men have labored, patiently and tenaciously, to refine and perfect them. Year by year, century by century, guns became more accurate and dependable. They loaded faster, shot farther, and hit harder. And they became beautiful. Their lines were graceful, their proportions just. They were functional, first of all. But like all things man has valued, they also were decorated, ornamented, and embellished. Stocks were carved and inlaid, locks and barrels chased by the finest artisans of their time.

With each improvement guns had greater impact on events. Feudalism fell at least in part because of firearms. They determined whether campaigns of

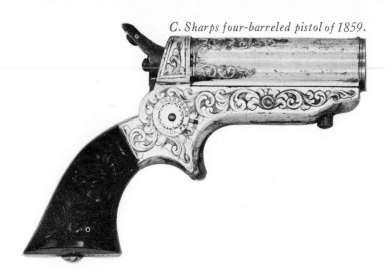

conquest triumphed or were beaten back. They wrested the American wilderness from the Indians, helped win independence for the colonies, and fought to preserve the union of the states. Perhaps more than any other implement, the gun has shaped the course of nations and the destiny of men.

The story of the gun is highly dramatic, yet strangely obscure. Despite its vital importance in the affairs of men, there are many fundamental facts we do not know about who invented what gun, or when, or where. Who, in fact, invented gunpowder? Did Leonardo da Vinci, in fact, design the wheel lock? Many such questions are insoluble at this late date. Some are subject to a reasonable guess based on careful evaluation of the available evidence.

Sometimes the evidence itself poses as many problems as the mystery being investigated. A dismaying number of documents purportedly substantiating one point or another have themselves proved to be false—for instance, those describing the achievements of the fictitious Black Berthold in inventing both gunpowder and guns. Other puzzles for the historian are contradictory reports by witnesses to the same event, documents in code, and the inexplicable disappearance of records known to have been in existence. Above all, guns themselves have often been altered. Names, dates, and other markings have been changed, and sometimes complete weapons of unusual design have been faked. Yet none who have pursued the story would have the task easier than it is. Its gaps and confusions add to its fascination.

This book is an effort to trace the story from the discovery of gunpowder to the late Nineteenth Century, when the appearance of smokeless powder began a new era of firearms history. Technical advancement supplies the thread of the narrative, but there have been technical books before. Here there is an attempt to relate these achievements to history and, above all, to people, and to indicate some of the excitement, the humor, and the curious lore that is as much a part of the subject as the improvement of a lock mechanism. It is a book done for fun with the hope that the reader will find it entertaining, too.

Only the most personal of books can be solely the product of one man's work. A broad subject such as the history of firearms is well beyond the capacity of any single specialist. Help in this instance has been sought and freely given by many of the world's leading students of firearms. It would be impossible to name all who have assisted, but special thanks are due to some whose generosity was far above anything that might reasonably have been expected.

First, my British colleagues, Howard L. Blackmore, Claude Blair, and William Reid, have been pillars of strength. They have read the entire manuscript, made suggestions for additions in the interest of better balance or accuracy, corrected errors, helped with the assembly of pictures, and made available the products of their own extensive and original research in European archives and museums. In the United States, Herschel C. Logan, James Serven, and Samuel E. Smith, leading students all, provided a similar review of the completed book to help guard against inaccuracies or omissions.

Walter J. Howe and the technical staff of the National Rifle Association of America were helpful in many ways. Inquiries on moot technical points always elicited prompt responses and specimens in the N.R.A. museum were made available for study and photographing.

Illustrations were a particular concern and help in acquiring the appropri-

Sharps & Hankins four-barreled pistol.

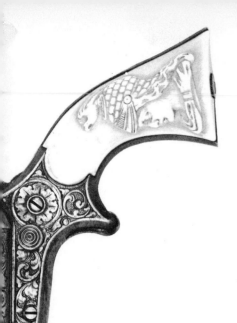

ate guns was given by many people. Owners who graciously permitted us to reproduce a piece from their collection are credited elsewhere, but there were several persons who rendered extraordinary assistance, and these I should like to thank more specifically:

Mrs. John Nicholas Brown, of Providence, Rhode Island, not only opened her vast collection of military art for our use, but also spent hours helping to find the most suitable pictures for our purposes;

William O. Sweet, of Attleboro, Massachusetts, gave us free run of his fine collection, including the interesting revolvers of the James brothers, and with his assistant, Clarence Falley, assisted materially in setting up and executing many of the special color portraits that grace the book;

Joe Kindig, Jr., of York, Pennsylvania; Robert Abels, of New York City; Drs. Charles Hendricks and Jack Strassman, of Altoona, Pennsylvania; William Locke, of Cincinnati, Ohio; William Renwick, of Tucson, Arizona, and Bluford W. Muir, of Washington, D.C., supplied pictures and lent specimens from their extensive collections;

Colonel Frederick P. Todd and Gerald Stowe of the West Point Museum, Craddock Goins, Donald W. Holst, and C. Malcolm Watkins of the Smithsonian Institution, Thomas E. Hall of the Winchester Museum, Francis Wilshin and David Thompson of Manassas National Battlefield Park, and Dr. Francis S. Ronalds of Morristown National Historical Park were all extremely co-operative in making their facilities available to us.

To all of them, many thanks. If any errors should survive this expert screening, they are, of course, my own.

Harold L. Peterson

*Preceding pages: Armor and weapons
used in the 14th and 15th centuries when
the first firearms appeared.*

CHAPTER 1

FRIAR BACON AND HIS SECRET POWDER

There was a new noise in the world. A brilliant orange flash leaped from the tiny package of black dust. Thunder smote the ears of the bystander and a cloud of white smoke filled the air. There was a strong smell of sulphur, too, a hellish atmosphere that signified the presence, and perhaps the directing hand, of the Devil himself. Altogether it was enough to frighten any inhabitant of the Thirteenth Century. For this was an age when magic, both black and white, was an accepted fact, when Beelzebub was believed to intervene personally in human affairs, and when thunder and lightning were terrifying evidence of divine power.

16 *Yet this time these mysteries had been invoked at the bidding of man.*

Roger Bacon did not scare easily. He accepted all risks. Contentious and rash, he spoke his mind without fearing the consequences. Other scholars with whom he disagreed felt the lash of his tongue even if they were his superiors in the Franciscan Order. Frequently in trouble, sometimes confined and denied writing materials, Bacon carried on, insisting that the experimental method was both valid and vital for all science. This was a radical stand to take in the middle 1200's, when even a man who lived in Oxford was likely to cite an earlier scholar's writings as evidence that such a place existed. But Friar Bacon was ahead of the times in many ways as he recognized the magnifying possibilities of convex lenses, insisted on the possibility of creating flying machines, of building mechanically powered boats, and of sailing clear around a world that all sensible people knew was flat.

Above all, he caught some vision of the significance of gunpowder. Some say he actually invented it himself. Others maintain he discovered the formula in some of the obscure Oriental or Arabic treatises he was fond of studying. No matter which is true, there is no doubt that he knew what gunpowder was. With his passion for experiment and testing, he must have tried it out himself, blackening his hands and his brown habit with the crude mixture of saltpeter, charcoal, and sulphur as he wrapped a small amount in parchment, and unsettling his brother monks with the din as he set it off. Here was sheer power, and he wrote:

This powder is enclosed in an instrument of parchment the size of a finger, and since this can make such a noise that it seriously distresses the ears of men, especially if one is taken unawares, and the terrible flash is also very alarming, if an instrument of large size were used, no one could stand the terror of the noise and flash. If the instrument were made of solid material the violence of the explosion would be much greater.

The understanding of the propulsive force of gunpowder had not yet come. If it had, the conscientious monk would have had even more fears than he did. As it was, he considered the discovery far too dangerous for general knowledge. As a scientist compiling an encyclopedia of all knowledge, he could not ignore it. He had to write the formula down, but to protect mankind (and perhaps himself as well), he did so in a code so complex that parts of it still baffle students today. Significant words and phrases were hidden and mingled with ramblings about chalk, cheese, "philosophic eggs," and Tagus sand. But enough has been deciphered to prove that it was true gunpowder he described.

This was in about the year 1250, or a little before. Bacon was in his middle thirties. In the next quarter-century he was to learn that his secrecy had been to no avail. The world did not learn of gunpowder from him, but learn of the new substance it did. By 1267, when he wrote his last comment on the subject as an older man in declining health, the irascible friar observed that children were playing with firecrackers and that he could make rockets with bursting charges to amuse them as well. Gunpowder had come to stay. Worried scholars could not hold it back. Both a new noise and a new force were to help change the world.

But the world was not yet aware of all this. Outside the cloisters in which Friar Bacon and other members of the clergy lived, the secular side of feudalism held sway. Castles of the nobility dotted the landscape. Peasants tilled the fields and performed their menial tasks, while the noble knights and lords practiced their trade of fighting. Here and there stood small towns. In them could be found the seeds of a new class of merchants and artisans who would one day challenge the power of the nobles and make radical changes in the world. In the mid-Thirteenth Century, however, class lines were still fairly rigid. The peasants did the work, the clergy studied and prayed, and the nobles arranged the fighting.

The backbone of medieval warfare was the 17

mounted knight. Trained from youth as a warrior, he sought personal combat with other knights, despising infantry as beneath his dignity—especially when it was armed with projectile weapons. As a result, battles often broke up into a series of individual duels without any over-all tactical control.

Typical of the passion for personal encounter which pervaded medieval warfare was the clash between the Scottish King, Robert Bruce, and Sir Henry Bohun just prior to the Battle of Bannockburn. On a Sunday afternoon in June, 1314, Sir Henry rode with an English scouting party along an old Roman road looking for the enemy. Just as they reached the brook or "burn" which gave the battle its name, they spied the Scots arranged in combat order. Well in advance of his men, Bruce rode up and down inspecting the lines. The golden crown on his helmet proclaimed his identity to all the English. Here was a chance to end the war with a single lance thrust. Sir Henry seized the opportunity. In an instant he set spurs to his horse and rode toward the king. Bruce was in a difficult position. He was on a small horse. His great charger, and his lance, shield, and other

arms were too far off to reach. His only weapon was the battle-axe at his saddlebow. Yet he scorned to shrink from the single combat. Warily he waited, axe poised, as the Englishman with leveled lance thundered at him. Timing the move perfectly, he threw his body to one side, caught the lance with his axe and deflected it. Then, as the momentum of the rushing steed carried Sir Henry past, Bruce pivoted, throwing the full weight of his body into a blow that cut through the back of the hapless Englishman's helmet and sank the axe deep into his brain. The individual attempt had failed and the Battle of Bannockburn was fought next day.

Sir Henry met his death a few years after Friar Bacon had also departed this vale of controversy. But the same sort of encounters had been occurring for centuries, although they did not always end fatally. A knight captured alive was worth considerable money in ransom; a dead one represented only the salvage value of his armor. Thus, when the English beat the French at the Battle of Bremûle in 1119, one hundred and forty French knights were captured and only three were killed. It was a happy era for a knight, in which he could fight

Catapult and longbow (below) are the only projectile
weapons in battle scene from 13th century French manuscript.
Right: Tournaments such as this one, shown in 15th century English
manuscript, hardened knights for grim realities of war.

1. *Italian plate armor of about 1400.*

2. *Roger Bacon's formula for gunpowder from 13th century manuscript.*

3. *Traditional portrait of Friar Bacon.*

4. *Demons assist invention of guns and gunpowder in 16th century cartoon.*

bravely and well with others who appreciated his skill and gallantry.

As an aid to his physical skill in protecting his hide, the medieval knight carried a shield and wore armor. At the time when Bacon was recording the composition of gunpowder, these shields were triangular, perhaps three feet long, and made of wood covered with leather. The armor, of the type called "mail," consisted of thousands of tiny interlinked rings, each made separately and then riveted together. It was completely flexible but offered no protection against the bruising force of a blow. For this reason, a quilted or padded garment was often worn underneath, and here and there reinforcing plates were coming into use to protect exposed areas of the body. Lastly, there was the helmet, perhaps merely a steel skullcap, perhaps a great helm, to protect the head. Fully equipped, a knight's armor might weigh sixty pounds, but the weight was well distributed, and he was completely mobile. (In contrast, a modern soldier frequently carries more than ninety pounds on his back, with much poorer distribution of weight.)

For weapons, the knight relied on his sword and lance, or occasionally an axe or dagger. These were the honorable arms—direct, deliberate, and personal. But there were other arms in the world as well. The lowly infantry, mostly recruited from the peasants and freemen of the towns, carried pikes, clubs, and cudgels, agricultural tools, and, in certain districts, bows and arrows. And there was a growing class of professional soldiers, many of whom were armed with crossbows.

These projectile arms were particularly despicable. Armor offered excellent protection against most of the infantryman's weapons. And the fact that the knight was armored while the peasant wasn't, gave him a great advantage—as did the fact that he was trained to use his arms and was naturally much more adept than the average infantryman. The projectile weapon greatly reduced these odds and was therefore hated. The sword knew where it struck. Thus, it was an honorable arm. The arrow knew not whom it might injure. It was a scoundrel's weapon.

There were three principal types of bows: the short bow, the crossbow, and the longbow. The first was not a very fearsome weapon, although the Normans had used it effectively at the Battle of Hastings in breaking the Saxon shield wall and striking King Harold in the eye to shatter the defenders' command. It was tolerated by the knights, however.

The muscular crossbow was much more dangerous. It consisted of a short but powerful bow mounted crosswise on a stock. By 1250 this crossbow was compounded of whalebone or horn, wood and sinew, so stiff that it could not be bent by hand but required a mechanical advantage. Slow to load, its power commanded respect as its short iron-headed arrow could pierce the finest armor. It was too powerful. At the Second Lateran Council in 1139 the Church forbade its use (except against infidels) under pain of anathema "as a weapon hateful to God and unfit for Christians." Still the crossbow caught on and professional Genoese crossbowmen were found in many armies. When they could, the knights struck back. Just a few years before Bacon's first treatise, England's epic Magna Carta forbade the employment of foreign crossbowmen on that island, at least.

The crossbow was no sooner restricted in England, however, than a new weapon, even more efficient, began to take its place. This was the longbow, which was just beginning to make its existence known at mid-century. The years from 1250 to 1300 saw its popularity rise in England, and in the next century it became a national weapon. Inexpensive and unprepossessing, this great bow was an arm any man could afford. A six-foot staff of elm was all that was needed. With the string pulled taut to the ear, it could hurl its three-foot arrow with amazing force. At the siege of Abergavenny in 1182, Welsh arrows are said to have pierced an oaken door four inches thick. They were left as souvenirs of the attack, with their iron points protruding on the inside. Giraldus Cambrensis saw them there still in 1188. He remembered well that a knight of William de Braose had been struck by such an arrow which went through the skirts of his mail shirt, then through his mail breeches, then through his thigh, then through the mail on the other side of his leg, then through the wood of his saddle, and finally penetrated deep into his horse's flank. The average crossbow could do no better than this and the longbow was much faster shooting. It took years of practice to make a skilled archer and only the Welsh and English ever mastered the art on a national scale. Well used, with pikemen and cavalry for support, it could be the arbiter of victory. At Crécy and again at Poitiers it struck down the flower of French chivalry. Armored knights of the noblest blood, who had devoted their lives to the study of fighting, had been slaughtered by yeomen and artisans. War was becoming democratized.

Onto this scene came gunpowder. The good Friar Bacon wrote the first description of its appearance in Western Europe. For many years it was thought that he actually discovered the powerful substance himself, but modern scholars generally feel he merely recorded something that was secretly known to other students, alchemists, and magicians. There are tales that gunpowder was known to the Chinese, the Indians, and the Arabs centuries before Bacon recorded it in Europe. But the lack of contemporary documents, difficulties in translation, and changes in the meaning of words have made it impossible to prove to scholarly satisfaction that these peoples discovered explosives before the Europeans.

The Arabs were perhaps the most likely discoverers. While Europe languished in the Dark Ages that followed the deterioration of the Roman Empire, learning and science flourished across the Mediterranean. The writings of Aristotle, Euclid, Ptolemy, and other Greek

Left: Crossbowman's gear of 15th
century: Pavise (shield),
sword, bow with quarrel in place,
dagger, helmet. Upright shield
gave cover as archer bent his bow.
Right: Painting believed to
date from 1430 shows exceptionally
early use of cannon in siege.

scientists and philosophers, were translated into Arabic and preserved. Moslem scholars were making great progress in medicine, chemistry, and mathematics. They invented the zero and presented the world with the Arabic numbers still in use. Their search for a magical substance that would transform base metals into gold produced a tremendous library of recipes. Some of these were for wildly improbable or superstitious compounds, but some were valid and practical. Gunpowder may have been among them.

Books containing these secret recipes circulated among European scholars and Roger Bacon read them. So did the gentle Dominican Albertus Magnus of Germany, who taught St. Thomas Aquinas, and who may also have described gunpowder a very few years after Bacon's first reference to it. The famous *Book of Fires* attributed to one Marcus Graecus, or "Mark the Greek," was such a collection of recipes. It circulated before 1300 and included both gunpowder and rockets among its other incendiary compounds. And there were other references, all following quickly—too quickly, it

would seem, to have sprung from one man at Oxford.

The gunpowder which all these treatises described was a simple mixture of sulphur, charcoal, and saltpeter. Hazelwood was recommended for the charcoal. This was pulverized and mixed with powdered sulphur. Then came saltpeter. This was the critical ingredient, for it contained the oxygen which permitted the other two substances to burn rapidly even when cut off from any other air supply. Combustion of the compound was almost instantaneous. If it took place in the open, there was merely a sudden burst of flame, quickly over. If it were confined, however, it produced an explosion as the gases demanded room to expand.

It is this expansion that provides the force to push bullets, although the potential was not appreciated by the earliest scholars. Bacon sensed that there was power in gunpowder, but he was more concerned with the noise and the flash as agents for terrifying an enemy, or perhaps even destroying him through the concussion of the explosion. The idea of hurling a projectile came later, perhaps as late as 1300. **23**

No one knows who first thought of using gunpowder as a propellant. It may well have occurred to a number of people independently. Many legends have grown up about this epic achievement, none provable—although one of the obviously impossible stories has acquired the greatest distinction, with statues, portraits, stained-glass tributes, and "scholarly" biographies of the supposed inventor. This legendary figure was Berthold Schwarz, or the Black Berthold. He is called *Berchtoldus niger* in Latin and *der schwarze Berthold* in German in

---

Below: Gothic compound crossbow of about 1450 is made of wood, horn, and whalebone. The crannequin underneath provided the leverage to bend the bow. The group of bolts, or quarrels, at bottom is not to scale. Opposite: Knightly swords of the 10th to 16th centuries. As projectile weapons increased in effectiveness, the sword declined in importance as a weapon, although even today it is a symbol of power.

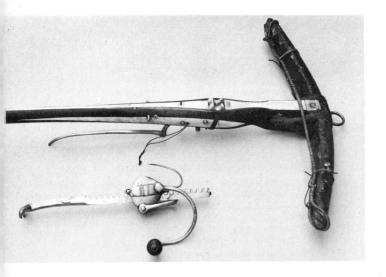

24

the early documents. According to which account one reads, he was a Greek, a German, or a Dane. He was a monk (Franciscan, Dominican, or Augustinian, depending upon the writer), or an alchemist, or both. The "Black" in his name may have referred to his complexion, his habit if he was a "black Dominican," or to the fact that he practiced the black arts, for he is called a "nigromanticus" in one early reference. (The modern rendering of Schwarz as a surname is a mistranslation.)

As with almost everything else about Black Berthold, there are at least two choices of the manner in which he invented the gun. In one, he is described as an alchemist who had found a way to make mercury into a malleable metal. Mercury held a great fascination for the medieval scholar. It was a puzzling substance. It looked like metal, but evidently it wasn't. Alchemists thought it might be the mysterious "First Matter." If it could be hardened and colored yellow it would probably become gold; if colored white it might become silver. In its natural state, First Matter was black and the process of solidifying and coloring it was, therefore, a black art.

As a practitioner of the black art, Berthold thought he had a way to solidify mercury and take the first step toward making gold. As every wise alchemist knew full well, mercury was inhabited by a Basilisk, a fearsome serpent whose breath and look were fatal. Before the mercury could be solidified, the beast had to be exorcised. Berthold tried heat first. Then he added sulphur, thought to be hot by nature, and saltpeter, believed to be cold, in the hope that the serpent would be killed in the struggle between these substances. Instead, Berthold himself was very nearly killed as the closed mixing vessel exploded and blew down the walls of his laboratory.

This story is told as early as the Fifteenth Century. The same source gives another version as well. Perhaps Berthold needed two experiences before he understood. In the second

version, the worthy alchemist mixed sulphur and saltpeter in a stone mortar to test the statement of Aristotle that substances with hot and cold natures were antagonistic. To this mixture he added a little charcoal or linseed oil, put the mortar over a fire, and was immediately flattened by an explosion which scattered pieces of stone all over his room.

From these experiences Black Berthold is supposed to have conceived the idea of guns for shooting projectiles—and some say he even invented gunpowder. The only difficulty lies in the fact that the best dates for Berthold, if indeed he really existed at all, indicate that he probably worked about 1350 or later, a good century after Bacon described gunpowder, and more than twenty-five years after actual cannon had appeared upon the scene.

Legends die hard, however, especially if they start early enough. Berthold's story goes back to within a hundred years of his supposed life, and within the next two hundred years the references multiply. Earlier documents were altered to add references to him, and in at least one instance a date was mistranscribed from 1393 to 1313, adding to the confusion.

Whoever conceived the gun, or how many different people contributed to the conception, will never be known. Nonetheless, guns were in use shortly after 1300, democratizing war even further than the bow and arrow. They made little impression at first, and it was fully a hundred years before their impact was felt.

Then change came rapidly. Mechanical art meant more than valor. The man wielding the superior weapon was the more formidable foe, regardless of his birth or even of his courage. As Thomas Carlyle wrote later, gunpowder "makes all men alike tall." With the whole character of war changed, one of the basic principles of feudalism was destroyed. The idea that war was a trial of moral values by battle, in which the Church refereed for God, was ended. War became a means to political ends; chivalrous ideas and attitudes disappeared until

Fanciful drawing of 1598 shows Black Berthold inventing gunpowder with assistance from the Devil. The claim for Berthold is false, however; it cannot even be proved he existed. But whatever its origin, gunpowder eventually ended the techniques of waging war depicted in these contemporary illustrations.

Machiavelli could write, "Although in all other affairs it is hateful to use fraud, in the operations of war it is praiseworthy."

The changes did not come easily. Many of the great knights tried to hold them back and keep warfare on its older, honorable footing. Gian Paolo Vitelli, the Italian *condottiere* who died in 1499, was accustomed to blind and cut the hands off arquebusiers he captured. The Chevalier Bayard, model of French chivalry and known as the knight "without fear and above reproach," shot them when he could. Yet he himself was destined to fall in the Battle of Sesia, the victim of an arquebus bullet. Perhaps it was the doughty warrior Miguel de Cervantes, author of *Don Quixote,* who best expressed the feelings of his fellow chivalric fighters when he cursed guns as "the Devil's invention" which enabled a "base cowardly hand to take the life of the bravest gentleman. ... A chance bullet, coming nobody knows how or from whence, fired perchance by one that fled affrighted at the very flash of his villainous piece, may in a moment put a period to the vastest designs. ..."

This was the crux of the matter. Bravery, training, birth were no longer sufficient. A man who dared not face a knight sword in hand could shoot him from hiding. The world was turned upside down and many a trained warrior lamented the new force with the Italian poet Ariosto (1474-1533):

O! curs'd device! base implement of death!
Fram'd in the black Tartarean realms beneath!
By Beelzebub's malicious art design'd
To ruin all the race of human kind.

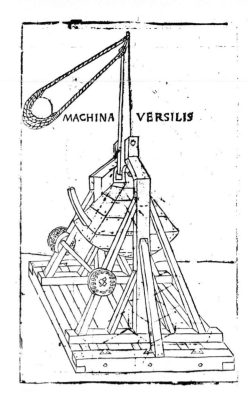

MACHINA VERSILIS

2

Preceding pages: Spanish explorers
of the New World wore morion and breastplate,
carried matchlock and cup-hilted rapier.

MARVELOUS MONSTERS

The first gun was fired. No one knows where, when, or by whom. If it caused consternation on the field of battle, with horses shying and men fleeing at the strange and fearsome explosion, history has not recorded the event. It was a local happening without apparent significance to the chroniclers of the age. Changes were to come, great sweeping transformations of warfare, society, and government, all brought on by this new instrument of death and power, but these would

30 *take centuries. The world of 1300 paid little heed to the newcomer—at first.*

Once the significance of a device has been well established, there are always claimants to the honor of having first used it. Guns are no exception, and there are forged documents, misinterpreted papers, and unsubstantiated boasts placing the first appearance of the gun in a number of different countries at a wide variety of dates. All are spurious. It can only be said that the gun was developed before 1326, when two separate documents from different countries indicate that it was in existence and widely known.

The more important of these documents is a royal instruction book for the youthful Edward III of England. Walter de Milemete, the prince's tutor, wrote the carefully illuminated manuscript in Latin and entitled it *De Officiis Regum*—On the Duties of Kings. He dated it 1326. Young Edward had need of such a book, for this was the same year that his mother and her friends arranged the murder of his father. Apparently she had conceived a dislike for the king because, among other things, he had neglected his royal duties and let himself and England be ruled by a succession of "favorites." In any event, his manner of death was highly imaginative and spectacularly sordid, and the new king would do well to study such a book lest he, too, suffer a similarly dramatic end.

Along with good advice on how to be a successful monarch, de Milemete's book contained an illustration of a gun, the earliest dated picture to have survived. There is nothing in the text itself to explain the picture, but it is evident from a study of the manuscript that its illustrations were painted first and the text lettered in afterward. Thus, the pictures are actually somewhat earlier than the date of the completed book. Another manuscript by the same hand also contains a drawing of a cannon and may even be earlier. But it is not dated and so is of less importance.

Meanwhile, on the continent of Europe, the city of Florence ordered the manufacture of cannon and projectiles in 1326, and a manuscript relating to the transaction still survives. There is no indication in it that such guns were a new invention or that the order was anything out of the ordinary. Thus, it must be assumed that guns had been in existence for some time.

Nothing is known of the form of the guns that Florence ordered, and unfortunately de Milemete does not describe the gun shown in his manuscripts. Still, it is possible to learn something from the pictures themselves. In the instruction book, the gun is shaped like a large vase lying on its side on a flat table. There is a touchhole on top, near the breech, and a knight fully armored in mail is touching it off with a red-hot firing-iron. There is no indication of any device for controlling the recoil of the gun, which must surely have been thrown off the table by the force of the charge. Perhaps this explains why the knight wears a worried expression and stands well to one side. More likely, the artist merely overlooked this technical detail.

The form of the gun is most interesting. It undoubtedly explains the origin of some of the early names for cannon. The French, for instance, used the expression *pot-de-fer,* or iron pot, while the Italians used *vasa,* again meaning pot or vessel. Despite the contour of the gun, however, the bore was probably a simple cylinder, as it is in modern firearms. A smaller gun of this sort has been found at Loshult in Sweden with such a bore, and the Japanese actually were still casting cannon of this shape as recently as the Nineteenth Century.

The undated manuscript, also believed to be by de Milemete, shows a similar gun. It is bigger this time and is lying on the ground with stone supports, while four men are grouped around it. Still no device for controlling the recoil is shown.

An especially interesting feature of both these pictures is the projectile. Instead of the ball which one might have expected, it is an

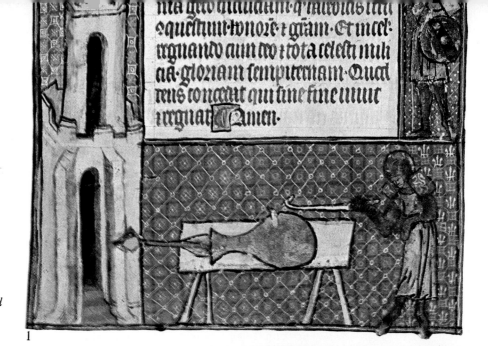

 nita quo mimmnum q̄ micolus ieu
ꝯqueſtumt honoꝛe ⁊ gꞃam. Et meet
ꞃgnanꝺo aim ꝺeo ⁊ tota celeſti milt
ua · glonam ſempuernam · Qual
reus concedut qui ſine fine uuuut
ꞃꞇgnat ꝗꝛ Amen.

1

2

1. De Milemete's manuscript of 1326 contains earliest dated picture of a gun.

---

2. Another de Milemete picture, undated, may be even earlier.

---

3. Actual gun dating from the mid-1400's, found at Loshult in Sweden, resembles closely the type which is shown in manuscripts.

---

4. Cannon with more fully developed carriages and stone cannon balls are employed against besieged city in picture from 15th century English manuscript.

arrow. The head is four-sided, like the usual crossbow quarrel, and probably it was made entirely of iron—including the "feathers." The colors in the painting are somewhat fanciful, so it is difficult to tell.

Since both of the earliest pictures of firearms show similar vase shapes, it is tempting to conclude that this was the form of the very first gun. But this would be rash. Guns had been in use before either of these pictures were drawn. They were being made in far-off Florence, and probably other places as well, at that very moment, and there is no indication that any of them resembled these firearms.

Actually, there were probably at least two different kinds of guns. Those just described were called "vessels" or "pots," while other guns were called "cannon." The word cannon itself is supposed to come from the Latin *canna*, meaning reed. If so, this gives a clue to their design: a long, hollow tube of the same general form as cannon today. Certainly, tubular guns were being made within a few years after de Milemete inscribed his lesson book for the young king, and they may even have been the first to appear.

Educators maintain that illustrations in school books have a great influence upon children, and Edward III seems to offer proof of their theories. Whether de Milemete's gun pictures were responsible or not, Edward soon became interested in the new weapon and he is a key figure in the early use of firearms. Numbers of guns, both large and small, were made at his command, as were stores of powder and different kinds of shot.

At this time, theories of ballistics had not even begun to evolve and Edward thus had a variety of projectiles to choose from. Metal arrows, such as those shown in de Milemete's book, were plentiful. Balls of brass, lead, and iron were cast for use in small guns or as scat-

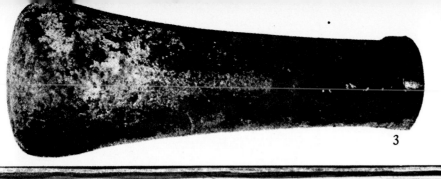

3

4

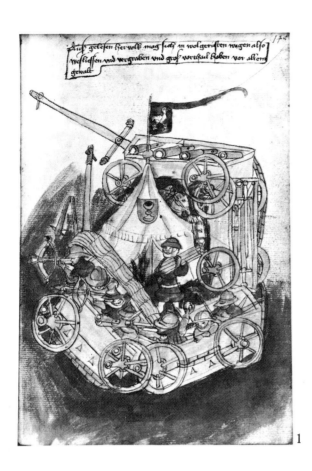

1

2

3

ter shot for large pieces. Big balls, however, were usually made of stone. Such balls were lighter than those made of metal and did not put as great a strain on the breech of a gun when it was fired. They were also easier and cheaper to make, and so they remained standard from Edward's reign until the end of the Fifteenth Century.

Edward III is perhaps best remembered for starting the great Hundred Years' War with France, an epic struggle which absorbed the attention and drained the resources of both countries. During this contest guns first began to achieve real prominence on the field of battle under the sponsorship of the English king. Of all the early actions in the war, two of Edward's successes stand out as milestones in military history: the Battle of Crécy and the siege of Calais. Both have a bearing on the history of firearms.

Crécy was a small French village near the

border of Flanders. Edward's grandmother had ruled the land in which it lay and as the retreating English army reached the area, the king decided to accept battle. It was the evening of August 26, 1346. A sudden thunderstorm had drenched the area. Then the air cleared. Edward's army, strong in its infantry, many of whom were experts with the longbow, was drawn up on a gentle slope. In the center were two groups of dismounted men-atarms with archers flanked out on either side. In the rear was a reserve.

The French attack was disorganized from the beginning. First came Genoese crossbowmen, sent forward to counteract the English archers. But the bright rays of the setting sun were directly in their eyes and the rapid, accurate shooting of the English quickly demoralized them. They stopped in confusion, then panicked, cutting their bowstrings, throwing their weapons away, and pressing back upon

4

the main French army. King Philip of France was infuriated. Shouting, "Kill me those scoundrels; for they stop our road!" he sent his first wave of heavily armored knights crashing into the milling mob. As soon as the horsemen cut their way through their unfortunate comrades, they, too, felt the sting of the English arrows which pierced their armor and drove their horses out of control. The second wave of knights tangled with the debris of the first, and the third with both its predecessors. Comparatively few ever reached the English lines, and these were soon beaten back. The yeoman's arrow had defeated the armored knight.

The longbow was the victor in this classic battle, but it may well have been aided by guns. Four early sources maintain that two or three English cannon opened against the Genoese and hint that the noise may have begun the panic of the crossbowmen and caused the French knights' horses to shy. Other writers assert that these guns existed only in the minds of apologists seeking excuses for the French defeat. At this late date, it seems impossible to prove one way or the other.

Nevertheless, Edward definitely did have cannon available at the time, even if they were not present on the battlefield. Immediately after Crécy he made use of some twenty of them in his siege of Calais. Here there is no room for doubt. Large and small guns were propped on their wooden frames and fired over the double walls and moat surrounding the French port. Cut off from all help, the beleaguered city held out for eleven months before surrendering to become an English stronghold on the Continent and the sole gain for England from the whole Hundred Years' War.

It is difficult to judge the importance of the guns in this successful siege. The noise, flash, and smoke of their explosions undoubtedly were of psychological value, and their great stone balls must have caused some destruction. As one early chronicler commented:

*Gonners to schew their art
Into the town in many a parte
    Schot many a fulle great stone.
Thanked be God and Mary mild,
They hurt neyther man, woman nor child;
    To the houses, though, they did harm.*

Despite this lukewarm report, the use of cannon gradually increased. References are scarce before 1350, but thereafter they multiply rapidly. By 1400 guns appear to have been part of every major military establishment.

Gunmaking was a crude and uncertain art throughout this century of battle. Relatively small guns could be cast in brass or bronze, and those of the pot form had to be made in that way. Tubular cannon, however, were usually made of wrought iron. To do this, staves of iron were laid side-by-side around a wooden core and welded together with heat and hammer. This was no mean task. It was difficult to control the heat in such an operation, and metallurgy was a matter of chance and guesswork.

Musketeer below is from Jacques de Gheyn's famous
manual of arms of 1607. Engravings of matchlock arquebus and of horsemen
firing them are from Wallhausen's Art Militaire au Cheval *of 1616.*

36

As a result, the joints were weak and unpredictable. Thus, a series of hoops was next wrapped around the staves, welded, and shrunk into position. A cooper made wooden barrels in substantially the same way, and this may have been how the term barrel came to be applied to the tube of a firearm.

It took courage to be an artillerist in that era. Even with the strengthening hoops there often were weak spots in a wrought-iron barrel. Cast guns might have pits or flaws undiscovered by the gunner. Powder also varied in strength. The basic ingredients often were carried separately and mixed fresh before using, and a little extra saltpeter could make a lot of difference. Gunners did well to pray to their patron, St. Barbara, as they rammed the charge home, for it was never certain that the gun would not explode and do its killing in the wrong direction. Ordinary soldiers and laymen maintained a respectful distance from these weapons. Gunners were a class apart. There were rumors that they were in league with the Devil. Some folks even said artillerists did not loot, pillage, and drink on campaign. This in itself was good cause for suspicion. And there was the example of Scotland's King James II. Fascinated by the big guns, James had been personally supervising their work in the siege of Roxburgh Castle in 1460. As he inspected a huge, hooped bombard named "The Lion," it exploded, and a fragment struck him in the chest, killing him instantly. If this could happen to kings, lesser men might well take warning.

Despite all the dangers, cannon increased in number and in size. The search for more power led to larger and larger guns, some of them bigger than anything that has been made since. A gigantic wrought-iron bombard, known as "Duille Grete," or "Mad Margaret," and still preserved in Ghent, has a mouth thirty-three inches in diameter and weighs 33,606 pounds. It threw a six-hundred-pound stone cannon ball. A huge gun, seventeen feet long and weighing more than seventeen tons, was cast in bronze for the Sultan Mohamet II of Turkey when he laid siege to Constantinople in 1453. According to tradition, it could throw a half-ton ball for almost a mile. Now called the Dardanelles Gun, it is displayed at the Tower of London, a latter-day gift from Sultan Abdul Aziz to Queen Victoria.

One of the more famous of all the big guns, however, was "Mons Meg." This wrought-iron gun, now resting on a restored carriage at Edinburgh Castle, was also associated with the luckless James II, whose interest in artillery proved fatal. Legend has it that it was made by Molise McKim, hereditary smith of Threave. For his efforts he was supposedly given the estate of Mollance (pronounced "Mowans"). And the gun was thus named after his nagging wife, "Mowans Meg" or "Mons Meg," who also made a loud noise. Modern scholars feel the origin of the name was probably much more prosaic. Nonetheless, its thirteen-foot, four-inch length and twenty-inch bore must have gladdened the king's heart.

Even after its days of active service were over, its career was colorful. It was used to fire salutes on state occasions and it was carted about in ceremonial processions. For some of these parades it was painted with red lead and Orkney butter in what sounds almost like a fertility rite. And this may not have been too inappropriate for the colorful cannon. At any rate, one Eighteenth Century picture of the gun bears the sole caption: "An antient bombard or gun, called Mons Meg. Tradition says a woman was got with child in it." Finally, in 1680, the ancient piece burst in the midst of a salute to another James, soon to become King of England and Scotland. For years it lay neglected until Sir Walter Scott aroused national interest in the relic. Then, in 1829, King George IV ordered the huge piece returned to Edinburgh. Pipers marched before it, heralding its approach, and the 73rd Foot, with three troops of cavalry, provided escort as the venerable cannon was hauled up the steep hill to the castle and its final home.

Size might be important in battering down walls and buildings, but it was a hindrance if one wanted to use a gun against an opposing army. Big guns were too cumbersome, too slow, and their one huge ball did relatively little more damage than a smaller one. What was needed was a gun firing a number of smaller balls. Gunmakers were already producing it.

The first attempt to gain increased firepower was the ribauld or ribauldequin. In a sense, it was the direct ancestor of the mitrailleuse and the machine gun. A number of small barrels was fastened together in a straight line. Usually the touchholes, which communicated with the powder charges inside, were so aligned that a single sweep of the burning coal, or whatever igniting device was used, would set all of them off almost simultaneously. Here was a gun that was strictly antipersonnel. It was of no value in battering fortifications. From now on guns would be used against enemy soldiers as well as their strongholds.

Although they were rapid-firing, ribauldequins were slow to load, and so their use was limited. Each barrel had to be loaded separately and this took time. They could deliver

one devastating volley, but the battle might be over before the second one was ready. They were particularly useful for defending gates and barricades where the enemy would be concentrated in a narrow area. In such positions the guns could be mounted and aimed in advance, waiting for the proper moment to fire.

The earliest known mention of a ribauldequin lists one at the city of Bruges in 1339. In 1340 one is described as covering the gate at Tournay. Then the fascination with size again took over and in 1387 the biggest ribauldequin of all was constructed.

This huge monster was the project of Antonio della Scala, Lord of Verona, and he had three of them built in all. Each mounted one hundred and forty-four barrels in three stories, one above the other to a height of twenty feet. Each story was divided into three compartments and each compartment held twelve tubes which could be fired simultaneously. A gunner was stationed in each story, ready to fire his complement of thirty-six shots in three volleys. With all three of these huge machines operating together, della Scala could command an almost simultaneous discharge of four hundred and thirty-two shots. Four powerful dray horses could pull each tower—if the ground was suitable. This was the drawback. In 1387 the Veronese set out to fight the Paduans at the Battle of Castagno. With them went their prized ribauldequins. But the ground was wet. The lumbering monsters never reached the field and without their secret weapon the Veronese were soundly beaten.

There was a way to overcome the double drawbacks of cumbersome size and slowness of reloading. A gunner could be assigned to each barrel. And these barrels need not be all joined together on a wheeled frame. If they were small enough, each man could carry his own individual gun. It would be a cannon carried by hand—a hand cannon or handgun.

This may not have been the actual reasoning behind the invention of the first hand firearms.

Bodyguard of Emperor Rudolf II of Bohemia carries musket with sharply curved butt in de Gheyn engraving. His elaborate equipment contrasts with simple gear of early 16th century knight (at right).

The shape of these primitive guns and the timing of their appearance, however, would seem to indicate such a line of thought. Ribaulde-quins came into use shortly before 1339. Handguns were known by 1350 and are recorded throughout Western Europe in the succeeding half-century.

The first of these handguns were little more than ribauldequin barrels fitted to a wooden haft. They were simple tubes of iron or brass, closed at one end and with a touchhole on top through which the powder could be set off. Sizes varied, but most early barrels were apparently quite short. The town of Perugia, for instance, ordered five hundred of these new weapons in 1364. Each was to be no longer than the palm of one hand. A surviving specimen in Sweden is eight inches long, and another found in the moat of a robbers' stronghold near Tannenburg, Germany, still held a charge of powder and a lead ball in its twelve-and-a-quarter-inch barrel. This interesting specimen has a caliber of about .70 and weighs two and three-quarters pounds, exclusive of its wooden haft. Since the castle itself was destroyed in 1399, there is no doubt that the gun dates from the Fourteenth Century.

Small guns such as these would be extremely difficult to control when fired. The recoil would make them almost unmanageable. Also the metal would become hot after repeated firing. Thus, the wooden stock or "tiller" was a necessity. The first of these were simple poles. An English manuscript of 1374 compares them to the hafts of pikes, and tells how William de Sleaford, Keeper of the Privy Wardrobe, got thirteen shillings for making eight of them and attaching the barrels. Lengths varied somewhat, depending upon the size of the barrel and the preferences of the man for whom the work was being done. Four to five feet, however, was probably average.

There were several methods of fastening the barrel and stock together. The simplest and probably the earliest was to place the barrel atop the end of the tiller and bind them with iron bands. In more sophisticated designs, the end of the tiller might be shaped and grooved to receive the barrel before the straps were added. Later, some barrels were made with sockets into which the stock could be inserted, or with pointed tangs which could be driven into the end of the pole. All of these forms were undoubtedly in use before 1400.

A German manuscript of 1411 tells how these hand cannon were loaded. First came the powder, poured in at the muzzle. Gunpowder was likely to be weak in that era and an alarming quantity was used: three-fifths of the barrel was filled with it! Then it was rammed down. A space was left, and then came a wooden plug or sabot, and finally the ball, which was practically at the muzzle. There was really no bore left for the ball to travel down when fired and thus no guide for its flight. The gunner knew it generally would go forward when fired, but that was about all he could be sure of.

This lack of accuracy was not so distressing

Above: 16th century German matchlock is inlaid with bone and mother-of-pearl. At right: Gunners aid hard-pressed spearmen in bringing boar to bay. Engraving dates from 1580's. Far right: Kneeling Dutch explorer fires unusual left-handed matchlock from atop shoulder in 1663-1670 print.

40

as it might seem. The gunner couldn't tell exactly where he was pointing the piece anyway. In the first place, it was difficult to hold the gun steady against the expected recoil. Usually, the best a shooter could do was to grasp the tiller directly behind the barrel with his left hand and clamp the remainder of the stock between his left arm and his body. With his right hand he thrust a red-hot firing iron, or glowing coal, into the touchhole on the top of the barrel. This required him to keep his eyes fixed on the hole so that he would not miss it and perhaps apply the fire to his other hand or snuff it out against the barrel. It was impossible for him to look where he was shooting. At times he might brace the end of the pole against the ground instead of clamping it under his arm, and on heavier guns he might support the barrel on a forked rest, but still he had to watch the touchhole as he applied the fire. The only way to overcome this predicament was to use two men, one to hold the gun and one to fire it. This was sometimes done.

Changes came and the gun was improved. The touchhole was moved from the top to the right side of the barrel. A little ledge or pan was added beneath it to hold priming powder and make ignition more certain. Then a hinged cover was placed over the pan to protect it from the weather. Barrels were lengthened. Stocks were shortened and widened. The general contours of a modern gun began to appear.

Most important was the development of a wick called a "match" and a device for holding it. The match was a loosely twisted rope of hemp that had been dipped in saltpeter and spirits of wine, so that it would burn slowly and steadily and hold a coal, much like modern punk. With both the red-hot iron and the fresh coal held in tongs, a shooter was forced to stay near a fire and pick up his iron or coal at the last possible minute. With match he was free to move about. A moderate length would burn for a considerable time and a shooter could always light a new piece from the old. The gun was now a practical weapon for use in the open, outside of a fort or other fixed positions.

The next significant development came with the invention of a device for attaching the match to the gun. A clamp was fashioned on

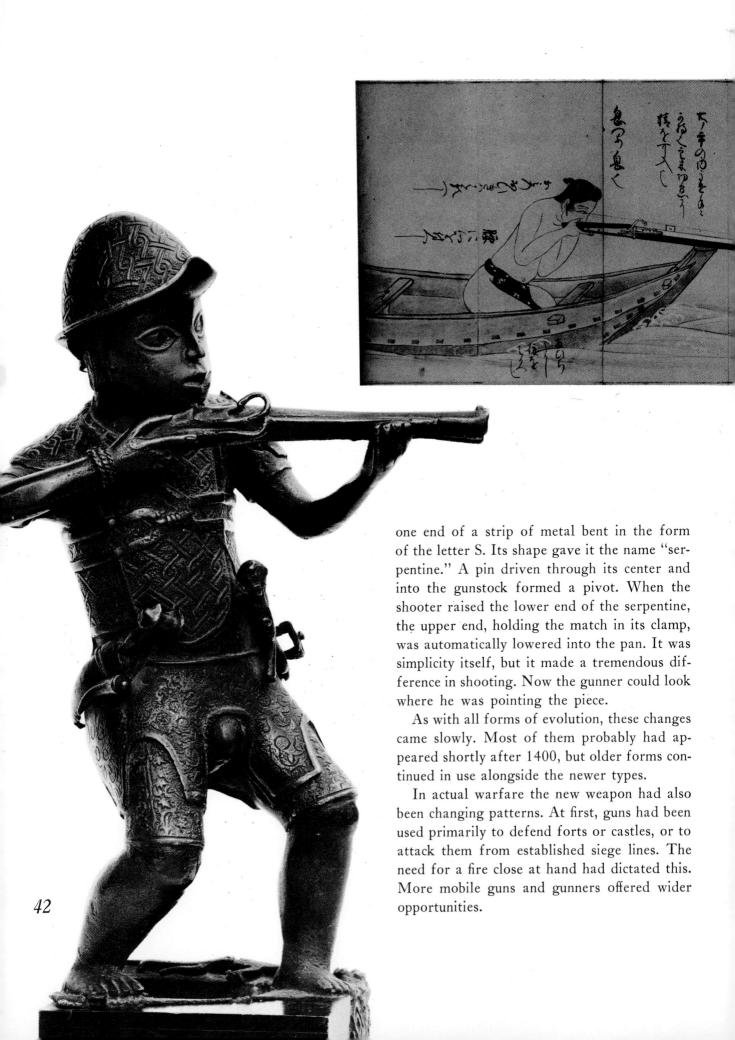

one end of a strip of metal bent in the form of the letter S. Its shape gave it the name "serpentine." A pin driven through its center and into the gunstock formed a pivot. When the shooter raised the lower end of the serpentine, the upper end, holding the match in its clamp, was automatically lowered into the pan. It was simplicity itself, but it made a tremendous difference in shooting. Now the gunner could look where he was pointing the piece.

As with all forms of evolution, these changes came slowly. Most of them probably had appeared shortly after 1400, but older forms continued in use alongside the newer types.

In actual warfare the new weapon had also been changing patterns. At first, guns had been used primarily to defend forts or castles, or to attack them from established siege lines. The need for a fire close at hand had dictated this. More mobile guns and gunners offered wider opportunities.

*At left: 16th-17th century East African bronze
statue of soldier with matchlock is
probably a native representation of early Portuguese
explorers. Above: Japanese scroll of 1612
shows proper approach to wild fowl with matchlock.*

No one understood this better than the Bohemian hero, John Zisca. A devout follower of the religious leader John Huss, he had a lion's courage and tremendous tactical genius. Under his command an army of poorly equipped peasants beat back the finest German and Hungarian armies in victory after victory during the Hussite Wars of 1420-1434. A veteran even before the wars began, Zisca had only one eye, but this was enough to tell him his men could not fight on even terms with the power of the Holy Roman Empire. He needed a new approach to warfare, and he found it in the wagon fort and the handgun. Wagons had been employed to form movable forts before. The Russians had used them against the Tartar cavalry, for instance. And wagons continued to be used in the same way by American pioneers in the West more than four hundred years later. Zisca brought the idea to Central Europe. He developed a special wagon, with a heavy wooden

shield that could be hung on the side toward the enemy. When danger threatened, he would select an easily defensible position and form the wagons quickly into a fort. There he awaited attack. In the intervals between the wagons were men equipped with polearms and peasant weapons, some crossbowmen, and an occasional cannon. Behind these defenses were his few mounted troops ready to sally forth if the enemy panicked or retreated. In the wagons themselves were more crossbowmen—and with them were the handgunners.

The new tactics worked wonderfully well. The Hussites could never attack. They had to provoke the enemy to attack them in their wagon fort, and this they succeeded in doing with great skill. Fully armored German and Hungarian knights charged the peculiar-looking arrangement. They were met by a well-directed flight of crossbow bolts and a thundering volley from the handguns and the cannon. The effect was devastating. The few knights with sufficient luck and stamina to reach the wagons were despatched by the defenders with their polearms, cudgels, and swords. The broken remnants who retreated were struck by the small band of Hussite cavalry, quickly followed by the defenders of the wagons who ran after them on foot. The imperial armies were too demoralized to offer effective resistance.

Time and again the same thing happened. The wagon and the gun became national symbols. Zisca lost his one remaining eye to an arrow, but still he led his motley army until his death in 1424. His successors carried on, not only defending their own country but also invading foreign territory, always increasing the number of gunners in their wagons. By the end of the war, nearly a third of the Hussites were armed with handguns, and later Bohemian mercenaries serving in other armies were usually noted as handgunners.

Handguns were becoming an important part of the military scene, but changes were to come which would make them even more significant. **43**

The hand firearm of the 1450's would have been immediately recognizable as a gun to a shooter of today. It had a stock and a barrel, but one important part was missing—the lock. There was no mechanism for discharging the gun. The serpentine moved directly by hand was a step in the right direction, but the hand used for that purpose could not help to steady the piece at the same time. Within twenty-five years this lack was remedied with the first true gunlock, the matchlock, which is illustrated in a German manuscript dated 1475.

The first matchlocks were simple and direct. The serpentine was cut in half, right below the pivot. This pivot passed through a metal plate on the side of the gun and was linked on the inside to a long lever or sear, itself pivoted in the middle. A second long lever, attached to the free end of the sear, formed the trigger. This looked and operated much like the lever on the contemporary crossbow. When it was squeezed upward against the stock, it acted through the sear to move the serpentine down toward the pan and fire the gun. When it was released, a spring pushing against the sear raised the serpentine and held the match away from the pan. All working parts, except the serpentine and trigger, were inside the lock plate, protected from weather and accident.

The complete gun—lock, stock, and barrel—had now appeared. Instead of an extended sweep with the right hand, a slight pressure of the fingers would fire the gun. There was less chance of moving the piece and disturbing the aim. The right hand also could be used partially for supporting the gun and holding it steady. With a heavy piece and a noticeable delay in firing, the shooter needed all the help he could get.

Very shortly another form of matchlock appeared. This one required even less movement of the fingers to fire it. The action of the spring was reversed and it was made to act directly against the serpentine. When a soldier was ready to shoot, he inserted the match in the

jaws of the serpentine and pulled it back, or "cocked" it, until it latched in place. The pressure of a thumb against a button trigger on the side of the plate would then release the catch. The spring would snap the serpentine and match down into the powder in the pan.

Shooters liked the idea of a gun that could be fired with such a light pressure. But there were other features of the lock that were not so desirable. The force with which the serpentine was thrown forward often put the match out instead of firing the gun. Since it took some time to rekindle the wick, the game or enemy might well be in the next county before it could be accomplished—or, worse still, might be at the shooter's throat. The light touch also had unfortunate side effects. There was no safety except for the pan cover, and this was uncertain. Accidents could happen easily, and unexpected

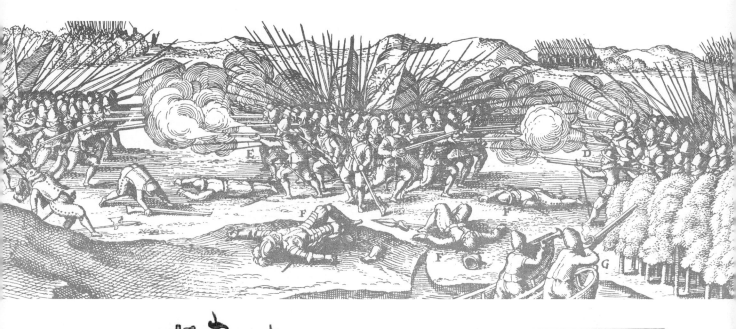

Top: De Bry engraving of battle between French
and Spanish is notable for what appears to be a bell-muzzled
gun being fired by soldier in right foreground.
Above: Early 17th century German wall gun inlaid with bone
plaques. At left: Powder flask for a musket.

or premature discharges were dangerous and troublesome. The snapping matchlock, therefore, was not popular in Europe for long. Before 1550 it had all but disappeared, except in small areas of Germany and the Low Countries.

By odd coincidence, however, these two primitive forms of matchlock have outlived all the later improved versions in actual use. It was in these formative years of the lock that European explorers were setting out to find new ways to the Orient. In 1498, Vasco da Gama reached India, and in about 1542 other Portuguese sailors landed on one of the islands of Japan. With them went the new guns. Firearms were a marvel to the ancient cultures of the East. A letter believed to describe the first sight of the wonderful weapon sounds as if even gunpowder was unknown in the outer islands of Japan:

...they carried with them one article...which was about two or three shaku [feet] in length, straight, heavy and hollow. One end, however, was closed, and near it there was a small hole through which fire was to be lighted. The article was used in the following way—some mysterious medicine was put into it, with a small piece of lead and, when one lit the medicine through that hole, the lead piece was discharged and hit everything. When it was discharged light like lightning was seen and noise like thunder was heard, so the bystanders invariably closed their ears with their hands.

Obviously, here was something marvelously powerful. Even as they covered their ears, the Japanese coveted the "article." The Portuguese were traders and an exorbitant profit could not be overlooked. They sold two guns to Tokitaka, lord of the island on which they had 45 landed. Tokitaka was delighted and practiced with his new acquisitions until he was so skillful he could "nearly hit" a target placed "almost one hundred steps" away.

With their great copying skill the Japanese set out to produce more guns on their own. Legend has it that the favors of a beautiful maiden induced a lonesome Portuguese to impart some of the secrets. Be that as it may, the Japanese gun industry was launched within the year. The gun they preferred was the snapping matchlock and for three hundred years this was the standard firearm of Japan. Further European refinements did not penetrate that isolated kingdom until the middle of the last century.

Less is known about the introduction of the matchlock to India, but it must have happened under somewhat similar circumstances. Here the preferred type was the most primitive of the sear forms, with the serpentine falling forward, away from the shooter. This would have been the type carried by da Gama's men in 1498, or by their immediate followers. With minor modifications it, too, has been made in remote areas of India until very recent times, centuries after it disappeared from Europe.

Meantime, in the mainstream of firearms development, the matchlock continued to improve.

The serpentine was turned so that it fell toward the shooter rather than away from him. This way he could keep an eye on the coal to see that it was lit and that it was properly adjusted. From the safety standpoint, a smaller trigger was developed which could be placed inside a trigger guard to protect it against accidental bumps.

Stocks became more sophisticated in design as shooting techniques changed. The early straight stocks, which were particularly popular in Germany and Switzerland, had been held against the cheek with the butt resting atop the shoulder. The shooter had to absorb most of the recoil with his arms and hands. The French developed a sharply curved butt which was held against the chest. With this shape, the force of the recoil was directed upward and a gun could be made lighter. In Spain the butt was broadened; here men first began to use the shoulder itself as a brace when firing. By 1600, the Spanish fashion had won over most of Europe, especially for heavy military arms.

With all the different types of stocks and different sizes of guns being made, a myriad of names developed which have plagued students ever since. There were hackbuts, hakbuchsen, harquebuses, arcquebuses, calivers, petronels,

and muskets, to name a few. Although they apparently were intended to mean specific types of arms, they came to be applied carelessly to different forms at different times. To complicate things still further, there were different usages in different countries.

Take the group of words hackbut, hakbuchse, harquebus, and arquebus (and other variants), for instance. In German *hak* meant hook and *buchse* gun. Thus, a *hakbuchse* was a gun with a hook. Illustrated inventories of the late 1400's show clearly that the hook was a small projection on the underside of the barrel that could be hooked over a wall to help take up some of the recoil when the gun was fired. Arquebus probably derived from the same meaning, but within a few years it was used to indicate a light gun fired from the chest or shoulder without a rest. Still later it came to mean a wheel lock, as opposed to a matchlock. And there were other meanings as well. It all depended on who used the word and when.

Other terms were a little simpler. The petronel was a light gun fired with the butt against the chest. A caliver was normally a light gun fired from the shoulder, and a musket was a heavy military arm fired from the shoulder, but requiring a forked rest to support the barrel.

This was a Spanish invention—the name deriving from the Spanish *mosquete*. The word appears at least as early as 1535, although tradition has it that the famous Duke of Alva developed the gun and introduced it into the Spanish service about 1550 for the bloody fighting in the Netherlands. Here it was seen by all of Western Europe and quickly adopted, along with its Spanish butt. These first muskets were indeed guns to be reckoned with. They had bores of eight or ten gauge and weighed up to twenty pounds. There was good reason for the forked rest. As the years passed the musket became lighter, the rest was abandoned, and by 1650 there was no longer any distinction between it and a caliver or an arquebus.

Arquebus or caliver, musket or petronel, the matchlock was a difficult gun to shoot. Its mechanism might be simple, but its operation was complex. Here is what a shooter had to do. First he removed the match from the jaws of the serpentine to reduce the chance of acciden-

*At left: Detail of early 17th century
engraving of Battle of Dalen shows sharply curved
musket butt still in use (left foreground).
Below: Dutch musket of the early 1600's is inlaid with
engraved staghorn and mother-of-pearl.*

Early 16th century landsknecht *loads his matchlock, which has straight German stock designed to be fired from the cheek. Note that artist has reversed the gun, making it left-handed.*

paper, and all was forced home with the rammer. Then he primed the piece by filling the pan with fine powder from a second flask, closed the pan cover, and carefully blew away any loose powder.

Now the gun was loaded, but much still remained to be done before it could be fired. The match had to be returned to the serpentine and adjusted so that the end would strike the pan. The coal on its end had to be blown into activity. If a shooter needed to wait any length of time before firing, he had to change the adjustment of the match to keep it from burning back to the jaws of the serpentine and going out. All this had to be done with two glowing coals never far from his supplies of powder. It took considerable skill—and patience—to be a successful shooter.

The martial laws of Virginia for 1611 give an excellent description of such a shooter as he manned his post on the frontier:

...he shall shoulder his piece, both ends of his match being alight, and his piece charged, and prined, and bullets in his mouth, there to stand with a careful and waking eye, untill such time as his Corporall shall relieve him.

The warning about a "waking eye" was completely unnecessary. It is difficult to imagine a sentry falling asleep with a mouthful of bullets, a handful of burning match, and a flask full of gunpowder. If he did, there might be little left to court-martial.

The gunpowder the Virginia sentry used in his gun had improved greatly over Roger Bacon's crude mixture. Early powder was a simple combination of the three basic ingredients ground to a fine powder. This resulted in a dusty black substance about the consistency of fine coal dirt and variously known as "meal" or "serpentine" powder. It was explosive—under the proper circumstances—but it had many drawbacks. It was unstable. It collected moisture and formed lumps which would burn but not explode. If rammed down the barrel too hard, it would also form slow-burning lumps.

tally igniting his powder. The match was kept lighted at both ends, so that if one went out it could be relit from the other. The match was held by the last three fingers of the left hand; the thumb and forefinger of the same hand were employed to hold the barrel while the gun was loaded. Next, with his right hand, the musketeer poured a charge of powder from his flask or bandolier down the barrel. A ball from his pouch (or from his mouth if during a battle) was followed by a wad of tow or

Even under the best of circumstances, all of the powder would not be burned, and a gummy residue was left which quickly fouled the barrel.

Once again it was a simple operation that brought improvement. It was found that adding a small amount of water to the mixture and then squeezing the sticky mass through sieves produced hard little grains that burned much more quickly and cleanly. Most of the disadvantages of the older powder were overcome and more force was added to the explosive at the same time. This "corned" powder, as it was called, was discovered about 1550 and it supplanted the earlier type almost immediately. Black powder had now reached its fullest development. There would be no more important improvements until the chemists of the Nineteenth Century produced explosives of an entirely different sort.

Bullets, too, developed slowly. The sphere of lead known to all muzzle-loaders today did not come to the fore immediately. Hand cannon sometimes fired projectiles of lead, it is true, but they also shot stone, iron, steel, brass, copper, and tin missiles as well. Sometimes these objects were spheres, but this was an age of experimentation in ballistics. There were cylindrical, pyramidal, rectangular, rhomboidal, and barrel-shaped bullets. Arrows were popular, too, as soldiers and sportsmen sought the most effective projectiles for their new arms. Notions of magic and philosophy often played as important a part in determining the choice as scientific observation. The diversity of forms and materials, therefore, continued for many years. Iron and steel balls were especially esteemed for armor piercing and, at least in France, they came to be known as *stuardes* because a Scot named Stuart is supposed to have killed the redoubtable Constable Anne de Montmorency with one during the Battle of St. Denis in 1560.

For a time it was even suggested that the material for the bullet should be dictated by the quality of the proposed target. And with this in mind, a French warrior who set out against the Emperor Charles V took along a half-dozen balls of gold for his arquebus. John Graham of Clavorhouse was likewise supposed to be impervious to ordinary bullets and was reputedly killed at the Battle of Killiecrankie only after an enemy tore a silver button from the coat of one of Graham's servants and fired it into the doughty warrior. Some of the same superstition has come down to modern times in fiction: for instance, the Emperor Jones, who could be killed only with a silver bullet, and the Lone Ranger who shoots only silver bullets.

Gradually, lead superseded all the other materials. Here was a metal with a melting point low enough to enable each shooter to cast his own bullets and yet with a high enough specific gravity for good ballistic results. By 1600 the lead ball was in almost universal use.

The matchlock, with its improved powder and bullets, had come a long way from the first crude firearms of the early 1300's, but it was still far from the perfect weapon. As has been noted, it was slow to load and fire. This could be an important failing in time of battle. Hernando de Soto had some arquebuses with him on his heroic trek through the wilderness of the southeastern United States in 1539-1543, and he became so disgusted with their weaknesses as weapons that he had them broken up and the barrels used for making nails. Before he did so, however, one of his companions complained bitterly about their slowness when pitted against a fast-moving enemy armed with bows and arrows:

[*The Indians*] *never stand still, but are alwaies running and traversing from one place to another: by reason whereof neither crossebow nor arcubuse can aime at them: and before one crossebowman can make one shot, an Indian will discharge three or foure arrowes; and he seldom misseth what he shooteth at.*

It could not be said of the arquebusier that he seldom missed his target. The gun was still inferior to the bow in accuracy as well as speed. **49**

The worst disadvantage of all was that there always had to be a lighted match. This was a constant hazard in the presence of powder, and Captain John Smith, for one, accidentally set off a pocketful of powder with his match and burned himself severely. The necessity for a live coal was also a liability in other ways. It was impossible to maintain one on a windy or rainy day, and on these occasions a gun was useless. Henry Hudson and his men were badly cut up during a fight with Indians in 1609, when rain put their matches out. A glowing match in the dark immediately indicated a soldier. It made him a prime target for an enemy and kept him from surprising anyone else.

Unless the matches were kept lit at all times, it was necessary to have a fire close at hand to light them. Even then there might not be time in an emergency. The history of warfare in the Sixteenth and Seventeenth Centuries is full of instances in which soldiers of one army or another were caught with their matches out and suffered severely for the oversight.

Even in America the wily Indian soon came to recognize the significance of the glowing coal. In what is now South Carolina, a group of twenty Spanish soldiers marched on an In-

dian village to force the natives to give them some corn. Just outside the village they were met by a group of Indians who assured them they could have all the food they desired if they would only put out their matches, which made the women of the village terribly nervous. The gullible Spaniards gallantly complied—and all but one especially fleet recruit were massacred.

The picture was not all bad, however. The matchlock did have some good qualities. Its noise, flash, and smoke were potent psychological factors. It could be loaded with several

balls at once, and when one of these struck a target the effect was fearsome. A ball almost an inch in diameter crushed flesh and shattered bones in a way no arrow ever could, and the force of its blow was almost certain to knock a man down, even if he received only a flesh wound. A man could learn to use it with acceptable skill far more quickly than he could become a skilled archer. The matchlock was also cheap and relatively simple to repair. Because of this, it remained the standard military firearm in Europe until about 1700. Warfare here was a rather formal affair, usually fought between small segments of the population in good weather. In such circumstances it served relatively well. In America, where everyone was involved in Indian fighting and warfare was total, day or night, regardless of weather, it was not good enough. Expense and simplicity were secondary to people whose lives depended on their firearms. If better guns were available, they wanted them just as soon as possible. Europe had been developing better guns and America demanded them.

53

CHAPTER *3*

*Preceding pages: German wheel
lock of mid-1600's. Lever at top was used to
pull back doghead to prime the pan.*

THE MECHANIC'S DELIGHT

*If a really efficient gun was to be made, some means had to be found to ignite the
powder without that accursed glowing match. Nimble minds throughout Europe
gave their attention to the problem. They knew, of course, that men had been lighting fires for centuries by striking stones, usually flint or iron pyrite, against steel
and catching the resulting sparks in tinder. Could gunpowder perhaps be set off
the same way? It could. A self-igniting gun now awaited only the proper mechanism to make use of the principle. As often happens when many persons are
working independently on the same problem, several solutions developed almost*

56 *simultaneously. Probably the first practical one was the wheel lock.*

Wheel locks were a mechanic's delight. The principle of producing sparks by striking stone against steel was simple enough, but the wheel lock did it the hard way. In general, it worked like the modern cigarette lighter. A disc of hardened steel was fashioned into a wheel and notches were cut into its rim. A short length of chain connected the spindle of the wheel with a powerful mainspring. When the wheel was wound with a key, the chain was wrapped around the spindle, and tension was put on the spring. When the wheel was released, the spring pulled back on the chain and spun the wheel. A little portion of this wheel intruded into the priming pan, where a piece of iron pyrite was held against it by spring pressure. When the wheel revolved, the friction of serrated wheel and pyrite produced sparks in the pan itself.

So far it was relatively simple, but there was more to come. A latch was necessary to hold the wheel in its wound position until the shooter was ready to fire. Then there had to be a release from the trigger. Another device had to open the pan cover automatically and let the doghead holding the pyrite bear against the wheel. In a typical, fully developed wheel lock, there were from thirty-five to fifty separate parts. Complicated double locks, or those with special actions, might have even more.

Despite its complex construction, the new wheel-lock gun was relatively simple to use. First, the shooter wound the wheel with a key called a spanner. Then he primed the pan just as he had done with the matchlock, and finally placed his charge in the barrel. In the wheel lock, however, the pan cover slid instead of swinging open as it had in earlier arms. As soon as the piece was primed, the shooter closed this cover and pulled the doghead down against it where a strong spring kept it tightly in place. The gun was now ready to fire. It could be set aside or carried for an indefinite length of time, and unless it became wet it would still go off the moment the trigger was pulled. For safety, the doghead could be pulled up, away from the pan. Then, even if the trigger were bumped or pulled accidentally, no spark would be generated. Better wheel locks sometimes had an additional device which locked the wheel so it could not turn. These were doubly safe from accident. When the shooter did pull the trigger intentionally, the wheel turned, the pan cover slid open, and the pyrite showered sparks into the powder, igniting it almost instantly.

No one knows who invented the wheel lock. It may even have been devised by several mechanical prodigies independently. A knowledge of clocks would seem to have been in the background, for only in the world of clockmakers were the complicated wheels, springs, and keys common. Certainly it originated in the area between Nürnberg in southern Germany and Milan in northern Italy, for the earliest references to the new lock and the first datable specimens all come from these areas. And they continued to be the wheel lock's real home, the acknowledged center of production throughout the period of its existence.

Appropriately enough, the first datable reference comes from the hand of one of history's greatest all-around geniuses, Leonardo da Vinci. In his famous hodgepodge, *Codice Atlantico*, is a drawing of a complete wheel lock for a gun, a similar device for lighting fires in general, and several experimental drawings of methods for attaching the transmission chain between the spring and spindle of the wheel. These are obviously design drawings, not just representations of a sample lock. Old Leonardo was either trying to improve on a prototype, or—a more exciting theory—he may have been the actual inventor himself. To judge by his drawings, he was not entirely successful. Skilled modern mechanics report failures in models made from his pictures. The wheel spindle is too thin to be practical, they state, and kinked springs of the type shown break after only a few opera-

1. *Exquisitely chiseled French wheel lock, of early 17th century.*

2. *Italian pistol of early 1600's (top), with famous Brescian pierced metalwork. Gilded German pistol of early 1700's.*

3. *German pistol of late 1500's (top). Bavarian pistol of early 1600's.*

1

2

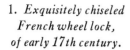

4. *German wheel lock of early 17th century.*

5. *Wheel-lock rifle by Hans Stifter of Prague, middle 1600's.*

6. *Tschinke from eastern Germany, early 1600's. Note characteristic stock and outside mainspring.*

7. *German rifle with stock carved by "Master H.N.," who is believed to have worked in Austria in the period 1625-1650.*

58

4

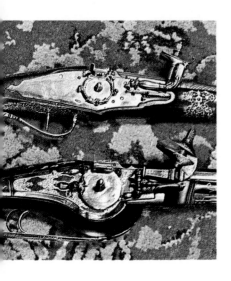

3

5

6

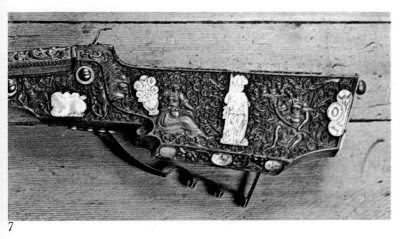

7

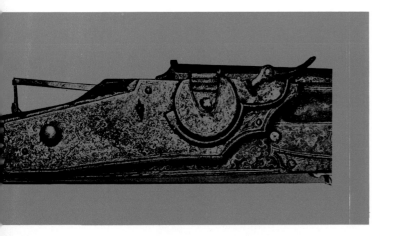

At left: The earliest datable wheel lock—
a combined pistol and crossbow made for Ferdinand II,
brother of Emperor Charles V, between
1521 and 1526. Below: Combined matchlock and
wheel lock made in Germany about 1630.
At right: Robert Dudley, Earl of Leicester, who
led English forces in wars against the
Netherlands in 1585-1587, is portrayed holding a
splendid wheel-lock petronel in right hand.

tions. Improvements were necessary and they came, either from da Vinci or others.

The date of Leonardo's primitive wheel lock is a matter of some dispute. The drawings in the various folios were made intermittently and there is no evidence of dates. Whatever information on time or sequence might originally have been given was forever lost when, after da Vinci's death in 1518, a collector cut and pasted them into a single volume. The best guess is that the pictures in the folio containing the wheel lock date from about 1508.

60   This is as much as we know for certain about the lock's origin. There are rumors and claims, of course, but none is provable. For many years it was asserted that one Johann Kiefuss of Nürnberg invented it in 1517. The stumbling block here, however, is the fact that nobody as yet has been able to find a record of such a person. Furthermore, since da Vinci's drawings were almost certainly made prior to 1517, and since there are other references to wheel locks before that date, Kiefuss must not only be established as a person, but placed before 1517 in order to honor his claim to being first.

When it comes to surviving examples of the

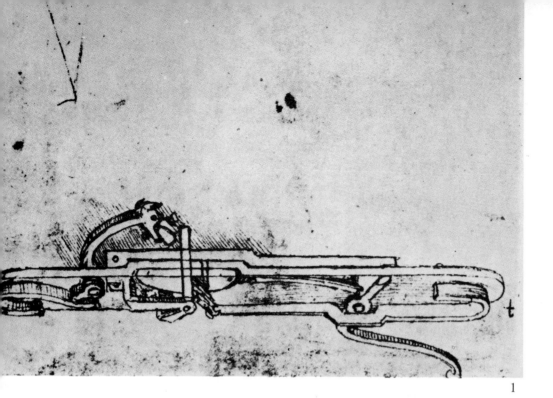

1

2

Der zornige   Juncker

Iohan Bussemacher excu.

62

3

1. *Leonardo da Vinci's design for a wheel lock from the Codex Atlanticus.*

2. *Combined spanner and priming flask.*

3. *German horseman with wheel-lock pistol, from a book dated 1601.*

4. *Carved staghorn powder flask with silver mounts by Jeremias Ritter of Nürnberg, 1605-1646.*

4

weapons themselves, there is a complete blank for the formative years. Students have yet to identify a lock known to have been made before 1520, although it is probable that a series of combined wheel locks and crossbows may have been made in Venice as early as 1510. The earliest provable wheel lock comes almost immediately thereafter, however, and it too is combined with a crossbow. This peculiar apparatus was made for Ferdinand, brother of Emperor Charles V. It bears his initials and those of his wife, and these, together with their coats of arms, indicate that it must have been made between 1521 and 1526. Several more conventional wheel locks made during the next decade for Charles V himself still survive, the earliest dated 1530. And there are a number of existing specimens of later dates.

The impact of this new gun upon warfare and upon society in general was tremendous. Here was a gun that was always ready to fire. No longer could one look for the telltale match as a sure sign of danger. Accidents could and did happen if someone "didn't know the gun was loaded."

Interestingly, one of the earliest references to a wheel lock involves just such an accident. It was recorded by Wilhelm Rem, who placed it in his *Chronica newer Geschichten* under the fascinating title, "How Laux Pfister Shot a Whore in Constance":

In the year of Our Lord 1515, on the day of the Three Holy Kings [January 6], there was a certain young citizen of Augsburg in Constance who invited a handsome whore. And when she was with him in a little room, he took up a loaded gun in his hand, the lock of which functioned in such a way that when the trigger was pressed, it ignited itself and so discharged the piece. Accordingly he played around with the gun and pressed the trigger and shot the whore through the chin, so that the bullet passed out through the back of her neck. So he had to compensate her and give her 40 florins and another 20 florins per annum for life. He also paid the doctor 37 florins, and the other costs amounted to some 30 or 40 florins.

Many morals might be learned from this adventure, not the least of which was that a wheel lock could be a very expensive toy to fool around with in certain circumstances.

Now for the first time a firearm could be carried concealed and yet be ready to shoot. As a result, the wheel lock began to supplant the sword and dagger as a weapon of sudden violence in civil life. As accidents and homicides involving the new weapon increased, the leading citizens looked on it with less and less favor. In 1517, the Emperor Maximilian I forbade the making of wheel locks, first in the hereditary Hapsburg lands and then throughout the Empire as a whole. Maximilian died the next year, however, and so it is doubtful if the ban was ever fully enforced.

Above: German petronel of 1560. Name evolved from French "poitrine," or chest—against which specially designed butt was held for firing. At right: Small wheel-lock pistol with all-metal stock, made in Nürnberg in the late 16th century.

In 1522, the city of Ferrara in Italy took action. No one was permitted to carry crossbows or firearms into the city, day or night, and wheel locks were specifically indicated. In 1523, the ordinances became more specific and more drastic still:

And since an especially dangerous kind of firearms have come to be used, which are called vulgarly stone guns [wheel locks] with which a homicide can easily be committed; in knowledge of this, His Excellency, knowing that these are devilish arms, prohibits ... their being carried ... without explicit authorization, under penalty of having a hand publicly cut off....

Modena, Milan, Florence, and other cities followed suit, "because these arms are being used more and more for murders and assassinations." Often, however, the ban came to be applied primarily to wheel locks short enough to be concealed under the clothing. Even these could usually be kept in the house and longer ones could be carried unloaded from one's home to the city gates. The authorities were definitely disturbed.

In warfare, the very features that perturbed the city fathers were considered the wheel lock's greatest advantages. A sentinel's gun could now be ready to fire at a moment's notice and the arms of all the soldiers so equipped would be equally ready. Wind and even a light rain no longer made any difference.

Most important was the fact that such prohibited small guns were now practical. With the matchlock it had been necessary to use both hands. Thus, a gun designed for use in one hand would have had very little advantage. In the Orient, matchlock pistols were made, but almost none in Europe. The wheel lock brought forth the pistol and made it an important weapon. Italy is often thought to be the pistol's birthplace and its name said to come from the city of Pistoia. The preoccupation of the Italian city fathers with these small guns early in the 1500's, and the fact that the word had spread to England by the middle of the century, seem to

1

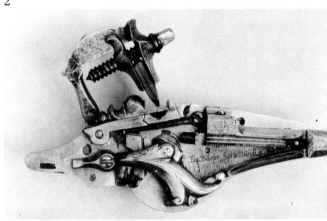

2

support this tradition. However, the Czechs maintain that it derived from the short Bohemian handgun known as a pistala, or pipe. And there have been other derivations as well as these.

Whatever its origin, the pistol now became a practical weapon for cavalry and restored the mounted warrior to a place of importance in armies throughout Europe. The series of humiliating defeats for cavalry which had begun with Crécy and continued through Poitiers, Agincourt, and the Hussite battles, among others, had led to an emphasis on infantry armed with pikes and projectile weapons. Gradually, firearms had come to dominate. Now horsemen could carry guns, too.

The German *reiters* of Charles V quickly seized upon the wheel-lock pistol and made it their own. Forming fifteen or sixteen ranks deep, they would dash up within range of the enemy but never close with him. The men in the first rank would fire each of the two pistols

4

5

1. *German patron,
or cartridge box, for wheel
lock of 1585.*

2. *Interior of a wheel lock.
The sear is between the leaves of
mainspring at right, the
chain behind the ornate bridle.*

3. *French pistol of about
1610 is inlaid with staghorn,
mother-of-pearl,
brass wire, and silver studs.*

4. *Duel on horseback with
wheel locks actually was fought
in Switzerland in 1659.*

5. *Youth fires wheel-lock
pistol into the air in late 16th
century German engraving.*

1. *German sporting gun dated 1668.*
2. *Cavalrymen armed with pistols clash in battle in the Netherlands.*
3. *Trooper fires wheel-lock carbine in early 17th century Dutch engraving.*
4. *The only English wheel-lock pistol thus far identified dates from about 1580.*
5. *17th century Dutch pistol with carved ivory stock.*

Combat de Mookerheyde.

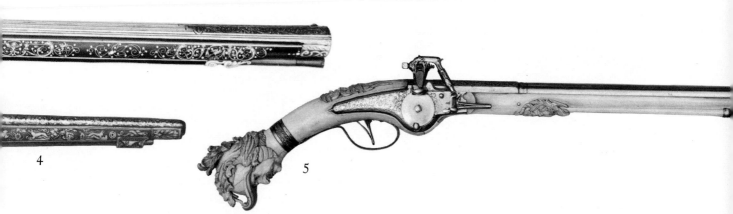

4

5

they carried in their saddle holsters, then wheel to the right or left and expose the second rank which fired in its turn. As they rode to the rear, they reloaded. Theoretically they could keep up a continuous fire in this fashion as long as necessary. For a time the tactic worked well, but the *reiters* came to put so much dependence on their pistols that they forgot the real value of cavalry as a shock troop. If the enemy charged them and insisted on fighting hand to hand, they were often defeated. Pistols were not enough to win battles by themselves.

Yet the proportion of horsemen rose and gradually great cavalry leaders such as Gustavus Adolphus of Sweden, Prince Maurice of Nassau, and, later, Oliver Cromwell of England, developed tactics that combined the shock of a mounted charge with the added strength of firearms. For all, the pistol added a new dimension of firepower for mounted men and the face of warfare changed once again.

The new lock also opened up a host of other possibilities for warfare or perhaps political use. Charges could now be exploded at a distance by pulling a string, or they could be set off by springs and a clock mechanism. Here were all kinds of opportunities undreamed of in less civilized societies. In 1573, Samuel Zimmermann of Augsburg described the possibilities of amusing fireworks and set pieces ignited by such a device. He then went on to pleasant speculation about chairs so rigged that if anyone sat in them he would be shot or at least badly burned. It would also be possible, he declared, to place in the street what appeared

to be a purse of gold, but which actually contained a device that would shoot the person who attempted to pick it up. The booby trap had arrived!

These were not just wild dreams. Such devices actually were constructed. In 1581, during the siege of Pskow, the defender, Ivan Petrovich Shujski, was sent a chest by a freed prisoner which exploded when it was opened and killed several bystanders. Explosive letters also were devised, as were trip-guns.

All of this naturally raised some question about the moral issues involved in such deceptions. It was pointed out that all of the machines were operated by their victims, who thereby gave impetus to their own demise. In 1599, the learned Jesuit Mariana dissected the niceties of the problem and ruled that although the destruction of a tyrant by putting poison in his food was sinful, since all men must eat, yet the placing of a poisoned nail in the seat of his chair was permissible, since he was not under any necessity to sit on it and did so of his own free choice. Presumably the same logic could be applied to the new infernal machines, thus adding another dimension to warfare.

In the field of ammunition and equipment there were other advances tied very closely to the development of the wheel lock. Flasks still were used for carrying the shooter's supply of powder, while a pouch held his bullets. In some instances, the spanner was mounted on the flask itself to reduce the number of separate pieces of equipment. Also, a strap known as a *porte tache* became quite popular. This device but-

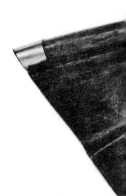

1

toned around the belt and hung down on the shooter's right side. Along it were hooks, pockets, and buttons to attach the bullet pouch, spanner, and flask, so that they might be carried more conveniently.

Most important, however, was the appearance of the cartridge. The exact date of this invention is unknown. Leonardo da Vinci mentioned cartridges a few years after 1500, and it is supposed that he was merely recording something that already had been developed. This was the first step in the practical packaging of individual charges of ammunition. The cartridges of the Sixteenth Century were simple tubes, of rolled paper, each holding enough powder for one charge. Sometimes the bullet was attached as well, but usually it was not. In order to use it, the gunner simply bit off one end, poured a little of the powder into the pan and the rest down the barrel. The ball followed and the paper itself was rammed down on top for a wad. Loading in battle was greatly speeded and much less powder was spilled. The Germans even developed a little box holding six cartridges which was worn on a string around the neck. It is known today as a "patron," from the German word for cartridge.

Throughout the Sixteenth Century these cartridges were used primarily by horsemen. It was not until Sweden's young Gustavus Adolphus ordered his infantry to use them early in the Seventeenth Century that any sizable group of foot soldiers was won over.

Still, the wheel lock did not supplant the matchlock as the principal weapon for infantry in Europe. And there were reasons, most of them related to the complex mechanism of the lock. With all its separate parts, a wheel lock was an expensive weapon. Each component had to be carefully made and skillfully fitted in place. The precision of workmanship required for a wheel lock was a far cry from the easy tolerances of the matchlock, and so it cost several times as much.

Wheel locks were rugged and dependable arms, it is true, but when trouble did develop a specialist was required. If a trigger, sear, or spring on a matchlock broke, the nearest competent blacksmith could mend it. Not so with the wheel lock. Special training and sometimes specialized tools were needed. These were not always readily available.

The iron pyrite used for making sparks was a problem. It was a soft mineral that wore

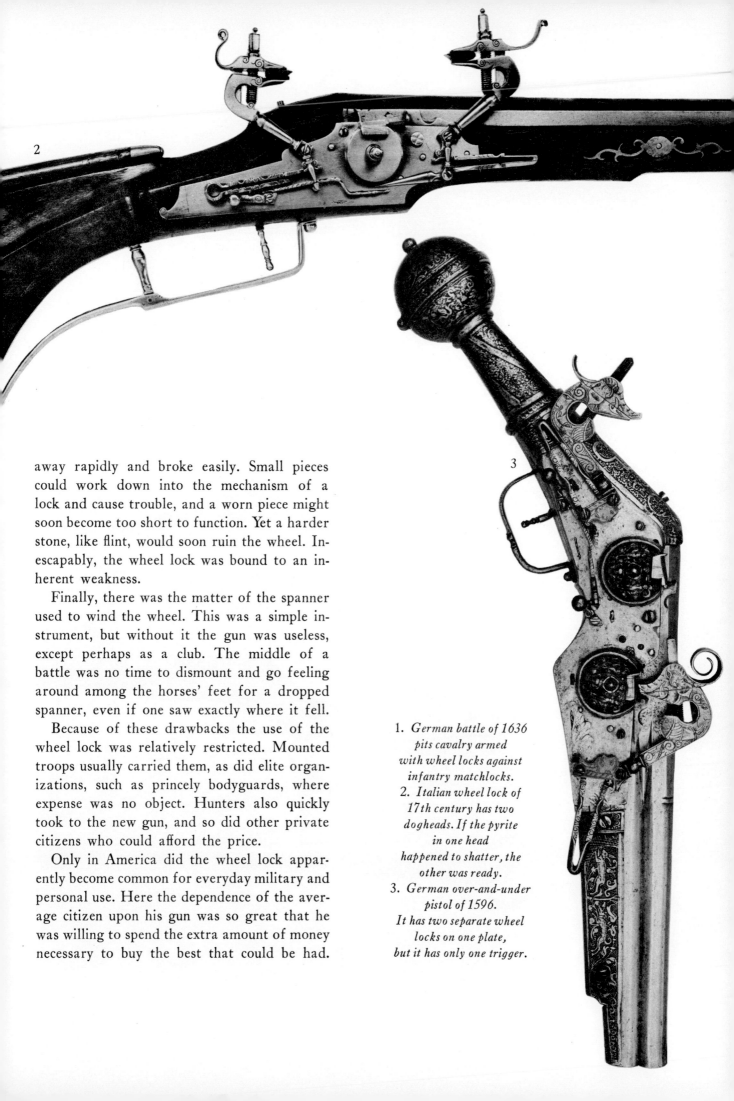

away rapidly and broke easily. Small pieces could work down into the mechanism of a lock and cause trouble, and a worn piece might soon become too short to function. Yet a harder stone, like flint, would soon ruin the wheel. Inescapably, the wheel lock was bound to an inherent weakness.

Finally, there was the matter of the spanner used to wind the wheel. This was a simple instrument, but without it the gun was useless, except perhaps as a club. The middle of a battle was no time to dismount and go feeling around among the horses' feet for a dropped spanner, even if one saw exactly where it fell.

Because of these drawbacks the use of the wheel lock was relatively restricted. Mounted troops usually carried them, as did elite organizations, such as princely bodyguards, where expense was no object. Hunters also quickly took to the new gun, and so did other private citizens who could afford the price.

Only in America did the wheel lock apparently become common for everyday military and personal use. Here the dependence of the average citizen upon his gun was so great that he was willing to spend the extra amount of money necessary to buy the best that could be had.

1. *German battle of 1636 pits cavalry armed with wheel locks against infantry matchlocks.*
2. *Italian wheel lock of 17th century has two dogheads. If the pyrite in one head happened to shatter, the other was ready.*
3. *German over-and-under pistol of 1596. It has two separate wheel locks on one plate, but it has only one trigger.*

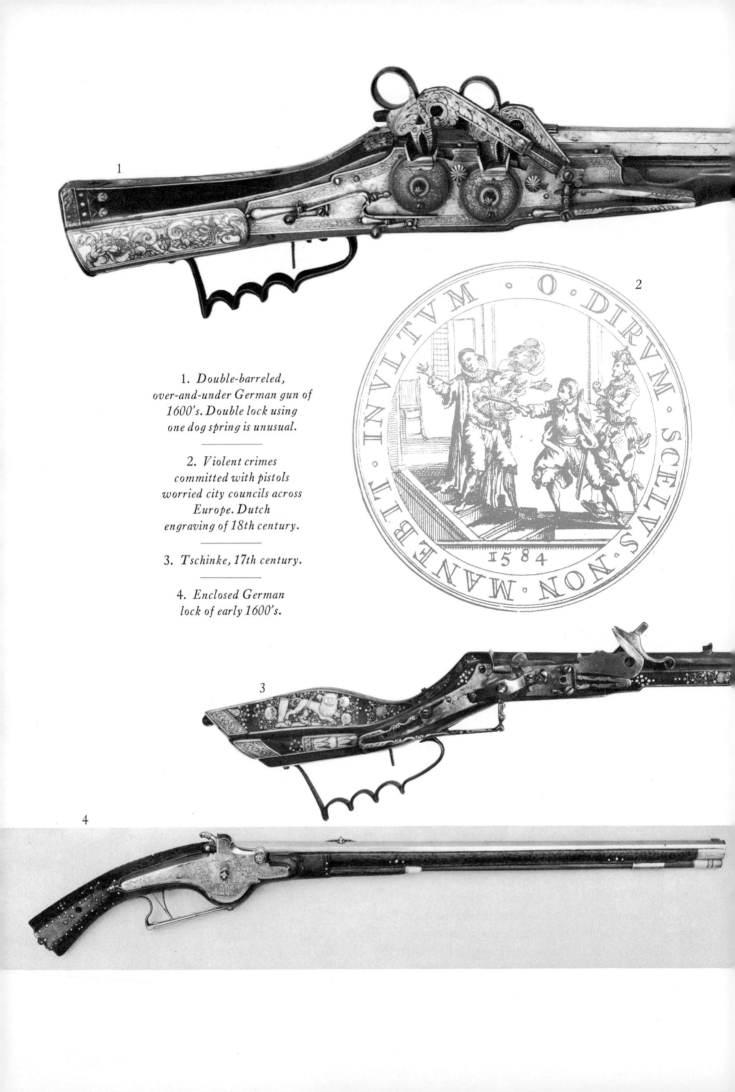

1. *Double-barreled, over-and-under German gun of 1600's. Double lock using one dog spring is unusual.*

---

2. *Violent crimes committed with pistols worried city councils across Europe. Dutch engraving of 18th century.*

---

3. *Tschinke, 17th century.*

---

4. *Enclosed German lock of early 1600's.*

Ralph Lane, governor of Sir Walter Raleigh's ill-fated "Lost Colony" on Roanoke Island, mentioned both pistols and a petronel in 1586. Far off in the arid Southwest, the expedition of Don Juan de Oñate, which wound its way north to explore and settle New Mexico, carried wheel-lock arquebuses, as well as matchlocks. Even in the English colonies, such as Jamestown, where there were few wealthy settlers, archaeological recoveries indicate that wheel locks were used to a considerable degree for both military and personal purposes.

Because the wheel lock was an expensive weapon, it developed differently from other arms. Most matchlocks were simple, crude affairs. A decorated one is a rarity. A crude wheel lock, on the other hand, is a rarity. Many were only competently made, it is true, but very few were poorly constructed. Decorated ones are common. As aristocratic weapons, care was lavished upon them to an extravagant degree and the artistry of firearms embellishment reached its zenith. Stocks were carved and inlaid with precious metals, ivory, horn, bone, mother of pearl, and fine woods, sometimes plain and sometimes colored. Metal parts were etched or engraved and sometimes chiseled in high relief. Bluing, gilding, and enameling accented the designs. Motifs ranged from scrolls, arabesques, and grotesqueries through illustrations and portraits. Classical mythology provided many themes, with Diana, Mars, Venus, and Leda among the most popular. Because of their association with guns and hunting, the Christian Saints Barbara, Hubert, and Stephen also appeared frequently. Historical, mytholog-

ical, military, erotic, or grotesque, the themes were tailored to the taste of the purchaser and the finest artists were available to create the design or execute the work. Schools of decoration developed and students of today can often recognize the court or family workshop that performed the work, and sometimes even the individual artist himself.

A little extra money was not especially important to the buyers of fine wheel locks and so they purchased these superb specimens. They also encouraged designers to devise "extras" in the hope of obtaining increased safety, greater certainty or speed of operation, more convenience, or perhaps just something different. Gunsmiths, clockmakers, and other mechanics seized the opportunity. Fearful and wonderful productions resulted. An extra doghead for holding a reserve piece of pyrite was added in case the regular one broke at an inconvenient time. More conservative designers or patrons sometimes added a serpentine for holding a match instead of the auxiliary doghead. After all, the entire mechanism might give out and then the old way would still be available. There were complete double locks, multiple barrels, and other arrangements for producing a volley of shot or repeating shots. Little chimneys were added to carry the smoke of the priming away from the shooter's eyes. The wheel and sometimes almost all the mechanism were moved inside the lock plate to protect it from the weather. There were locks that wound themselves by simply moving the doghead forward and back, thus eliminating the separate spanner and speeding the loading process.

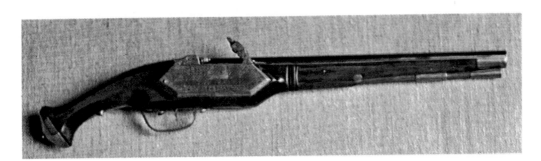

Above: Last-known wheel-lock pistol, one of a pair by Le Page, 1829. Left: Bergier's waterproof wheel lock made for Louis XIII.

Finally came the modern advertising man's dream: a wheel lock that would shoot under water! This mechanical marvel was designed by Pierre Bergier, a watchmaker of Grenoble. The lock was enclosed and hermetically sealed. The lock plate and all the mounts were gilded bronze to avoid rusting. It is assumed that the muzzle, at least, must have been left above water. Otherwise the barrel would have burst when it was fired. The shooter also would have had to emerge to re-span his wheels through the trap doors in the left side, reload, and prime, before submerging for another demonstration. Doubtless there must have been some advantage in a gun of this sort, even if it is not readily apparent.

At any rate, Bergier made several of these guns. To add to the complications, he normally made them capable of firing two or more shots, with the charges loaded one on top of the other in the same barrel and separate wheels and dogheads for each shot. In 1634, he made a four-shot arquebus in this fashion and presented it to Louis XIII. Louis, always

very fond of guns, was delighted and conferred royal letters of patent on the inventor. Two more arquebuses were presented to the king the next year and then, in 1634, a pair of two-shot pistols, all finely executed as befitted guns for a royal collection. With these arms the gadgetry of the wheel lock reached its apogee. There was no place else to go.

Even in its simplest forms, the wheel lock was made in a greater variety of shapes and sizes than the early matchlock maker would have dreamed possible. The muskets and lighter arquebuses continued. Then there were the pistols, clumsy angular things in the beginning, often with heavy, bulbous butts, then becoming slender and graceful in the early 1600's. At the other end of the scale were huge wall guns designed as a sort of light artillery to be fired from castle walls or from other fortifications. There were carbines for horsemen and variations catering to the preferences of the different geographical areas.

The most pronounced of these regional types was probably the *tschinke* made in the

German Baltic provinces. Large numbers have survived and are immediately recognizable, even by the layman, as an unusual gun. These were sporting arms, not weapons, as their slender, fragile-looking form immediately suggests. Most of the lock mechanism was mounted on the outside of the lock plate, thus making them even more frail. The most arresting feature, however, is the tiny, slanted butt. Such a gun is a reminder that even at the beginning of the Seventeenth Century many Germans still did not shoot with the butt braced against the shoulder, but held well above it.

In its myriad forms and variations, the wheel lock continued to be made for some two hundred years. From its center in southern Germany, Austria, and northern Italy, it spread throughout all German-speaking countries. Charles V brought some wheel-lock makers from his German domain to Spain after he became Holy Roman Emperor, and it was his delight to serve as an amateur gunsmith himself when he could afford the time. Other European countries imported wheel locks from these centers,

but gradually makers developed in France, Denmark, the Low Countries, and even in distant Sweden and England. By 1650, its popularity was on the wane as simpler, cheaper guns proved themselves just as efficient. Some Central European areas clung to it out of sheer tradition, even into the next century, but as an important arm its day had passed. Probably the last wheel locks ever made commercially were a highly refined pair of pistols produced by Le Page in Paris and dated 1829. By then they were anachronisms.

73

Preceding pages: English dog-lock
musket of about 1640 was a type widely used in
American colonies and English Civil War.

PECKING ROOSTERS AND BITING DOGS

Hard on the heels of the wheel lock came a whole group of ignitions that produced sparks by the striking of flint against a steel. It is not impossible that at least one of these may have developed at almost the same time as the wheel lock. Early references are often vague and could apply either to a wheel lock or a snapping lock. Both types were self-igniting and used a stone, and these frequently were the only elements noted by the commentators, who gave little heed to the problems of future arms historians. By 1547, however, incontestable documents from such diverse points as Italy and Sweden show that snapping locks were known and in use.

All of the snapping locks copied the actions of the householder in striking sparks with his flint and steel to start a fire. A carefully sharpened piece of flint was clamped in the jaws of a vise on one end of an arm. The other end was pivoted so that the jaws bearing the flint could be swung in an arc. Directly opposite was a bar of steel, also mounted on a pivoted arm, and just below this was the priming pan. A heavy, V-shaped mainspring supplied the power to throw forward the arm holding the flint, so that the stone struck the steel a sharp, glancing blow and sent a shower of sparks cascading into the powder in the pan. These were the basic elements in all flint arms, but regional preferences and evolutionary stages produced a half-dozen major types and a host of minor variants.

One of the more primitive and probably one of the first was the snaphaunce. It likely was developed in the Low Countries sometime before 1550, and its very name is indicative of its action. The sharp striking movement of the vise holding the flint reminded early Dutchmen of the pecking action of a rooster and they called it a *schnapp-hahn,* or pecking cock. The flint vise itself became known as a *hahn* or cock, and the bar of steel was sometimes called a hen. This analogy was also adopted in Germany, Scandinavia, and even in England, although the Dutch *schnapp-hahn* quickly became corrupted there to snaphaunce or snaphance, the terms still used today. These same countries also accepted the name cock for the flint vise, but usually preferred steel, battery, or hammer for the bar of steel it struck.

The origin of the name snaphaunce was much too prosaic to be accepted by the romanticists of the last century. With their gifted imaginations they soon devised far more interesting derivations. The most successful and popular of these maintained that the lock had been invented by Dutch chicken thieves who, it was claimed, were called *schnapp hähner,* or

chicken snatchers. The glowing coal of a matchlock was a liability in their profession. If the farmer himself didn't notice the glow or smell the burning wick, his dog was very likely to. The local gentry were remarkably unsympathetic to such activities and justice was harsh—if, indeed, the apprehended culprit survived to be accorded that honor. A more efficient and less visible gun was needed if the poultry pilferer hoped to achieve success and remain healthy. Thus, these clever chicken snatchers developed a new sort of a gun which was named after them. So goes the legend and it has been a remarkably hardy one. Even today it crops up from time to time, a tribute to the superiority of imagination over actuality.

The Dutch snaphaunce is quickly recognizable by its big S-shaped cock and the large disc usually found on the exterior end of the pan. The pan itself was generally formed as a half-cylinder with a sliding cover. The steel bore against a spring in much the same manner as the doghead of a wheel lock, so that it could be at rest in two positions — either directly above the pan or pushed forward out of the way. This second position of the steel provided a safety factor. Even with the piece loaded and primed, there could be no possibility of an accidental discharge if the steel was not in a position to be struck by the flint.

The inner mechanism was simple. The shank of the cock passed through a hole in the lock plate and was fitted with a lug called a tumbler. When the cock was pulled back to the "set," or "cocked," position, it rotated the tumbler and compressed the mainspring. At the same time, it allowed the end of a horizontally moving sear to slip through a hole in the lock plate and catch the tail of the cock, thus holding it in position with the mainspring compressed. When the trigger was pulled, this sear was retracted and the cock was driven forward against the steel. At the same time, a plunger automatically opened the pan cover to receive the sparks. This was a far cry from the complicated wheel

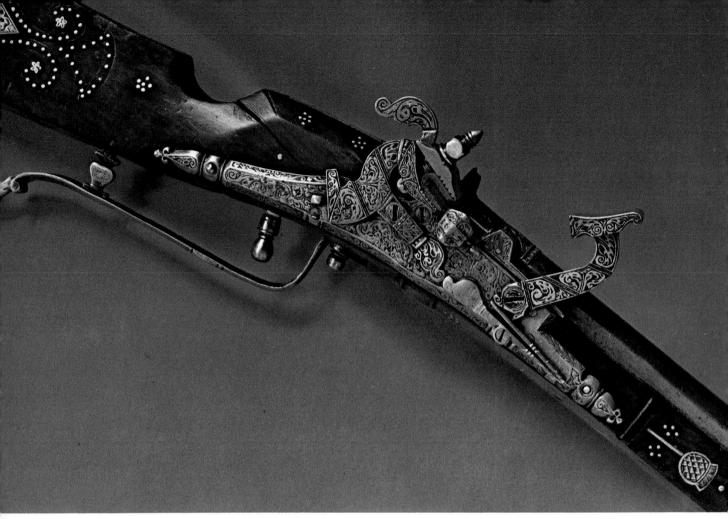

*Above: Scottish snaphaunce
lock on a birding piece made for King Charles I.
Trigger guard is unusual on a Scottish gun.*

*Below: Italian snaphaunce with finely
chiseled barrel and mounts, had separate steel and
pan cover, differed much from Dutch version.*

lock and permissible tolerances were much greater. Consequently, the snaphaunce was both cheaper to manufacture and easier to repair.

The Dutch were a great merchant people. Fat-waisted ships from the Netherlands carried goods from many nations. All of the North Sea was under their dominion in the middle years of the Sixteenth Century, and soon Dutch vessels were active in the Mediterranean, along the west coast of Africa, and in the Indian Ocean. With the Dutch ships and merchants went the Dutch snaphaunce. It influenced the design of firearms in other north European areas such as England, Scotland, and the Baltic and Scandinavian countries, which manufactured their own arms, and it became a popular trade item in parts of Africa, where there was no established gun industry. Later, when guns were made by native craftsmen, they either used imported locks or made copies as exactly as they could. Tradition and custom are most important in such areas of the world. The Dutch-type lock was the one they were used to and it was the type of lock they demanded on any new gun they might buy. In Morocco, for instance, the primitive snaphaunce was still being made as late as 1885, centuries after it had disappeared in the land which gave it birth.

Meanwhile, in the south of Europe quite a different form of snapping lock had developed. This was the miquelet, a much more sophisticated and efficient mechanism than the Dutch snaphaunce. It was popular in both Spain and Italy, and indeed there is considerable doubt as to which of them invented it.

The date of the miquelet's appearance also is a matter for conjecture. In 1547, the Duke of Florence forbade the carrying of firearms short enough to conceal, and he specifically mentioned both wheel locks and flint arms. As far as is known, the Dutch snaphaunce was never popular in Italy, so this must have referred to a native type, either the full-blown miquelet or its immediate forerunner. Unfortunately, no Italian flint arms of this period have

been identified and it is possible only to guess.

In Spain, the invention of the miquelet has been attributed to Simon Marquarte II, son of the Simon Marquarte the Emperor Charles V brought to that country to make wheel locks. Alonzo Martines de Espinar, who wrote about guns in 1644, while Marquarte was still living, was more cautious, however. He simply stated that Marquarte made more such locks than any other kind and that he was the greatest maker of them ever known. Once again, no Spanish miquelets made much before 1600 have yet been identified, and there are no earlier pictures or descriptions.

Such is the puzzle. But puzzles always invite a solution or at least a guess. With this in mind, a tentative nod might well go to Italy. The earliest documentary references to flint arms come from there. A combined wheel-and-flint lock which may date as early as 1550, and certainly no later than 1600, is preserved in Turin. The Italian lock is cruder than the Spanish form, and since Simon Marquarte II of Spain is credited with either inventing the lock or, more likely, improving it during the last years of the century, it may be that it was the Italian mechanism he refined. Not much to go on, but at least it is possible.

Dutch snaphaunce shows
classic form of
the lock, with circular shield
on the end of the pan.

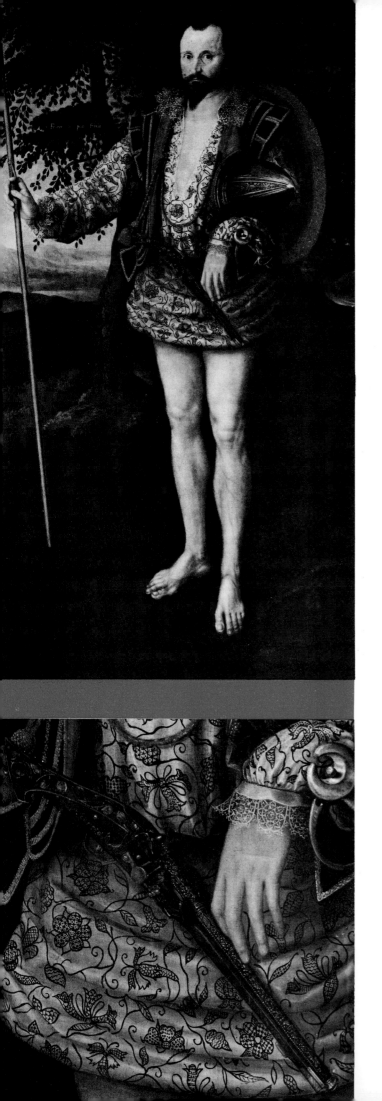

Both Italian and Spanish locks had far fewer parts than the snaphaunce. And they had other advantages. One important improvement was the development of a means of combining the steel with the pan cover into one L-shaped device which has come to be known as the hammer, or frizzen. This step in itself eliminated four moving parts, thus simplifying the mechanism and insuring that the pan cover would open properly the moment the flint struck the steel and knocked it back. Another characteristic of the miquelet was its exceptionally heavy mainspring, which was fastened outside the lock plate rather than inside, as in most other locks of the period.

The cock also was distinctive in form—only it wasn't called a cock. In the countries of the south its action reminded the people of a biting dog, and throughout Italy, Spain, and France a dog it was. Frequently it was even sculptured or engraved to resemble that animal. But, dog or cock, it had small projections at its base so that the mainspring could bear directly against it without needing a tumbler. Thus, one more part was eliminated.

The principal difference between the Italian and the Spanish locks lies in the way the mainspring acted upon the cock. In the Italian form, the spring pushed down upon the toe. In the Spanish, it pushed up against the heel. As in the snaphaunce, the sear nose still passed through the lock plate to catch the cock and hold it in position. Now, however, there were two separate sear noses because it was necessary to add an extra position—"half cock" as it came to be known in English. This was a safety position. The cock was drawn back far enough for the pan to be primed and closed, but supposedly it could not be fired until it had been drawn back to full cock. Then the action of the trigger withdrew both sears and let the cock move with the impulse of the spring. In the Italian locks the angle at which the flint in the cock struck the steel was not so efficient as in the Spanish version. Also, the manner in which the sear noses engaged the heel of the cock caused them to work out of adjustment after they had become a little worn. For these reasons the Spanish lock was much the better of the two.

The virtues of the Spanish miquelet were many. As was noted, it was even simpler than the snaphaunce. Therefore, it cost less and there was less chance for something to go wrong. Also, with its extremely powerful spring and the excellent angle at which the flint struck the steel, it was possible to produce sparks with almost any piece of flint. While other locks required carefully shaped flints with sharp edges, a Spaniard could pick up a fairly rough piece of almost any size, fit it into the adaptable jaws of the cock, and obtain enough sparks for ignition. The huge ring atop the jaw screw also was an advantage. It meant the screw could be turned by hand and did not require a screwdriver or other tool, as was the case with almost all other locks. Here was a rugged, serviceable gun and an inexpensive one, too. For

these reasons it remained popular in Spain until the era of spark-striking locks was past. None of the other European forms offered serious competition to the miquelet.

With all its advantages, one would have expected the miquelet to spread outside Spain and Italy. It did, but not to the north. Other Europeans had their own local mechanisms and were not sufficiently impressed with the lock from south of the Pyrenees to junk them. The route for expansion lay to the south. The Dutch snaphaunce was established in Morocco, but Arabia quickly accepted the miquelet. As the popularity of the lock moved eastward along the southern shore of the Mediterranean, it spread over to Sardinia, then on to Turkey, Persia, and up through the Caucasus to southern Russia. There were regional variations, but all were essentially the miquelet.

The very name miquelet is actually a misnomer, and many students today prefer to call it the "Mediterranean lock" because of its dominance along the shores of that sea. Like the snaphaunce, the miquelet also has a romantic legend to account for its beginning. And as in the case of the snaphaunce, the tale is false. In fact, it is generally the same story with just a change in locale. In the northern parts of Spain, along the Pyrenees, in Aragon and Catalonia, lived a band of cutthroats and assassins known playfully as *Los Miguletes or Miqueletes*—the Little Michaels. These worthy fellows had the same problems with the matchlock as their chicken-snatching confreres in the Netherlands. What more natural, then, than that one ingenious member of the brotherhood should invent a new gun which eliminated the pesky match and made their lives simpler, safer, and more pleasant? Not knowing the name of this

clever cutthroat, the populace, it is said, identified the lock with the whole group—miquelet.

Actually, the term miquelet was not picked up and applied to the gun until well into the Nineteenth Century, when its days were almost over. In the period of its greatest popularity, it was known among the Spaniards themselves as a *patilla* lock, probably because of the small foot at the base of the cock. Outside Spain, gun enthusiasts of the Seventeenth and Eighteenth Centuries called it simply the Spanish lock. But once again it is doubtful that actuality will ever catch up with imagination.

Aside from their excellent lock, the Spanish gunsmiths also made one other notable contribution to gun construction. They produced the finest gun barrels in Europe. And the story of the discovery of the "secret process" (at least as recorded by the Eighteenth Century gunsmith Isidro Solér) is just as fascinating as the legends of the snaphaunce and miquelet locks.

According to Solér, the actual discoverer of the secret was not really a Spaniard, but a German, Nicholas Bis, who had been brought to Spain in 1691 by King Charles II, and who later became gunmaker to Philip V. Bis was disturbed by the quality of Spanish barrels, which

frequently burst when tested. The barrels had been well forged and should not have behaved badly. Bis decided that the material was at fault rather than the workmanship.

Better iron had to be found and Bis set out to look for it. Finally, he determined that the iron in Biscayan horseshoes was the most ductile in all of Europe and, therefore, the most suitable for making gun barrels. The roughness and lack of malleability of the raw iron that had been used previously had been its chief weaknesses. So Bis carefully selected a number of shoes that had been well worn and trodden on horses' feet. Starting with fifty pounds of horseshoes, he divided them into five piles, the first weighing fourteen pounds, the second twelve pounds, and the remaining three eight pounds each. Each pile was heated in the furnace, cut, folded, and welded over and over, a total of thirty-two times. Then the largest mass was forged into the breech of the barrel, the next into the section just ahead of the breech, and the succeeding pieces completed the tube to the muzzle. Welded together, they produced a barrel weighing about five pounds. Ninety per cent of the metal with which he had started was consumed in the fire.

1. *Neapolitan or Sardinian miquelet, 17th century.*
2. *Italian miquelet lock. Note that mainspring pushes down on toe of the cock.* 3. *Spanish miquelet of 19th century with spring pushing up on heel of cock.*
4. *A Spanish battle scene, done in 1806.*

It was a complicated process, and Bis was ridiculed at first. Then his success won over other gunsmiths, who began to follow the same procedure. The fiery Alonso Martinéz, a fellow apprentice with Bis in the early days, even went his friend one better by making a barrel completely from horseshoe nails. This was strictly a *tour de force* to show his skill. He never made another and no other gunsmith emulated him.

In addition to the miquelet, Italy also produced a snaphaunce. But it was far different from the Dutch version, and its period of popularity was later. It had a sear which acted vertically to engage a notch in the tumbler and hold the mainspring compressed in the full-cocked position, instead of a horizontal sear that passed through the lock plate and engaged the cock, as in the Dutch snaphaunce and the miquelet locks. In fact, its only similarity to the Dutch lock—and the reason for its being called a snaphaunce—was the fact that the steel and the pan cover were separate pieces. Most surviving Italian locks of this form are finely made, sophisticated pieces of the Seventeenth and early Eighteenth Centuries.

The Dutch snaphaunce had no connection whatsoever with the miquelet. It may or may not have influenced the Italian snaphaunce. But it certainly did color the development of snapping locks in England and Scotland, with both of whom the Dutch had very close trade ties.

In Scotland the influence was most direct. Dutch arms and locks were imported and used in quantity. Then, as the Scots developed their own arms industry late in the Sixteenth Century, they began to copy the guns with which they were familiar. The Dutch mechanism was adopted completely, although the Scottish craftsmen looked to their own Celtic tradition for ornamentation and design. For some reason, the Highland gunsmiths and shooters seem to have had an aversion to trigger guards. Almost none are encountered on Scottish-made firearms. In the era of the snaphaunce there was no chance of an accidental discharge if the steel was pushed forward. When the French, or "true," flintlock came along later, however, the exposed ball-trigger was a distinct hazard —especially on those arms which had no half-cock position. There must have been many unpleasant accidents, a high price to pay for tradition—or so it must have seemed to the average Sassenach, at least.

Although in the beginning, the Scots adopted the Dutch mechanism intact for their arms, the stocks and mounts were completely indigenous and it is by these features that a collector usually first learns to recognize a Scottish firearm. Long guns with Scottish locks are extremely rare. Perhaps no more than twenty-four survive today—and some think they always were rarities. After one has seen such a gun, however, it is almost impossible to mistake it for anything else. No other area in Europe produced such light, curving butts with fluted channeling and carved Gothic traceries. Sometimes the uninitiated identify them as Arabian or Moorish arms, but this is the only possible confusion.

The pistols also are most distinctive and there is no chance of misidentification. The earliest snaphaunces sometimes had wooden stocks with brass or silver mounts. But even in the beginning there were stocks made completely of brass, and soon the all-metal stocks became a Scottish characteristic, universally used. Generally the stocks were made of iron, but brass was also used occasionally. Inlay and engraving enhanced the decorative effect of pol-

ished metal and graceful design. Butts resembling hearts, ram's horns, lemons, or kidneys flowed smoothly from the grips. In the center of each was screwed a metal pricker for cleaning out the touchhole if it should become clogged with powder fouling. Since Scottish pistols were usually carried on the person rather than in saddle holsters, a hook was placed on the left side, opposite the lock, so that it could be fastened to its owner's belt.

In some early documents, these Highland pistols are called "cutthroat's pistols," which raises an interesting speculation about the number of such gentry in Scotland. Certainly there were far more of these pistols than there were long guns—if any comparison of respectability was intended.

Indeed, the references to violence with this weapon are frequent, and the butt was used just as often as the muzzle. On January 28, 1596, for instance, a citizen of Edinburgh was set upon by rogues who "dang him with pistolettis on the heid and...sair hurt him." A few years later, in 1622, a messenger named Adam Scott had experience with both ends of the gun. On

July 22, he encountered Sir Robert McClennane of Bambie. Apparently, Sir Robert had no desire to see him, for he promptly thrust a pair of pistols against Scott's chest and pulled the triggers. From the poor courier's point of view, the providential double misfire undoubtedly made up for all the misfortunes that had ever befallen him. But still he suffered sore wounds from Sir Robert's pistol butts and sword before he could get away. With such hard usage, the Scottish pistol had need of its all-metal construction.

As the years passed the Scots modified their locks. The tail on the cock was removed. The sear still moved laterally, but sometimes it engaged a notch in the tumbler and sometimes it passed through the lock plate and held the front of the cock instead of catching the rear.

South of the border, the English also imported many arms from the Low Countries and Germany. They, too, borrowed the Dutch snaphaunce action, but usually they combined the separate steel and pan cover into a frizzen. This was an improvement over the Dutch lock, although it also increased the bugaboo of accidental discharges. Unlike the Scots, the English were not willing to risk this. They devised a little hook to catch the rear of the cock and hold it safely at half cock until it was pulled all the way back just before firing. This little hook was called a "dog," and collectors have come to call locks that have them "dog locks,"

while the older locks are identified simply as English locks. Sometimes an extra notch was cut in the tumbler to form a half-cock position instead, but this never worked well with a laterally acting sear. The notches could not be cut deeply enough or sharply enough, and with a little wear the sear tended to slip out of position and let the cock fall forward unexpectedly. When this happened the piece "went off half-cocked." The frequency of such unpleasant events added a phrase to the language that is still used to describe any premature or ill-prepared venture. The miquelets, with their better-designed safeties, seem seldom to have had this difficulty. At least there is no comparable expression in Spanish or Italian!

At this time, the ownership of firearms in England was still controlled by an ancient law of Henry VIII, passed by Parliament in 1542. Just as the Italian states had recoiled in horror at the use of firearms for crimes which somehow seemed worse than those done with such tried-and-true weapons as sword or dagger, so the English took note that diverse persons of

... malicious and evill disposed myndes and purposes have wilfully and shamefully commytted, perpetrated and done diverse detestable and shamefull murthers, robberies, felonyes, ryotts and routes with Crossbowes, lyttle shorte handguns and little hagbutts, to the great perill and contynuall feare and daunger of the Kings most lovinge subjects....

85

To remedy this unfortunate situation, Parliament decreed that no one could shoot one of these weapons, or even keep it in his house, unless he had lands or income with a yearly value of over one hundred pounds. Evil purposes apparently could be expected to disappear when one had crossed that financial threshold. There was, however, one interesting exception—everyone who lived along the seashore or near the border of Scotland was encouraged to obtain firearms and practice with them. Qualifications of income or social standing could be waived for persons residing in such perilous locations.

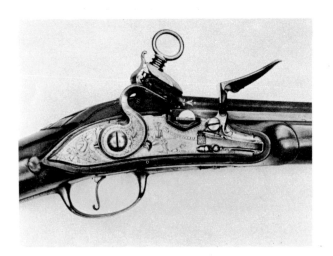

Despite vigorous enforcement, this income-geared legislation did not entirely correct the situation. For one thing, marksmanship was apparently rather poor, and for another the enthusiastic English sportsman could not seem to resist a good target no matter where he saw it. Birds were especially fine objects to shoot at and sometimes good to eat, as well. The trouble was that they were often found perched on a house, church, or other building, and even if the fowler's aim was excellent, the building was bound to suffer, especially when bird shot was used. One Sixteenth Century London tailor, for instance, chanced to spy a likely bird through his window. Having his gun handy, he leaned out over the sill and let fly. Unfortunately, he potted a fellow citizen instead, and this led to much unpleasantness. Finally, in 1549, Parliament decreed that:

. . . noe person under the degree of Lord in Parliament shall henceforth shote in any hand-gunne within any citie or towne at any fowle or other mark, upon anie church, house or dove-cote, neither shal any person shote . . . any hayl-shot [bird shot] or any more pellets than one at a tyme, upon payne of tenne pounds. . . .

Passersby might now be safe from sporting tailors, but they would still do well to avoid the residences of the nobility.

Nevertheless, the popularity of birding increased. The poorer classes found in it the means of increasing their food supply, both through consuming the birds themselves and also through preventing the birds from consuming their crops. Wealthier Englishmen at first apparently considered birding only a form of target practice, but later it became a sport to be enjoyed for itself.

This was the period that gave birth to the famous Seventeenth Century English birding piece, the first gun to be so specialized. It was a huge affair, too, with its English or dog lock and a barrel five or six feet long. The British sportsman of that era believed that the longer the barrel, the greater the charge he could use, and hence the longer the range and the flatter the trajectory of the bullet's flight. In this theory he completely overlooked the braking action of the increased friction between ball and bore, but this knowledge would not come until much later. There were some short birding pieces, too, usually distinguishable from muskets or calivers by a slight flare at the muzzle and ornamental moldings.

The long pieces were more popular by far. They brought sport and food along the streams and marshes of England, and when Civil War broke out between Parliament and Charles I, they saw service defending castles and manor houses, where their size was no hindrance and their supposedly greater range was considered an advantage.

SEARCHING the PHEASANT

*Opposite page:
Spanish flintlock
with sear nose
in front of cock.
Left:
Pheasant
hunting, from
a sporting book of
1686. In
silhouette are
two views of
long fowler with
English lock
used in colonial
Connecticut
in 1625-1630.*

87

English dog-lock pistol with cast-brass barrel was brought to Plymouth in the year 1622, by John Thompson.

The English settlers of America brought their long fowlers with them. In 1621, Edward Winslow wrote home from Plymouth to people who might be planning to join the Pilgrims, telling them to be sure to bring such guns and advising: "Let your piece be long in the barrel; and fear not the weight of it, for most of our shooting is from stands [blinds]."

Within a few years there were a good number of such pieces in the new land, providing food and defending garrison houses against Indian attack. One early colonist even succeeded in bringing down a crow on the wing, a feat which impressed the Indians as much as it probably surprised the shooter.

Other firearms with English and dog locks came to America as well, especially muskets and pistols. More efficient than the matchlock, cheaper and simpler than the wheel lock, they soon supplanted both in the English colonies.

In England itself the change was slower. There were large supplies of matchlocks on hand and a change-over would have been expensive. The matchlock's disadvantages were not so damaging in formal warfare as they were in sport, thievery, or on the frontier. Then, too, there were the long years of civil war that absorbed the country's energies and drained its finances. Thus, the English lock and dog lock remained just two of several systems in use, until the French flintlock superseded all other locks at the close of the Seventeenth Century.

While English and Scottish locks followed in the pattern of the Dutch snaphaunce, and the miquelet locks of Spain and Italy dominated the shores of the Mediterranean, still another snapping lock developed in the far north of Europe. Students today call it the Scandinavian snap lock. Sweden probably first produced the new mechanism shortly before 1550, and from there it spread west to Norway and east and south through Finland and the Baltic provinces, picking up minor variations along the way.

This lock from the far north combined details of both the Dutch snaphaunce and the miquelet. An external mainspring pushed up against the heel of the cock, just as it did in the Spanish miquelet, while steel and pan cover were frequently made in two pieces as they were in Dutch locks. Sometimes, however, steel and pan cover were combined. Then the lock closely resembled a miquelet in mechanism, but not in shape. Scandinavian locks had an appearance all their own. The slender angular or straight cocks were like nothing found in any other area. They are the distinctive feature that immediately stamps a lock as being Scandinavian. Minor details of the jaw attachment

tell students whether a lock was made in Sweden, Norway, or the Baltic provinces.

The Scandinavian snap lock was hardly a sophisticated mechanism. Occasionally a well-made specimen is found on a fine sporting gun, but most of those that survive were made for muskets or simple hunting guns. Wheel locks were imported for many of the fine arms during the Sixteenth Century, and later the French flintlock became more popular. In the far reaches of the northern and eastern forests, however, professional hunters and peasants clung to the traditional lock until modern times.

Thus it was that from the frigid wastes of northern Sweden to the arid sands of Arabia, from the western tip of England to the remote villages of the Caucasus, flint arms were bought, traded, or manufactured. Within a short span of years, all of these different locks and their variants had developed. All were simple. All worked. The principle was sound. What was needed was refinement.

Swedish snaplock rifle
of late 17th century, with barrel
signed by Samuel Ridderspore.

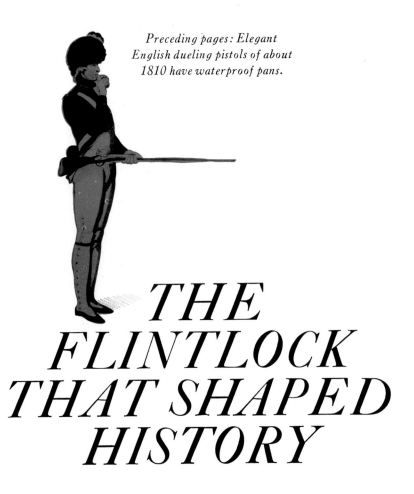

CHAPTER 5

Preceding pages: Elegant English dueling pistols of about 1810 have waterproof pans.

THE FLINTLOCK THAT SHAPED HISTORY

The gunlocks of Northern and Southern Europe met on the middle ground of France. Here the best of each was combined to bring the spark-striking mechanism to its highest development in the "true" flintlock. From France the flintlock spread to most of Western Europe, and for two hundred years it was the finest gunlock made. More than any previous gun, it played a decisive role in events that shaped the world. With it were fought the great wars of the Eighteenth Century that determined the rulers of Austria and Spain, and made France pre-eminent on the Continent. In North America, the French and British fought with flintlocks for a colonial empire. American revolutionaries used the gun to gain independence in the 1770's and to defend it in 1812. And French and English 92 flintlock muskets brought the era to its climax in the epochal Napoleonic Wars.

ost of the great early firearms inventors are unknown. Their names are lost beyond even the wildest guess. Not so with the father of the flintlock. Here for the first time it is possible to point with reasonable certainty to the exact man, and to the place and date of the new lock's origin. True, there is no absolute proof of authorship, but the circumstantial evidence is overwhelming. And it is unanimous. Every clue points to Marin le Bourgeoys as the inventor, the little village of Lisieux in Normandy as the place, and the years 1610 to 1615 as the time.

Marin le Bourgeoys was born in this village. The date is not known for sure, but it was about 1550. There was little in his appearance to suggest the genius that lay within. He had a peasant's face with high cheekbones and a broad, heavy nose. In later years a luxurious white beard and mustache hid the thick lips and lent dignity to his countenance. But the bulging, frog-like eyes were keen despite their heavy lids, and his hands were deft.

Le Bourgeoys was descended from a line of skilled craftsmen. His ancestors had been locksmiths, clockmakers, and armorers. As was usual in that age, young Marin followed in their footsteps, but soon he displayed a wider-ranging genius that raised him far above the usual level. He was a superior workman and innovator in all of the family trades. Before inventing the flintlock, his arms production had included wheel locks, snaphaunces, crossbows, and at least one air gun. He was also a sculptor, a painter, and a maker of musical instruments, planetariums, and "other mechanical inventions."

Such outstanding talent gained him recognition and honors far outside his native town. In 1589, the Governor of Normandy appointed him to be his official painter. By 1598 his fame had spread to the capital in Paris and King Henry IV made him a *valet de chambre*. In 1608, further honor followed with a warrant of lodgings in the Grand Gallery of the Louvre Palace as "painter and *valet de chambre*, worker in moving globes, sculptor and mechanical inventor" to the king. This was a signal distinction for the provincial Norman, but still he preferred to dwell in his native village, journeying only occasionally to Paris to deliver a gun or one of his other productions to the king. After Henry's death in 1610, Marin continued to work for his successor, Louis XIII, and it was for that monarch that he made the first known flintlock. By this time le Bourgeoys was well into middle age, but he had productive years still ahead and he fashioned many more of his new guns in the Lisieux shop before his death in 1634.

Like most French gunsmiths, le Bourgeoys was thoroughly familiar with Dutch snaphaunces and Mediterranean miquelets, both of which had been made in France before 1600. Le Bourgeoys' inspiration was to join the two to produce a hardy French hybrid. From the miquelet he took the combined steel and pan cover, and from the snaphaunce the inside mechanism with the mainspring bearing on a tumbler. Then he added his own touch. Instead of having the sear move laterally, as it had in the wheel locks and all the other flint arms, he redesigned it so that it moved vertically. Here was an extremely significant improvement. It strengthened the action and, most important, it permitted a really safe half-cock position.

So good was the new arm that its fame spread quickly. Well before le Bourgeoys' death, his brother Jean and his apprentices were making true flintlocks. By the mid-1630's, books of decorations suitable for the new lock were being published in Paris as knowledge of the the invention spread throughout France.

Here was the gun that finally supplanted the matchlock as the standard military arm. It eliminated the hazards and unreliability of the lighted match, avoided the expense of the wheel lock, and overcame the crudities of the early flint arms. Change took time, but by 1700 every

93

*Preceding pages: Muskets of
Revolution (top to bottom) are Charleville,
the Brown Bess, American, and German.*

major power had adopted the flintlock musket.

Dozens of different models appeared as each nation developed the musket that best suited its tastes. The English seized upon the vertically acting sear and applied it to their own locks, which already had the one-piece frizzen.

From Hesse and Hanover in Germany came heavy-butted monsters with calibers of .80 and more. Potsdam arsenals boasted narrow-butted Prussian patterns with equally big bores and the iron ramrods that Frederick the Great insisted upon. Austrian or Dutch, Scandinavian or Italian, each was distinctive. And each played a role in the turbulent years from Blenheim to Waterloo—more than a century of formal warfare on three continents in which the flintlock musket reigned supreme.

Of the many shapes and sizes of muskets to belch smoke and ball in these critical years, two stand out above the rest: the British Brown Bess and the French Charleville. These were guns of destiny, celebrated in legend and verse —and in actual history as well. From the early 1700's through 1815, they dominated the battlefields of Europe, America, and India, and even later small numbers of them continued to hurl their huge lead balls with deadly effect in minor actions around the world.

Brown Bess was the affectionate nickname given to his musket by the British soldier. No one knows how the name originated. Some have tried to link it with Queen Elizabeth, but there were more than a hundred years between the death of the one and the birth of the other, so that such an association would have been remote indeed. More likely, the "Bess" was simply a pet name such as men have often applied to guns, and the "Brown" stemmed from the artificial browning of the barrel and the color of the walnut stock, which was no longer painted black as it frequently had been in the past.

96   This browning was put on the barrel for a

purpose, just as guns are often blued today. It was supposed to help prevent rusting and to avoid glare in the bright sun. This was sound reasoning and the ordnance people liked it. Not so the soldiers. Many of them apparently believed the dull tubes did not go well with their handsome scarlet coats and gleaming buttons. Bright barrels made a much braver show and they proceeded to polish off the offensive brown.

Ordnance officials protested in vain. They could not halt the practice and finally had to content themselves with pleading that if the soldiers felt they must polish their guns, they should do it in a way that would not injure them and impair what accuracy they had.

Like the derivation of its name, the origin of the gun itself is somewhat of a mystery. There has long been a tradition that it was developed and adopted at the instigation of the great John Churchill, Duke of Marlborough, during the reign of Queen Anne (1702-1714). Indeed "Corporal John," as his men called him, did set great store by his infantry and was particularly interested in musket drill. If he did have any connection with the Brown Bess, however, it must have taken an uncommonly long time to get it into production, for the first fully developed and datable specimens come from the late 1720's.

No matter what its origin or how it got its name, the Brown Bess was a superb weapon for its day. Actually, there were several models made over a period of some one hundred and twenty years until the flintlock was abandoned. All were similar, however, and all carried the same famous name. They were brass-mounted guns with .75-caliber barrels pin-fastened to sturdy stocks. They balanced well despite their long barrels, and their rugged locks were not easily broken.

This was the arm of the British soldiers as they extended and solidified the empire in India and America. American colonists came to know it through service with British troops in the principal French and Indian Wars, and it was a common arm in American arsenals. Thus, when America began to produce its own muskets at the beginning of the Revolution, it was the Brown Bess that the various Committees of Safety selected as the model to be copied. It was the main weapon of the British during the American Revolution. Wellington's men carried it on the Peninsula and at Waterloo. Americans faced it once again during the War of 1812 and finally in the hands of Mexican troops during the campaigns of 1846 and 1847, by which time it was an obsolete weapon sold by Great Britain to the government of Mexico.

The adversary of the Brown Bess throughout this whole era was almost always the French musket. While the British musket underwent three minor modifications or models, its French counterpart experienced more than a dozen. Each was a slight improvement over its predecessor, until finally the French musket was the finest in the world.

Although the name Charleville is generally used by collectors to refer specifically to the model of 1763, its only validity lies in its handiness and the custom of popular usage. The Royal Armory at Charleville did indeed manufacture muskets of that model, but the armories at Maubeuge and St. Etienne also produced it. And Charleville made later models as well. Still, the name has stuck and in America, at least, it is the recognized term.

Standardized French flintlock muskets had been adopted about the same time as the British, with the model of 1717 as the very first. From the beginning they were lighter than their British adversaries, with a caliber of .69 and a slender, more graceful stock. After 1728, the barrels were fastened to the stock by iron bands instead of pins, and this again permitted a lighter stock without loss of strength. Later improvements brought brass pans, which were less subject to corrosion, and reinforced cocks for greater strength.

In America, the French arms were known first as enemy weapons. Then, when the shifting alignments of the War for Independence found France supporting the colonies, French muskets began to flow into the United States and Americans became more familiar with them. Their light construction and smaller caliber, as well as their availability, appealed to military men, and the British pattern of the Committee of Safety muskets was abandoned in favor of the French. After the war, when the new United States government began arms production in its new national armories, it selected the 1763 Charleville as a pattern for its first muskets and continued to follow French models as long as flintlocks were used.

Four factors combined to make the flintlock musket the important weapon it was: strength, reliability, speed of loading, and the bayonet. The sturdiness of these guns has already been

97

noted. The other factors were, if anything, even more important.

It has long been the fashion among fiction writers to comment disparagingly on flint ignition and to emphasize misfires and flashes in the pan. This distorts the picture unfairly. The flintlock was a highly dependable weapon if properly cared for and used. If the flint was dull or the frizzen worn or greasy, there would be few sparks and possibly the priming powder would not be ignited. If the touchhole between the pan and the bore became plugged, the priming powder could flash brilliantly in the pan without setting off the gun. And this performance, spectacular but leading to no result, has kept the expression fresh in the English language today. If the shooter took care to see that his flint was sharp, his frizzen in good condition, the touchhole open, and the priming powder fresh and dry, he had no real worries about misfires. Only the weather could really give him serious trouble.

One very interesting invention of the Eighteenth Century showed just how capable the flintlock was of firing under the most trying circumstances and with most unusual hazards. This was a gun with the lock upside down, underneath the barrel. Apparently the designer had been trying to get away from the distracting flash and smoke in the line of sight by putting all the mechanism on the bottom. The pan cover, of course, held the priming powder in place as long as it was closed, but the moment the flint struck the frizzen and drove it open, the powder started to fall out. Nevertheless, the sparks ignited it in mid-air, and since powder burns upward, it still managed to set off the charge in the barrel through the vertical touchhole. Improbable as it seems, modern experiments with one of these guns have shown that it almost never misfires. The flintlock was a reliable arm.

Speed also was important. The faster a soldier could shoot, the more balls he could pour in the general direction of his enemy. With the complete paper cartridge which became almost universal during the early Eighteenth Century, loading became a very quick process. One military treatise of 1768 states that recruits were not to be released from practice until they were skilled enough to load and fire fifteen times in three and three-quarter minutes—in other words, a sustained rate of fire of one shot every fifteen seconds. In actual battle this rate might be slowed somewhat, but there is no basis for the modern notion that it took minutes to prepare each shot.

Four shots a minute left little time for aiming, but that was not so important in Eighteenth Century warfare. The basic formation for an engagement was the line of battle. This consisted of two, or sometimes three, rows of men drawn up shoulder-to-shoulder, one line close behind the other. About six feet behind these lines was a row of "file closers," or reserves, to take the place of casualties. From this formation soldiers advanced to the attack, marching to within sure range of the enemy, delivering a volley and then charging to decide the issue hand to hand. It was also in this formation that the soldiers received an attack. Standing steady, they waited until the enemy was within range, fired a volley, loaded, and if possible fired one or two more volleys before the enemy was on top of them. There was no aiming at specific targets. The idea was to lay down a field of fire through which the enemy had to pass and to get just as dense a concentration of bullets in the air as possible. Much the same theory is applied today with modern automatic weapons, but since guns fire faster now, the solid lines of men are not needed.

When the two forces closed for hand-to-hand combat, it was often the bayonet that decided the day. According to tradition, the bayonet first appeared in Bayonne, in southern France, and took its name from its birthplace. This may well be true. Daggers from that area were called bayonets in the 1500's, and the earliest references to the use of specific daggers with guns come from Bayonne in the 1640's. At first these bayonets were simple daggers with tapering handles that could be driven into the gun muzzles. These plug bayonets, as they were called, left much to be desired. If they were pushed in too tightly, it was difficult to remove them. If they were not pushed in tightly enough, they might fall out or be left in the body of an enemy. And, of course, as long as the bayonet was in place, it was impossible to shoot the gun. Even so, they gained some popularity. A few British regiments were equipped with them as early as 1663, and the French fusilier and grenadier regiments raised in 1671 also carried them.

Ways were soon tried to improve such a handy weapon. First, loose rings were fastened on the hilt to loop over the barrel, but this did not work well. Then, about the end of the Seventeenth Century, the socket bayonet was devised and quickly adopted throughout Europe. It consisted of a sleeve which fitted over the barrel and locked in place with a stud and slot, an elbow bent out at right angles, and a straight blade, usually triangular in section. It could not be used for cutting, but it was a magnificent stabbing instrument. This was the appendage that made the flintlock musket so versatile. Every man was now both musketeer and pikeman. With one weapon he could fight at long

range and hand to hand. It was a fine combination and military men from all nations were greatly attached to it.

Since volley fire was so effective for massed formations, it was a natural conclusion that a single gun firing a volley all by itself would be a most useful weapon for an individual in a more personal encounter. Gunsmiths and designers brought forth multibarreled guns in small-scale imitations of the old ribauldequins and organ batteries. These were expensive, however, and it was hard to ignite a series of charges from a single lock. The best answer seemed to be a gun that would fire a number of projectiles in a wide pattern from a single barrel. A short barrel with a wide flaring muzzle, they thought, might serve the purpose, and the blunderbuss was born.

Here was a gun to attract immediate attention in any group. It had a short, convenient length. Its huge muzzle was frighteningly impressive when viewed from the wrong end, and on some of the later versions there was a wicked little bayonet which flew up into place when a spring was released. Small wonder that romantic legends grew up about it.

In America, particularly, almost every schoolboy is convinced that this was the arm of the Pilgrims who came from England to found the Plymouth colony in 1620. The figure of

Right: Breech and locks of
Joe Manton sporting piece, London, 1810. Left:
In the field with flintlock fowlers.

the staunch colonist, with his big hat, his bland smile, his Bible, and his blunderbuss with its muzzle flared out like a trombone, has been a stock subject for November magazine covers, calendar pictures, and book illustrations for more than fifty years. Yet the blunderbuss did not really develop as a weapon until several years after the Pilgrims set sail. And even if it had been known in England, it would have had little use in the wilds of the New World.

There is the repeated myth that the blunderbuss was a wonderfully practical arm because it did not require regular bullets. All the shooter had to do was to scoop up a handful of old nails, broken glass, sharp stones, scrap iron, or any other debris that might be handy, and drop it down the muzzle of the murderous monster. Such projectiles may indeed have been used in extreme cases when other ammunition was not available, but they certainly were not standard. Just think what those items would do to the bore of a gun, and imagine what would happen if one nail or piece of scrap iron got caught crosswise with the weight of the charge behind it. This was emergency fodder only. The contemporary manuals all called for a load of musket or pistol balls, or buckshot—and as many of them as would chamber conveniently.

Finally, there is the belief that the spread of

the shot was directly related to the flare of the muzzle. This one fooled even the early blunderbuss makers themselves, and they sought to alter the shot patterns by varying the size and shape of the muzzle. Some bells were made huge for a wide spread. Others were formed as a flattened oval in the hope of obtaining a horizontal pattern. Actually the dispersion of the shot was controlled more by the size of the bore at the breech, the length of the barrel, and the uniformity of the bore expansion from breech to muzzle. After all, shot can only spread out at a certain rate, and a barrel that widens more rapidly than this rate will have no effect whatever on the projectiles.

Modern tests conducted under the auspices of the National Rifle Association have indicated that almost all blunderbusses had a fairly consistent pattern, no matter what the size or shape of their muzzles. At forty feet there would be a spread of twenty to thirty-six inches; at sixty feet, forty to fifty inches. And the test gun with the widest spread had the largest breech diameter and smallest muzzle diameter of the lot. The Eighteenth Century gunmakers came to recognize this fact also, and gradually the exaggerated flares of the early blunderbusses gave way after 1750 to short, large-caliber arms with almost cylindrical

Doolittle engraving of Battle of Lexington has Major Pitcairn on horse at right. Americans retreat at left. Right: Paul Revere's picture of the Boston massacre was an effective propaganda piece for American patriots. In both scenes the British troops fire volleys according to approved 18th century tactics for infantry armed with smoothbore muskets.

bores, the flare being simulated by a thickening of the metal with decorative moldings at the muzzle. These were not decadent specimens as is often charged. Instead they represented the blunderbuss at its functional best.

When the blunderbuss was properly used it was a highly effective weapon. A large one might take a load of sixteen buckshot and a charge of one hundred and twenty grains of black powder—a fearsome load that made the blunderbuss a magnificent arm for defending a street, a door, a staircase, or for repelling boarders from the decks of ships at sea.

Householders were fond of it. A two-inch muzzle thrust into the face of a burglar produced an effect wonderful to behold.

Stagecoach guards also liked the blunderbuss, just as their descendants in the late Nineteenth Century had a fondness for the shotgun. The bell muzzle made it easier to load on a swaying coach, and since the lurchings and joltings of the vehicle over the rutted roads made accurate aiming impossible, a gun that sprayed its slugs was the best possible weapon.

Upon occasion, the blunderbuss was on the other side, too. Probably the most celebrated case of assassination by blunderbuss occurred in 1681 with the murder of Thomas Thynne in London. The notorious Swedish adventurer John Philip, Count of Königsmark, is supposed to have arranged the bloody deed. According to the scandal of the day, Königsmark became the great and good friend of Mrs. Thynne, so much so, in fact, that one day he invited her to go traveling with him. The lady demurred, protesting that it would be a scandalous thing to do while her husband was still alive.

The charming lady had also hinted, however, that she would be willing to have such an unfortunate obstacle removed, so the count proceeded to hire three professional killers to help smooth the path of romance. They intercepted Thynne's carriage on a Sunday evening in February, just as it entered Pall Mall from St. James' Street. Two of them covered the coachman with their pistols, while the third disposed of the surplus husband by blazing away through the coach window with his blunderbuss. Its terrible charge left no doubt of the outcome and Mr. Hobbs, the surgeon, reported he "found in Thynne's body four bullets which had torn into his Guts, wounded his Liver, and Stomach, and Gall, broke one Rib, and wounded the great Bone below." And he needlessly added: "Of which Wounds he dyed."

So much for the effectiveness of a blunderbuss at close range. The actual killers were arrested and hanged. Königsmark tried to flee the country, but was caught and tried. His usual luck or influence got him off, however, and he left England for further adventures, both martial and marital.

Blunderbusses were highly popular throughout most of the civilized world. In Europe they ranged in size from huge monsters on swivels, designed to be mounted on the gunwales of ships, to relatively small pistols.

The bulk of these picturesque arms were flintlocks. A very few of the first ones may have been wheel locks and there may have been some with earlier flint systems. Later, some percussion models were manufactured, especially large ones for naval use. By this time, however, the day of the blunderbuss was past and the short shotgun was taking its place.

The Eighteenth has often been called the most civilized of centuries. In some ways it was, but it showed another side, too. Violence lurked just beneath the surface. Clubs of young rakes roamed the streets of London with mischief in mind that far outdistanced the juvenile delinquent's activities today. It was their delight to inflict both indignity and pain on complete strangers who merely chanced to cross their paths.

Sober citizens did well to stay home nights. If they went abroad, they were wise to travel in groups and to carry weapons—a sword, of course, and perhaps a pair of pistols that would fit conveniently in a pocket.

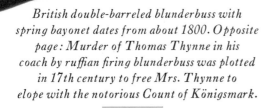

British double-barreled blunderbuss with spring bayonet dates from about 1800. Opposite page: Murder of Thomas Thynne in his coach by ruffian firing blunderbuss was plotted in 17th century to free Mrs. Thynne to elope with the notorious Count of Königsmark.

It was the flintlock that had made the pocket pistol really practical. There had indeed been a very few small wheel locks, but these were mostly extravagant pieces a gunsmith made to show his skill in shaping the necessary parts on a small scale. The earlier flint systems were just not practical in small sizes either, but the flintlock was well suited for such purposes and pocket pistols began to appear in quantity soon after that mechanism became popular. These ranged in size all the way from six- or seven-inch specimens suitable for a greatcoat pocket down to tiny four- or five-inch weapons that could fit unnoticed into almost any garment.

One very popular form of pocket pistol at the beginning of the Eighteenth Century had a barrel which screwed off, so that it could be loaded at the breech. This idea had been applied earlier to larger pistols, but it was better suited to the tiny ones because it eliminated the need for a ramrod and, indeed, for any wooden stock ahead of the trigger guard. To make the lock even more compact, the frizzen spring was curled backward under the pan instead of sticking forward in the more common position. This pattern has been called "Queen Anne" by modern collectors, even though its greatest popularity came after that sovereign's death in the year 1714.

An interesting quality of these "turn-off" pistols was their surprising range and accuracy. Because the shooter filled the chamber to the brim with powder, he always obtained the same charge and this was one factor in increasing the accuracy of his shooting. More impor-

tant, since the ball did not have to be rammed down the barrel, it could be made to fit tighter, and thus shoot truer. Also, turn-off pistols were frequently rifled. Dashing Prince Rupert, nephew of King Charles I and his cavalry leader during the English Civil War, had demonstrated the capabilities of the large version of these pistols many years before. As the royal army halted at Stafford on September 13, 1642, the handsome prince drew one of his screw-barreled pistols and fired at the weathercock of St. Mary's Church, some one hundred and eighty feet from where he and King Charles rested. The bullet pierced the tail of the cock. The monarch was astounded and declared it a lucky accident, whereupon Rupert promptly repeated it with his other pistol.

As the century progressed, pocket pistols became more and more refined. The lock mechanism was moved inside, with just the cock and frizzen protruding above the center of the barrel. This made the contour smoother and less likely to catch and tear a pocket or leave the owner struggling to free it while his target of opportunity rapidly disappeared. Placing the lock inside also reduced the amount of wooden stock necessary and again diminished the bulk of the gun. About 1800 another development became popular. This was a folding trigger that fitted into a recess on the underside of the piece and only popped out when the gun was cocked.

Some pistols, however, concentrated more on "extras" than small size. For those who wanted more firepower, there were additional barrels. In the most common model there were two, one above the other, with a valve in the bottom of the flashpan so that a shooter could select whichever one he wanted to fire. But from all standpoints the most astounding piece of equipment was the spring bayonet. This tiny dagger folded back along the underside of the barrel until a latch was released and a spring swung it out into stabbing position. Since most of these implements had triangular blades

only a little more than two inches long, they can hardly have been intended for deadly work. Perhaps they were effective in clearing a path through a Mayfair crowd.

There were larger pistols as well for those who rode horseback, traveled by coach, or wanted protection about the house. Every man of property owned at least one pair and sometimes several. Pirates and highwaymen were especially noted for the large number of guns that filled their pockets, hung from their belts, or were tied to ribbons. There was no time for reloading once a ship had been boarded or a fight begun, and it was a good idea to have several shots available.

But even a single opponent was sometimes more than a match for the heavily armed highwayman—if his mind was sharp enough. There is, for instance, the tale of the legendary Welshman, Twm Shon Catti. Sir John Devereux, it is said, once gave this worthy the task of carrying a large sum of gold to London. Declining the offer of an escort, Twm put on the oldest clothes he could find in the hope that he would appear to be a poor prospect for any self-respecting knight of the road. Nevertheless, it seems he attracted the eye of the notorious Tom Dorbel, who rode up bristling with an arsenal of pistols. Feigning the terror of a country lout, Twm begged the great highwayman to put several bullet holes through his coat, so his master would think he had fought a good fight before yielding his treasure and perhaps would not be too harsh with him. The highwayman obliged. Twm capered with delight and pleaded for just one more hole, this time through his hat. And so he continued until the gullible thief had fired his last pistol. Whereupon Twm drew his own and proceeded on his way with all of his own gold plus every penny the furious Dorbel had been carrying.

There is some doubt about the historical actuality of the Twm Catti story, but it appealed to the travelers of a day when heavily armed marauders might halt them on their own journeys, and they delighted to hear the tale.

Something of a record for the number of consecutive victories in a short space of time may have been set by the worthy Duke of Chandos in 1720. On Monday, January 25, his coach was set upon by a party of five robbers as he rode home in Cannons to London. With the aid of his servants he beat them off and gained his destination safely. On February 1, he was again held up and this time not only thwarted the highwaymen but managed to capture them as well. The very next day he surprised and chased off a party of three knights of the road who were in the act of robbing a postboy. All of this within a period of nine days.

With life proceeding at this pace in the most civilized of centuries, it is small wonder that gunsmiths prospered.

Of all the personal arms of the flintlock period, however, probably none arouse as much interest today as the dueling pistols. There is a macabre fascination both with the practice itself and with the magnificent guns made for the purpose. And there is a real admiration for the skilled workmanship that produced weapons of such precision.

At first, duels were hand-to-hand encounters. Swords were the usual weapons, but other arms also were employed — maces, axes, daggers, clubs, and sometimes a combination of weapons. With all of these the antagonists' physical strength and dexterity were most important. 103

Preceding pages: English coaching blunderbuss has brass barrel and cannon moldings at the muzzle, about 1780. Seen in pocket is a greatcoat pistol by Adams of London, about 1800. Above: Queen Anne turn-off pistol of early 18th century.

Then, shortly after 1650, firearms began to come into general use for dueling.

Duels were fought for any cause and sometimes for no cause. There was, for instance, the case of the Neapolitan nobleman who fought fourteen duels to "prove" that Dante was a greater poet than Ariosto and then admitted on his deathbed that he had never read the works of either. Intemperate language, an affair of the heart, an insolent gesture—almost anything might produce a challenge. Such personal encounters uselessly took the lives of men throughout Europe and America, although perhaps France and Italy held the record. There was, in fact, a saying that if two Englishmen were shipwrecked on a desert island, they would quickly find something to gamble on, but if two Frenchmen were wrecked they would duel.

Not all duels were fatal. Frequently an exchange of shots was sufficient to satisfy both parties; sometimes it was necessary to draw blood; but in bitter cases only death could end the affair.

The early duels with firearms were relatively informal affairs. There was none of the ritual that marked the later "code duello." Correspondingly, the guns used were not rigidly prescribed. Any handy firearm might be pressed into service. It was not even considered necessary for the two adversaries to be armed alike. Long guns, as well as pistols, were used, and all sorts of unusual conditions were agreed upon. In one bizarre incident, an Englishman traveling on the Continent was challenged to a duel by a wealthy resident of the area in which he found himself. Unable to escape the en-

counter, the Britisher agreed to a meeting with pistols in the challenger's baronial hall—in complete darkness. Resolved not to hurt his adversary no matter what the provocation, the kindhearted Englishman waited until the challenger fired. Then, slowly and carefully feeling his way along the wall until he found the fireplace, he discharged his own pistol up the chimney. To his amazement there followed a sickening thud as the body of his too-cautious opponent dropped to the hearth.

The most common duel in all countries, however, was the face-to-face meeting at a given distance. Usually this was ten to fifteen paces. The trained duelist was careful to show only his right side to his opponent, to keep his stomach drawn in, and his right arm shielding as much of his chest as possible. In this position he presented the smallest possible target and shielded his vital areas in the best manner. He was trained to shoot immediately upon taking aim and to move only his forefinger so that he would not deflect his aim. Above all he was counseled not to be alarmed or distressed if hit! As one instructor of the period put it:

I cannot impress upon an individual too strongly the propriety of remaining perfectly calm and collected when hit; he must not allow himself to be alarmed or confused; but, summoning up all his resolution, treat the matter coolly; and if he dies, go off with as good a grace as possible.

Although he had never had any formal training in such niceties, Andrew Jackson followed this advice perfectly in his celebrated duel with Charles Dickinson in 1806. The .70-caliber ball from Dickinson's pistol struck the future president in the left breast, broke a rib over the heart, and then deflected. It was a severe wound, but Jackson gave no indication of it. Deliberately, he dropped his adversary and walked from the field without giving either the dying Dickinson or his seconds any indication that he had been touched.

As pistol duels became both more frequent

and more formal, special arms were developed, reaching the height of their perfection between 1770 and 1810. Because they were designed for such a specific purpose, they had definite characteristics which enable them to be recognized immediately for what they were.

First of all, the dueling pistol had to be quick and accurate. Often rules or custom precluded deliberate aiming, and besides, there usually wasn't time. The man who fired first had a tremendous advantage—if he fired accurately. For this reason, the well-made dueling pistol will "point" almost automatically. It is a good test of such a pistol to hold it down at arm's length, then suddenly raise it and point it at a target long enough to check the aim with the sights. If it is a true dueler and well made, it should be right on target.

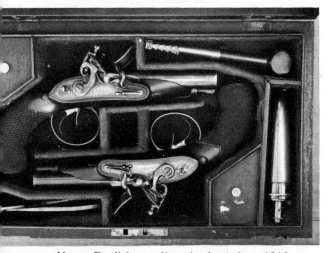

Above: English traveling pistols of about 1810.
Below: Highwayman makes a score.

The bore also had to be true and finely polished to carry the ball directly to its destination. French duelers were usually rifled, but the great majority of English dueling pistols were not, since custom frowned upon it. Some, however, had "blind" rifling which stopped a few inches from the muzzle and so gave the impression of a smoothbore. Either way, a good pistol would carry the usual dueling distance without deviation. In fact, one English smoothbore pistol of about 1790 was tested recently and found capable of hitting a man-sized target three times out of four at eighty-five yards.

The outsides of the barrels also received attention. Normally, they were about ten inches long, octagonal, and exceptionally heavy, so that a nervous and jerky trigger-pull would be less apt to affect the aim. Also, they were browned or blued to avoid glare.

The desire to avoid glare and distraction carried over into the gun mountings as well. Silver was almost never used, and brass only rarely. The standard mounts were iron or steel and they were browned or blued just like the barrels. The stocks were made without ornament or carving except for fine checkering of the grips. It was felt that other decoration might be detrimental to a sure, steady grasp or might possibly distract the eye at a critical moment. There might be a little engraving on the barrel tang, on the lock plate, or on the trigger guard, but that was all.

Finally, the mechanism of the gun was refined and speeded to its ultimate degree. Special pans were designed for fast ignition. Frizzens were made to operate against light springs so that they opened quickly and easily. Set or hair triggers were added, with screw adjustments so that they could be adapted to the preference of the individual user and fire with just the touch he wanted.

When finished, these superb guns were cased in pairs with all their accessories, just as were other fine pistols of the period. The box was walnut, oak, or mahogany, with the interior *107*

*Cased set of pistols
by Nicholas Noël Boutet
of Versailles has
pocket model as well as
large traveling
size, plus full array
of accessories.*

divided into compartments and lined with felt or velvet. Again, there was no ostentation, just a simple but well-made case with a lock, a handle, and possibly a plate for the owner's name or monogram.

Despite the popularity of the pistol and the rigidity of the "code duello," individualists still continued to fight with other weapons and under more imaginative circumstances. This was particularly true in America where such formalities often were held in contempt. But it is to the French that credit must be given for perhaps the most spectacular duel ever fought.

As might be expected, the quarrel concerned a woman, a Mademoiselle Tirevit, of the imperial opera, whose two suitors agreed to fight a duel to settle their respective claims to her affection. M. de Grandpré and M. le Pique were men of imagination, and since the lady had signified her willingness to bestow her

smiles upon the survivor of such a contest, they determined that the encounter should be decisive and in the grand manner befitting so important a dispute. At their order, two identical balloons were constructed. On the day selected, de Grandpré and his second entered the car of one balloon and le Pique and his second the other. The setting was the garden of the Tuilleries amid a great crowd of spectators who had gathered for the occasion. The gentlemen were to fire at each other's balloon only, not at their respective persons. Since pistols would hardly have served the purpose, each aeronaut took a blunderbuss. At a given signal, the ropes were cut and the ascent began. The winds were moderate, and the balloons remained about eighty yards apart. As they reached a height of about half a mile above the earth, the signal to fire was given. Le Pique somehow managed to miss his opponent's balloon completely, but de Grandpré scored a direct hit. The wounded balloon collapsed and plummeted to the ground, killing both its passengers. De Grandpré, however, triumphantly continued his ascent, eventually landing some seven leagues from Paris and the charms of Mlle. Tirevit, whose mind presumably was now made up.

Advances in firearms were not confined to dueling weapons. All guns shared them. Except for minor improvements in design, the flintlock had remained relatively the same from the time of its general adoption until about 1750. Stocks had been improved and locks had been strengthened, but that was about all. Then there came a sudden spurt of activity which brought great strides in gunmaking just as the flintlock period was drawing to a close.

Two major changes helped the lock itself. The broad, flat pan, which had collected water whenever there was even a light rain, was redesigned. The closure was made tighter. Water was shunted away from the opening and drains were added to make a "waterproof" pan, or so it was claimed. The other big improvement came with the addition of a roller bearing between the frizzen and frizzen spring. This reduced friction, made the pan open faster, and helped produce a better shower of sparks.

Probably the biggest improvement of all, however, was perfected by the celebrated English gunmaker, Henry Nock. In almost every gun ever made before, the flash from the pan had hit only one corner of the main charge in the barrel. From this point, ignition spread relatively slowly to the rest of the charge. A long barrel was needed to let the entire charge burn inside and so exert its maximum force. Late in the Eighteenth Century, attempts were made to lead the flame into the bottom center of the charge by a long channel. This did not work well. A little fouling clogged the channel and caused frequent misfires. Even when it did work perfectly, there was such a noticeable delay between the igniting flash and the eventual explosion of the charge that it was

almost impossible to hold an aim. Nock solved the problem by devising a breech with only a short channel and a little chamber for an igniting charge. This in turn set off the main charge all at once and added considerable force to the explosion. The two discharges were so rapid it was impossible to differentiate between them. What's more, the thoughtful Nock had provided a clean-out screw for easy maintenance of the breech.

The effects were far reaching. Guns could shoot further because the explosion was more efficient. Since the charge did not take so long to burn, barrels could be made shorter and lighter. Before this, most sporting guns had had barrels about forty inches long. Now they were reduced to thirty or thirty-two inches with just as good results, and they were easier to handle. Because of this shortening and lightening, the side-by-side double-barreled gun became practical. A few had been made before, but they had been heavy and clumsy. Now they became a major factor in the sporting scene.

Englishmen were still as avid sportsmen as they had been in the days of the long fowler. Hereafter, they could argue the merits of the new double gun against their tried-and-true single-barreled fowling pieces. Joe Manton greatly boosted the standing of the double gun by inventing the elevated sighting rib to make aiming easier. But the consensus was that the new guns were useful only for targets between thirty and sixty yards away. Beyond that, the single barrel was the only bird-getter. Manton made both, and made them so well that the early years of the Nineteenth Century have often been called the "Joe Manton period" as far as English sporting guns are concerned.

English guns of the late flintlock period were noted for their fine workmanship and mechanical perfection, their gold or platinum linings for pans and touchholes, and a quiet elegance. France led in exquisite decoration. Continental flintlocks had always been more highly decorated than English ones, on the average. But

whereas the Germanic areas generally clung to styles reminiscent of the wheel-lock era, the French moved forward in a lighter, very different vein, reaching a climax with the products of the Versailles Manufactory.

Guiding light of this splendid enterprise was an artist and craftsman of the first order, Nicholas Noël Boutet. Descended from a line of famous gunsmiths, young Nicholas inherited the titles of "Gunmaker to the King's Light Horse" from his father and "Ordinary Gunmaker to the King" from his father-in-law. It was a turbulent time. Hardly had the skilled young gunmaker and goldsmith established himself in these positions when the French Revolution cost Louis XVI both his crown and his head, and terminated Boutet's appointment. The new government, however, was quick to recognize his ability and in the same year as the king's decapitation, he was authorized to recruit workmen to establish a manufactory for

arms at Versailles with a special workshop for *armes de luxe*. In 1799, Napoleon rose to power as First Consul and was so impressed with Boutet's work that the next year he granted him an eighteen-year concession at Versailles with specific instructions to make highly ornate firearms for presentation, as well as regulation military models. He was also to train artists to preserve the great traditions of French gunmaking.

This was the period from which the greatest of Boutet's work stems. Magnificent guns and swords were made for presentation to Napoleon's marshals and to the monarchs he placed upon the thrones of Europe, as well as to a host of others who shared the Emperor's favor. But this appointment, too, was of short duration. Before Boutet's eighteen years were up, the Battle of Waterloo and its aftermath put him out of work again. The victorious allies sacked his workshop, and carried off his models, equipment, and all his completed arms. Moving back to Paris, Boutet opened a private shop and revived his old titles, for the wheel had turned and the monarchy had been restored. He died in 1833, the respected *Arquebusier ordinaire du Roi et des Princes*.

So the flintlock reached the pinnacle of its development in both mechanical perfection and magnificence of decoration. At the same time a very cheap form of the gun was also being made for trade to the American Indians. Ironically, it was this form of the flintlock that sur-

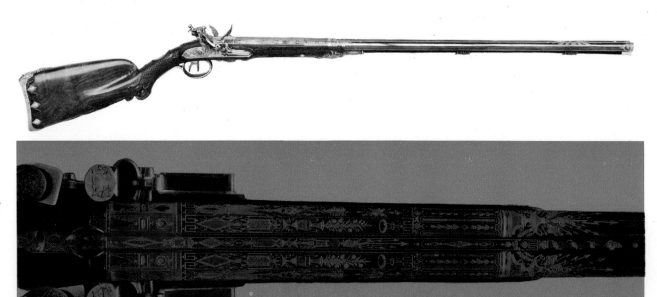

vived in active production and use long after the fine arms had become museum pieces.

Furs were the primary stimulus that brought forth this new arm. From the beginning, the European settlers and merchants had coveted the luxurious pelts the American Indian collected in his native habitat. Among other things, the Indian, in his turn, coveted European firearms and, the laws of economics being what they are, the two soon began to change hands. An active trade in guns had developed during the Seventeenth Century, but it was not until the early 1700's that a special trade gun was devised for barter.

The Indian knew what he wanted in a gun and the trading companies strove to produce it at a price that would permit a pleasingly exorbitant profit. Long, heavy guns were completely unacceptable to the aborigines. They demanded short, light pieces they could carry through the woodlands of the East or manage easily on horseback over the western plains. Smoothbores were preferred because of their greater versatility and larger calibers. And there were unimportant details the Indians insisted upon because they were used to them: a serpent-shaped side plate opposite the lock, a deep trigger guard, and even British proof marks. Trade guns made in America or in Belgium frequently had to bear imitations of these marks before the Indians would accept them.

There are many names for the trade gun. Some are old, some have been devised by later writers and collectors. They include Northwest gun, Hudson's Bay fuke, Mackinaw gun, and Indian musket or Indian gun. But they all refer to the same piece—a light flintlock with a caliber of about .58, a barrel thirty to forty-two inches long, a deep trigger guard, and a side plate in the form of a serpent.

For almost two hundred years it was the preferred gun of the American Indian, and it was made for that whole period without significant alteration. The flintlock suited the Indian perfectly and he insisted on it even though better arms which used percussion caps or metallic cartridges were available. He could make his own flint if he wanted to, whereas caps and cartridges had to be obtained from traders at high prices. A flintlock could be loaded more easily on a running horse than could a percussion arm. Placing a cap on a nipple was a delicate operation. But with a large touchhole, a flintlock could be primed by slapping the butt and jarring some of the charge out of the barrel and into the pan. It was customary to hunt buffalo, for instance, by riding alongside the great beasts and firing at close range, loading rapidly and firing again.

The trade guns were cheap, but they were sturdy. They had to be to withstand the treatment they received. An Indian seldom cleaned his gun or oiled it as a European would. If the stock broke, he wrapped it with rawhide. Usually he removed the butt plate and made a hide scraper out of it. Frequently he cut the barrel down to carbine length and made a tent peg or another scraper from the cut-off portion. He studded the stock with brass-headed tacks, decked it with rawhide, copper wire, scalps, and tinklers—did everything, in fact, but take care of it. Still, many of these sturdy flintlocks gave dependable service for years.

Trade flintlocks were made for the African natives as well as the American Indians. This trade, however, began somewhat later and continued until even more modern times. African trade guns resembled their American counterparts in being light, but they lacked the deep trigger guards and serpent side plates. Frequently their stocks were painted red and sometimes a mirror was set in the butt. They were cruder arms, but they were designed for similar circumstances. And they served well. Shops in Birmingham and Liége continued to make them until World War I ended the era.

With the passing of these rough descendants, the epic of the flintlock was finished. It had been almost exactly three hundred years since le Bourgeoys' invention.

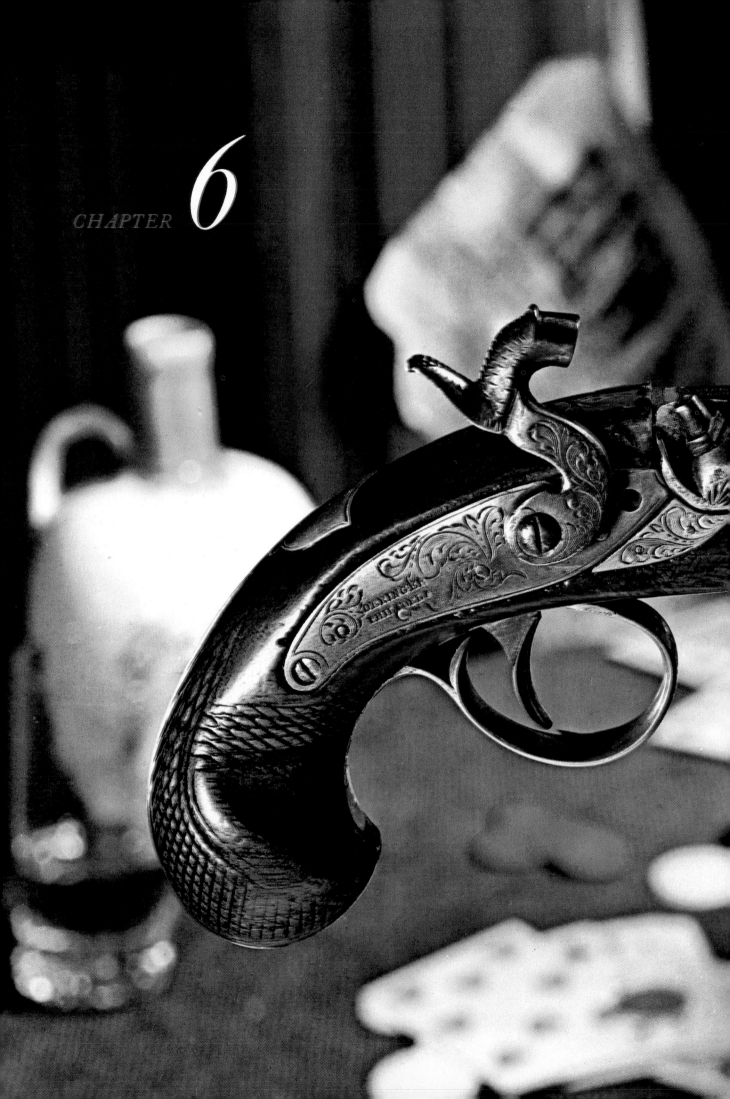

Preceding pages:
Henry Deringer's famous single-shot pocket
pistol was deadly at short range.

THE CLERGYMAN'S DISCOVERY

A Franciscan friar proclaimed the age of firearms with the first European description of gunpowder. A clergyman ushered in its modern era with the first successful percussion lock. Here was a real turning point in the history of firearms. Before this time, a gun needed live fire in the form of a coal, or free sparks struck by stone on steel. The new system did away with these hazards. It was more resistant to weather. It set off the charge faster and it provided the basic theory for all future developments in ignition, including the modern metallic cartridge.

116

Alexander John Forsyth was a Scottish minister with a passionate interest in science and a natural liking for shooting. Descended on both sides from clergymen of the Church of Scotland, he naturally inclined toward the church himself. He had barely obtained his license when his father died and the parish petitioned for his appointment as the new minister. Thus he was bound still closer to the family tradition and to the Belhelvie Parish. He had been born there in 1768. He was to spend almost all of his life in its comfortable manse and he was buried in its churchyard in 1843.

Belhelvie had much to recommend it for a man of Forsyth's tastes. It was a scant eight miles north of Aberdeen and the university. Friends of scientific bent could come and visit. And there was the seacoast nearby with its many fine opportunities for hunting waterfowl. The parishioners, too, were fond of the young minister they had seen grow up in their midst and they allowed him considerable freedom to pursue his scientific interests and experiments without serious complaint.

According to family tradition, Forsyth's interest in developing a new gunlock began on a hunting trip to a loch not far from the manse. He noticed that many of the wild birds escaped his fire by diving the moment they saw the flash from the pan of his flint fowling piece. The slight hesitation in the ignition was all that they needed to evade the shot. At first the young minister tried a hood which hid the flash and had moderate success. But he had heard of recent experiments with new kinds of gunpowder and primings, and these spurred his scientific interest. He believed there might be a way to produce a faster-firing gun and he set out to try to build one.

The new substances which attracted Forsyth's attention were called fulminates. They were salts produced by dissolving metals in acids. When struck they would explode violently. No one knows who first discovered the explosive qualities of the fulminates, but they are described at least as early as the Seventeenth Century. The indefatigable diarist, Samuel Pepys, mentioned fulminate of gold in 1663. Claude Louis Berthollet, the famous French chemist, experimented with both fulminate of silver and potassium chlorate during the late 1700's. It had been Berthollet's hope to substitute one of these substances for the saltpeter in gunpowder, but he was unsuccessful. In England, Edward Howard was working along the same lines with fulminate of mercury. None of these learned chemists, however, appears to have thought of using one of these explosive fulminates simply to set off a charge.

Forsyth not only thought it possible, but determined to build a lock that would do it. Long hours were spent in the little garden house known as the "Minister's Smiddy" where he performed his experiments and did his mechanical work. Still more hours were spent walking and thinking at the edge of the sea, so that servants, it is said, would turn away visitors with the explanation: "Och, ye micht he's awa' at the shore, thinking aboot his guns, and his locks, and his thingies, an he'll jist be back wi' wat feet, for he never looks when the sea's comin' up."

It was a long, slow process. Forsyth has been characterized as ingenious and observant rather than learned and intuitive. But tedious experiments succeeded where more scholarly minds had failed. At first, Forsyth tried simply to replace the priming in the flint pan with fulminate. The sparks frequently set off the new priming, but it was not so certain as the old powder had been, and what was more it often failed to explode the charge inside the barrel. Next he found that a sharp blow set off the priming better than a spark, but still it frequently failed to detonate the charge. The open pan of the flintlock was just not suitable for percussion ignition. He had to find some way to confine the fulminate in a small space

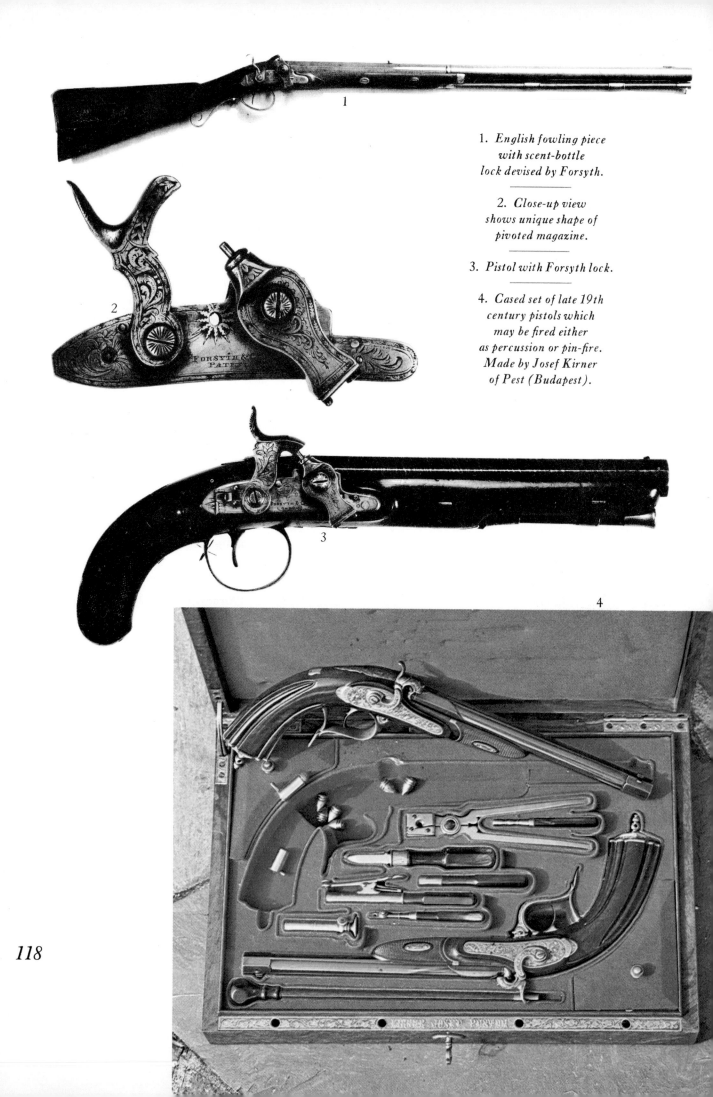

1. English fowling piece
with scent-bottle
lock devised by Forsyth.

2. Close-up view
shows unique shape of
pivoted magazine.

3. Pistol with Forsyth lock.

4. Cased set of late 19th
century pistols which
may be fired either
as percussion or pin-fire.
Made by Josef Kirner
of Pest (Budapest).

and direct its flame into the bore. In the spring of 1805 he succeeded. A pivoted magazine which deposited a small amount of fulminate in a channel leading to the bore, and a hammer which closed all other avenues for the flame as it struck, provided the answer he sought.

All that season he tested the new gun on the lochs and marshes near Belhelvie. Satisfied and proud, he took it to London the next year to show what he had done. Lord Moira, Master General of Ordnance, was impressed with the young Scot and his invention. The new gun offered definite military possibilities if it could be strengthened and perfected. He asked Forsyth to stay and work at the Tower of London and arranged a leave of absence for him from the Aberdeen Presbytery. A workshop and laborers were provided and the work proceeded on locks for both small arms and cannon. By the end of the year, however, the lock still needed improvement. The one official trial had proved disappointing and a new master general ordered Forsyth to settle his accounts and remove his "rubbish" from the Tower.

His association with the government ended, Forsyth turned to private enterprise. With help from his friend James Watt, inventor of the steam engine, he applied for a broad basic patent on the use of fulminate as a priming for firearms. All forms of fulminate were covered, as well as all methods of utilizing them for the purpose. The patent was granted April 11, 1807. With his invention thus protected, Forsyth formed a partnership in London to manufacture and sell his guns. Then he returned to his pastoral duties at Belhelvie.

The Forsyth lock used the fulminate in a loose powder form and the inventor apparently never considered any other approach to the problem. Some few guns were made with sliding magazines, but the pivoted form was most common. It was this magazine, shaped somewhat like the contemporary perfume bottle, which gave the lock its popular name — the "scent bottle."

These scent-bottle locks were popular among well-to-do sportsmen, but there were drawbacks that soon had other inventors and gunsmiths hard at work in an effort to improve the system. The careful finishing required to make the magazine and assure its safety made the Forsyth lock expensive. The lock alone cost as much as a complete, good-quality flint gun. The fulminates were highly corrosive and the lock had to be cleaned carefully after each use.

New solutions came rapidly, some good, some bad. Because so many men worked independently, and because the Forsyth patent was so broad that many were discouraged from patenting their discoveries, it is impossible to learn who was first with which idea. And just to make matters more complicated, a Frenchman named Prélat quickly copied and obtained a French patent on almost every new foreign gun he saw, from Forsyth's scent bottle on, with no indication of their actual originators.

Among the many inventions, were patch primers with the fulminate sandwiched between two pieces of paper. These were stuck to the nose of the hammer and exploded against a hollow tube or nipple at the breech of the barrel. They seem to have been made only in England. There were pill locks in which the fulminate was mixed with gum arabic, or some other binder, and rolled into little pellets. These were inserted in touchholes and struck by a sharp-pointed hammer. In America, Dr. Samuel Guthrie, one of the discoverers of chloroform, laid claim to the pill lock, but in England and on the Continent dozens of gunsmiths developed it almost simultaneously.

There was also the tube lock. This ingenious device made use of short, soft-metal tubes filled with fulminate. One end was inserted in the touchhole while the remainder of the tube rested upon the anvil for the hammer to strike. The tube was an efficient device, but it had several drawbacks if one happened to be standing next to a shooter using it. Sometimes flame spurted from the free end of the tube, and some- *119* times the force of the explosion would hurl the tube out of the touchhole in a most disconcerting manner. Joe Manton patented the first English tube lock in 1818, but others also claimed credit, and the variations and refinements were infinite from America to Central Europe. There were wedge primers, straw primers, disc primers, and a host of others.

The device which surpassed all the others, however, was the percussion cap. Pellets and tubes were used almost to the end of the muzzle-loading era, but the cap was vastly more popular and it was in many ways the direct ancestor of the modern metallic cartridge. Once again, it is impossible to be absolutely certain who invented it. There were many claimants, and possibly several of them did develop it independently. The earliest patent was Prélat's in 1818, but he certainly was not the inventor.

The list of possible fathers for the little cap is distinguished, and their stories of its invention are entertaining. Colonel Peter Hawker, a famous English sportsman, told how he conceived the idea after trying out one of Joe Manton's unsuccessful pill locks, and then convinced that reluctant gunsmith to make a few guns on his plan. Joseph Egg, a noted London gunmaker, claimed to have invented the cap and to have made the first one from a penny. James Purdey, who had worked closely with Forsyth, maintained that he himself had made the very first percussion cap of brass from an old umbrella tag, and that Egg's only claim was in making the first copper cap. His inspiration, Purdey said, was an inverted glass.

From the American viewpoint, however, one possible inventor stands out above the rest, an English artist named Joshua Shaw. Of a mechanical turn of mind, Shaw had just invented a "patent diamond" for cutting glass in 1814 or 1815 (he himself could not remember which), when his attention was attracted to the new percussion locks. Satisfied that the loose powder then used would never be fully satisfactory, he tried making a paste of the materials. He stored tiny amounts in little steel cylinders about three-sixteenths of an inch in diameter and three-eighths of an inch long. One of these cylinders accidentally became fixed on the ivory tip of an artist's pencil lying on his desk. By another fortuitous circumstance, it was struck a sharp blow. There was a small explosion and the pencil was shattered. This, according to Shaw, was the birth of the percussion cap. He immediately recognized its possibilities and conceived the idea of placing such caps on nipples similar to those used on the patch locks. In 1815, he produced a pewter cap as an improvement on the first ones of steel and iron, and in 1816 he switched to copper, the final material for all later caps.

A short time thereafter, Shaw decided to emigrate to America. He landed in Philadelphia late in 1817. Because of Forsyth's basic patent on fulminate locks, he averred that he had not obtained an English patent on his caps, and as an alien he could not obtain an American patent until he had lived in the United States for two years. For some reason which he never explained, however, Shaw waited five years—until 1822—before applying for a patent, and by that time there were several European patents on the device.

Thus, Shaw's claim is based only on his own

1

2

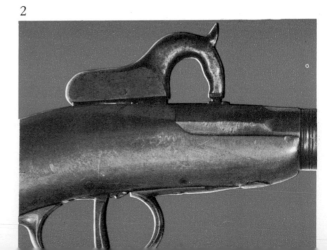

3

4

1. *Prussian tube-lock pistol.*

2. *American pill-lock pistol
of about
the period 1820-1825.*

3. *Three Deringers include
the largest (15 inches
overall) and the smallest
(three and three-quarters
inches) models the
master made.*

4. *Four copies of the
Deringer style: Counterclockwise
from top, they
bear the marks of Slotter,
J. E. Evans, Tryon, and R. Constable.*

5. *Another Deringer copy
carries the name of J. Jacobs
of Philadelphia.*

5

statements. No substantiating evidence that he invented the percussion cap has yet been found. Nevertheless, he was instrumental in perfecting and popularizing the cap lock in the United States.

As developed by Shaw and his European confreres, the copper percussion cap was a highly efficient primer. The thin metal casing was shaped somewhat like the top hat of the period. Inside, at the bottom of the cavity, a small amount of fulminate of mercury or potassium chlorate was covered with a disc of tin foil and sealed with a drop of shellac to make it waterproof. In use, the cap was placed on a tube or nipple leading directly to the charge in the bore. The hammer, acting like the cock of a flintlock, struck it a sharp blow, and the explosion sent a spurt of flame into the propellent charge. The system was impervious to the elements, and as long as the charge in the barrel remained dry, a percussion-cap gun could be fired even in a driving rain.

The first firearms to make use of the new cap locks seem to have been fowling pieces and pistols. The flintlock had champions among sportsmen who pointed out that it shot "harder" than the new percussion gun, but the advocates of the cap countered that their guns took fire faster. They did not have to lead a flying duck quite so far when they aimed. Thus, the

beginner could become a good shot more quickly and easily. In the end, the newcomers won and the flintlock disappeared. The double-barreled fowler also became more and more popular until it almost eclipsed the older single gun. For more than seventy years the double-barreled percussion shotgun was a standard item for sporting-goods stores throughout the world. It served military purposes as well. Major Levi Twiggs of the U. S. Marines was carrying one when he was killed beneath the walls of Chapultepec in 1847. Bushwackers and guerrillas carried them through bloody Kansas and Missouri. Many a Texas ranger and Confederate cavalryman rested one across his pommel, while stagecoach guards and peace officers of the Old West considered them indispensable.

One of the first of the pistol makers to adopt the new percussion system was a Philadelphia gunsmith soon destined to make his name synonymous with a whole class of firearms. Henry Deringer Jr. was a Pennsylvania German gunmaker noted for his fine craftsmanship. For years he had been making military arms and Indian rifles under contract to the United States government, and fine rifles and dueling pistols for private sale. According to his own statement, he switched to the percussion system about 1825 and began to concentrate on pistols. At first these were large weap-

ons, but gradually the smaller sizes began to predominate. The southern and western states were passing through an era much like that of Eighteenth Century Europe. Respected citizens and thieves, congressmen and gamblers all carried pistols and knives as a natural part of their costume. Deringer's new pistols, which could be carried inconspicuously in any pocket, fitted the times ideally.

Deringer held no patents on his pistols. His sole contribution lay in the structural design and workmanship of his guns. He produced a firearm that had great appeal for a large segment of the population. Imitators were quick to copy his pistols, but the fame of his design and craftsmanship spread so quickly that almost all of them were forced to do homage by trying to associate their names with his. Some copied his name exactly while others used variants such as Derringer or Beringer. But to the public all single-shot pocket pistols were derringers—and they didn't care how they spelled the name.

The typical Deringer pistol was a compact but lethal weapon. Some were as short as three and three-quarters inches; some were nine inches, and calibers ranged from .33 to .51. Because of their short barrels they were not accurate at long distance, but across a gaming table they were deadly.

One table-top encounter with Deringer pistols occurred in Los Angeles in 1852. A dinner party of eminent gentlemen had fallen to discussing heroes over their wine, and the question arose as to who was the greatest man in the country. Colonel John Bankhead Magruder nominated his fellow southerner, Andrew Jackson. Dr. William B. Osborn of New York, who was apparently further into his cups, declared in favor of his father and insisted upon challenging anyone who held a contrary opinion. "Prince John" Magruder, as the challengee, had the choice of weapons and selected "Derringer pistols across the dining-room table." There was no waiting. A pair of pistols was produced and carefully loaded under the supervision of the seconds. The principals took their places and the command "Ready!" rang out. Nervously the doctor fired without waiting for the next command. To his horror the shot took no effect and Magruder faced him, the muzzle of his still-loaded piece a scant four feet away. It was too much for Osborn. He dropped to his knees and begged for mercy, which the colonel accorded with a few suitable remarks and the toe of his boot. Only Magruder and the seconds knew that the pistols were loaded with bottle corks instead of bullets.

Unfortunately, most encounters did not end so harmlessly. Homicide followed homicide, and derringers figured in a large percentage of

123

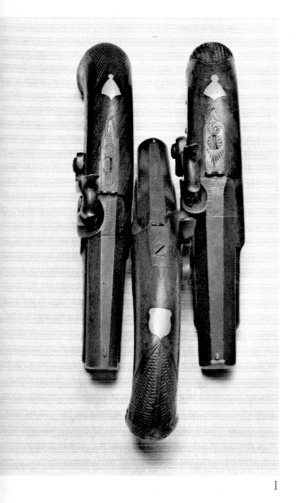

1

1. *Deringer-type pistols marked (left to right) by Gillespie of New York, Dimick of St. Louis, and Hoffman of Vicksburg.*

———

2. *Deringer copy made by Klepzig & Co., San Francisco.*

———

3. *Pair of Deringer pistols distributed by A. J. Plate of San Francisco.*

———

4. *Special primer on Deringer-type pistol fed pellets automatically over the nipple. Patented by Jesse S. Butterfield.*

2

3

4

them. Vigilance committees were formed to reduce murders and restore order, but if no blood was actually shed, the attitude toward shooting seems to have been remarkably lackadaisical. Thus, for instance, when "Long John" Cardinwell and an editor of the Columbia *Gazette* engaged in a shooting spree, the attitude seemed to be one of annoyance that they had disturbed the peace of that California town. Cardinwell, it seems, had a grudge against the editor. Standing in the doorway of a saloon one day, he saw the object of his ire approaching and decided that such a person was too much for a man of his character to put up with any longer. Taking deliberate aim with the Deringer, he fired at the unwary newspaperman. The shot went true, but the editor had had the foresight to be carrying a bowie knife inside his shirt. The ball struck the knife blade and inflicted only a flesh wound. Irritated by this unfriendly act, the intended victim returned the fire, and soon an impressionable bystander also joined the general shooting. Then the police arrived and arrested all three. Cardinwell was fined $20, and the others were duly released. The rival newspaper commented upon the severity of the punishment and concluded: "We therefore advise all persons who wish to shoot at others, to go outside the corporation limits."

The height of the percussion derringer's popularity was reached in the 1850's and early 1860's. It was already on the decline when John Wilkes Booth chose one to assassinate Abraham Lincoln as he sat in his box at Ford's Theatre on Good Friday, 1865. Henry Deringer himself died a few years later in 1868, a wealthy and respected citizen of eighty-two.

The advent of the percussion cap also made another form of single-shot pistol briefly popular. This was the underhammer, or bootleg, pistol. Underhammer guns were nothing new, but the method of igniting the priming powder as it fell from the pan had always appeared to be precarious. The percussion system, with the cap firmly placed on the nipple, seemed ever so much more reliable. The smooth silhouette of the new pistol made it easy to carry in the top of a boot, and some have maintained that this is how it got its name. Others say the silhouette itself resembled a boot and so suggested "bootleg."

The idea of combining the pistol and bayonet or dagger continued, but there was a difference. The tiny triangular spring bayonets of the flint pistols were replaced by larger fixed blades. A few wheel-lock and flint pistols had been combined with rapiers and hunting swords in earlier centuries, but now the practice was expanded to include cavalry sabers, artillery swords, and larger daggers in a variety of forms. In America, both the pistol and bowie knife were popular weapons, and these two arms were combined by George Elgin in his well-known cutlass pistol, one of the few such combination arms ever to have received a government contract. One hundred and fifty of them were ordered for an exploring expedition to the South Seas in 1838-1842. They saw action on this trip, too, for there is one report of a fight in which a sailor split the head of a hostile native with the heavy blade of his cutlass pistol. By the time the ships returned, however, the inventor was out of business, one of the makers was bankrupt, and another had died. Serviceable or not, they were impressive-looking weapons and the few surviving specimens are much sought after by collectors.

Along with the new percussion system came a whole new set of accessories. The old powder horns and the flasks of horn, wood, bone, or a dozen other materials were gradually replaced by flasks of stamped metal or pressed leather. A myriad of dies was cut to produce fanciful shapes and embossed designs. Graduated spouts were added to throw measured charges of powder according to the selected setting. There were containers for shot, too. Sometimes these were soft bags similar to those of earlier ages. In other instances they were long, snakelike affairs of leather with a metal scoop top; these were worn under the arm. Most often, how-

ever, they resembled the flask and were made of hard pressed leather with the same embossed designs. Caps could be carried loose in the pocket without danger, but there were also special cappers which provided both a container for the primers and an easy means for applying them to the nipples. The quality and artistry of the older handmade accouterments might have gone, but a well-equipped shooter of the mid-Nineteenth Century had a variety of machine-stamped gadgets to choose from.

While the percussion cap was making such inroads among civilians, the military men were not entirely idle. They, too, were interested. Because Forsyth was ordered out of the Tower with all his "rubbish," and because it was a number of years after the cap came into general use that it was adopted by any of the world's armies, it has long been the fashion to laugh at the slowness of the "military mind." But armies have special problems that are utterly foreign to those of the civilian sportsman. Just because a new lock works well in the hands of an enthusiastic shooter, who uses it only occasionally and takes good care of it, is no sure indication that it will also function well in the hands of a recruit, who wishes he were someplace else and does no more than is essential to maintain it. An individual can afford to take more chances. If his new gun does not work or keeps getting out of order, he can replace it reasonably quickly at a comparatively low cost. If a whole army has to replace its arms, it is a long, slow, and extremely costly procedure.

As long as there was no national emergency, ordnance officials were wise to move slowly and to make sure they were right before junking a system that had stood the test of time. Forsyth's official test had been disappointing. His lock was expensive and complicated. It required more care than the average soldier could be expected to give it. It was not yet a good military arm. (Besides, improvements were coming that would make it obsolete.)

Even after the cap was perfected, there was still need for information. Ordnance officers wondered how the new system would affect range and muzzle velocity, speed of ignition, and speed of loading. They were not sure a soldier could perform the delicate task of placing a cap on a nipple in the heat of action, or on a galloping horse, with any certainty of success. Tests were needed for all these factors and they proceeded to make them. When the answers were in, they found that the new guns lost a little in muzzle velocity. Although ignition itself was faster, it took a little longer to load. A soldier could only be expected to load and fire three times a minute rather than four, as he had with the flintlock. The new time factor was caused by the need to reach into a pouch for a cap and fit it carefully in place, instead of just pouring a little powder from the torn cartridge into a pan. And this could prove a difficult task with cold or nervous fingers. Still, the lower cost of the perfected cap lock, its greater resistance to the effects of weather, and its sureness of ignition outweighed its disadvantages for the soldier.

The only factor remaining was supply. As soon as it appeared that adequate supplies of the new caps could be obtained without the fear of a disastrous shortage in time of war, the

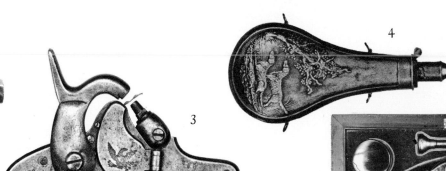

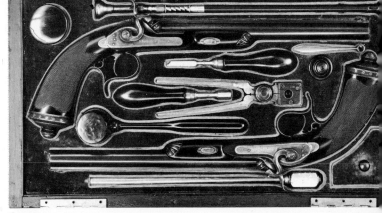

military establishments of most nations moved to adopt the new system. France issued a few percussion arms as early as 1829 and ordered complete adoption of the system in 1840. Sweden began its transition with naval arms in 1833 and also completed it in 1840. Prussia adopted percussion arms in 1839. In the United States, special percussion weapons were adopted in 1833, but it was 1841-42 before the new lock became standard for all troops. In Great Britain, various forms of percussion lock had been tested ever since the Forsyth and all had been failures until the cap. As early as 1831, a small number of percussion muskets and pistols made from converted flintlocks was issued. More followed in succeeding years until the Model 1842 musket completely superseded the older flint. Switzerland also adopted the system in 1842. And so on throughout Europe. The decision finally made, Forsyth was granted retroactive remuneration by his government, but most of it came after his death in 1843.

As early as 1817, a writer to the *Gentleman's Magazine* had considered the possibility that the world's armies might someday be armed with percussion guns and had recoiled from the prospect in horror:

If, however, this new system were applied to the Military, war would shortly become so frightful as to exceed all bounds of imagination. Future wars would threaten, within a few years, to destroy not only armies, but civilization itself. It is to be hoped that men of conscience will militate most vehemently for the suppression of this new invention.

The hope was vain. The detonating system had become standard for the civilized world.

1. *Dramatic but unsuccessful
Elgin cutlass pistol
was ordered by U.S. Navy in 1837.*
2. *Underhammer pistol.*
3. *Lock from U.S. Model 1855 rifle with
Maynard tape primer.*
4. *Typical stamped copper powder flask.*
5. *French percussion dueling
pistols, about 1845.*
6. *Lieutenant Hills attacked by Sepoy
cavalry during Indian mutiny
of 1857. From original water color.*

127

THE
SPINNING
BALL

*The date and place of the rifle's invention are lost in one of the byways of history.
And so is the name of the perceptive man who recognized—centuries before the
scientific principle was understood—that a spinning ball will travel straighter and
strike harder than one that sails without rotation. It may have been August Kotter,
a gunsmith of Nürnberg, or Gaspard Koller of Vienna; both have their advocates. Leipzig also has been designated as the birthplace. Dates range from 1450
to 1550. Unfortunately, there is no proof for any of these claims. The best we can
do is to set reasonable limits: The first rifle was the work of an unknown inventor
in Central Europe, probably eastern Germany or Austria, in the late 1400's.*

Evidence is sketchy, but the earliest references come from Central Europe, which was the hub of rifle production for at least two centuries. Nineteenth Century scholars said they had seen references to rifles in an Italian inventory of 1476 and in an invitation to a shooting match at Leipzig in 1498. But the interpretation of the inventory has been questioned, and no one has been able to find the Leipzig invitation despite careful searches.

There is one piece of evidence, however, that does establish the fact that rifles were in use at least as early as the opening years of the Sixteenth Century. This is an actual rifle of the period which can be dated precisely by the coat of arms it bears. It belonged to the famous Hapsburg ruler, Maximilian I, and the arms are those he used after he became King of Germany in 1493 and before he became Holy Roman Emperor in 1508. Maximilian was an avid hunter and fond of all forms of sport and military exercises. His prowess and his gallant attitudes toward war and life reflected an earlier day and led people to call him "the last of the knights." Firearms interested him greatly as military weapons, but for sport he much preferred the traditional crossbow.

Still, Maximilian did not completely overlook the sporting gun, at least for mountain game. There is a story in his *Hunting Book* of 1499-1500 that tells how he once used a firearm for shooting chamois. And there is the surviving rifle itself. The lock is now missing, but it appears to have been a snapping matchlock. The stock is decorated in the manner one would expect for the weapon of so august a person. The barrel is bronze, instead of iron. It is fitted with a peep sight for accurate shooting and the bore is rifled with twelve or fourteen grooves (two are indistinct) in a slow twist. It is in all respects a true rifle.

There is no reason to believe that this was one of the very first rifles ever made. There may have been others fabricated years previously that have not survived. Except for this gun, however, there is no concrete evidence of the rifle's existence until the middle 1500's. It is the only link between the disputed inventory, the missing invitation, and the wealth of references to rifles that appear half a century later.

It is interesting to speculate how this rifle and its predecessors came to be invented in the first place. Some students believe that grooves originally were cut into the bores of guns to collect the fouling residue that was the constant plague of all black-powder arms. At first these grooves were straight, they feel, and when it was found that they served their purpose well, someone attempted to increase their residue capacity by lengthening them and spiraling them around the bore. The fact that the gun then shot better came as a surprise bonus.

This is an interesting theory, but there is too much against it to grant it much credence. There are guns with straight grooves, it is true, but many of the earliest ones, including the Maximilian rifle, have spiral grooves. If the grooves were simply collecting places for fouling, there would be no need to make them parallel. But to shoot accurately this would be necessary. In order for a ball to "take" the rifling and spin properly in flight, it has to fit the bore tightly. In smoothbores the ball was usually considerably smaller than the bore diameter and fit quite loosely. Thus, if the grooves were designed merely as fouling reservoirs, the ball would still have been loaded loosely and the grooves would have had no effect upon it whatsoever. It is always possible that there occurred a series of lucky accidents that led to spiral fouling grooves and an oversized ball coming together with surprising and happy results, but the chances are against it.

It is much more likely that one or more gunsmiths deliberately set out to make the bullet spin as it left the barrel. For years the feathers on arrows and crossbow bolts had been set at an angle so that these projectiles would spin in

131

1. *Emperor Maximilian I of
Austria. The earliest known rifle was owned
by this Hapsburg ruler.*
2. *Although the lock is now missing,
Maximilian's rifle was originally a matchlock.*
3. *Shooting contests in the 16th century
were highly organized affairs. This one, held at
Prague in 1585, employs a moving target.*
4. *This Danish wheel-lock rifle was signed by
Wilhelm Hefflin in 1650.*

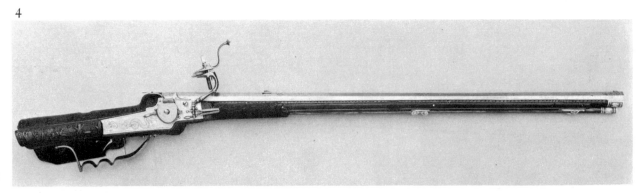

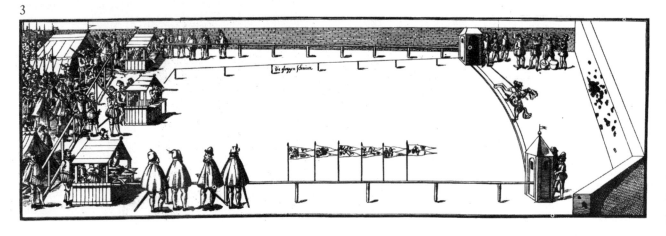

flight. It was known that this made them more stable in the air. Thus, it seems natural that some curious gunsmith should wonder if spinning bullets might not also shoot better.

The unknown inventor of the magical spiral grooves had no real idea why the spinning bullet flew straighter and struck harder. Nor had anyone else at the time. One group of savants theorized learnedly that a devil could not ride a spinning ball and interfere with its performance. As proof, they reminded their listeners that rotation was the fundamental motion of God's creation. They pointed to the spinning heavens which were agreed to be demon free, while everyone knew that the motionless earth was ridden with devils.

Another group took exactly the opposite viewpoint. They agreed with Maximilian, who sometimes referred to "devilish fire guns." If guns were indeed tools of the devil, then those which shot best must be in close league with the forces of evil. From this it was only logical to believe that a demon could ride a spinning ball better and guide it more accurately on its nefarious mission.

Actually, there were two reasons for the greater accuracy of rifled guns. The loose-fitting balls of the smoothbores bounced from one side of the bore to the other as they were propelled down the barrel. Their final direction was determined to a considerable extent by the nature of the last bounce they took before leaving the muzzle. A tight-fitting rifle ball always left the muzzle in a straight line. More important, no cast ball is ever absolutely true and uniform. The shape sometimes varies ever so slightly from the perfect sphere, and the density of the metal is never precisely the same throughout all parts of the ball. One area is always slightly heavier than the rest. This shifts the center of gravity away from the geometrical center of the bullet. As the ball flies, it has a tendency to turn its heaviest area forward. This causes a wobbling in flight and a tendency to drift. When the ball spins, the casting and weight differences do not remain in any one spot, but form concentric rings around the projectile as a whole and thus produce an artificial equilibrium. A gyroscopic effect is also created and this imparts even more stability.

It was three hundred years after the invention of the rifle before these actions were fully understood. The British mathematician, Benjamin Robbins, noted many of them in 1742, as did one or two other English scientists. But it was after 1800 that truly scientific ballistics came to the fore.

Even if they did not comprehend the physical principles underlying the rifle's accuracy, Sixteenth Century shooters were quick to recognize its superior performance. Few matchlocks were rifled, but quantities of the German wheel locks were manufactured with the new spiral grooves in their bores. Modern students would call them polygrooved rifles, for each barrel had many shallow grooves, usually between six and twelve. The early gunmakers seemed to feel that the more grooves a gun had, the better it could impart the desired spin to its bullet.

No matter how many grooves a rifle had, however, it could not impart its spin if the ball did not fit tightly. This matter of fit presented some difficult problems. Balls could be cast ever so slightly larger than the bore, so that when they were forced down the barrel they would intrude slightly into the grooves. To load a tight-fitting ball, it was usually placed in the muzzle and struck a sharp blow or two with the bottom of the powder flask or with a special light mallet to get it started. Then a strong push on the ramrod forced the bullet home. It was a tedious procedure and it led to further difficulties. Most ramrods were wooden and they sometimes broke under the strain of forcing the ball down the barrel. When the ball was struck for starting, it was usually knocked slightly out of shape, thus lessening its accuracy. Powder fouling quickly became a problem and the bore had to be swabbed out at least *133* every second shot or it would become impossible to force the bullet down. With such a bullet, a rifleman needed both patience and perseverance—or maybe stubbornness.

The use of the tight-fitting ball died hard. It kept cropping up even as late as 1800, although there was another and much better way. It had been found that if the ball were wrapped in a greased patch of thin leather or cloth, a smaller bullet could be used. In such instances it was the patch that was forced up into the grooves and imparted the spin to the ball. It was much easier and faster to ram a patched bullet down the bore, and this more than compensated for the extra time it took to cut and center the patch. Ramrods were not broken so often and fouling was not nearly so great a problem. Actually, the greased patch helped to soften and remove the powder residue.

No one knows when the advantages of the patched ball were first discovered, but it was probably at least as early as the Sixteenth Century. Greased patches have survived in rifle accouterments from about 1600 in the Royal Armory at Dresden; and far down in Spain, Alonzo Martínez de Espinar's *Treatise on Guns and Shooting* of 1644 describes the patching of rifle balls with a clear analysis of the advantages of doing so. Certainly by then, at least, it was a common practice, well known and accepted throughout most of Western Europe.

But skillful loading techniques included more than just the proper ball, whether patched or bare. For really accurate shooting, a marksman had to test his weapon until he understood its idiosyncrasies and had learned the powder charge that best suited it. Then he had to make sure to use that same charge consistently. The strength of powder was likely to vary considerably in that era, so testers were devised to measure the thrust of a given charge. Armed with this knowledge, the rifleman then decided upon the optimum quantity to use for his charge as long as that particular supply of powder lasted. This required measures and he proceeded to devise a variety of them. Sometimes the end of the ramrod was hollowed out and graduated for the purpose. Maximilian's rifle had that sort of measure. Others were made as parts of wheel-lock spanners, flask nozzles, or separate scoops that could be carried loose or tied to the clothing.

Such care was worth while, for marksmanship was a skill greatly admired in the area of the rifle's birth. For centuries there had been shooting contests sponsored by the leading cities of Central Europe. These were highly organized affairs with targets, weapons, distances, and techniques spelled out in detail. And there were valuable prizes, too, ranging from a maiden for the best bowman in the Magdeburg games of 1387 to a goat covered in red cloth

for the best shot at Ratisbon in 1586.

The first surviving record of a prize shooting for arquebuses dates from 1426, and as early as 1472 the practical Swiss held an all-gun meet. Usually these guns were smoothbores. For many years after the first rifles appeared they remained comparatively rare weapons. Their performance was so much better than the smoothbored pieces that mixed contests would have been manifestly unfair. Thus, these rifles were usually banned, or, upon consent, relegated to special all-rifle matches. After 1560 such special classes became more and more common, until by 1600 they were standard. At Basle in 1605, for instance, there was a dual meet. The smoothbores competed at five hundred and seventy feet with a two-and-a-half-foot target, while rifles were assigned the astounding range of eight hundred and five feet with a three-and-

135

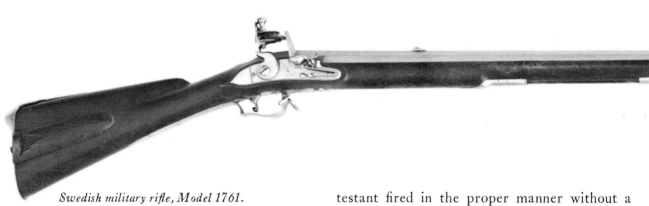

a-half-foot target. When it is realized that all shots were fired offhand, without supports of any kind and with a definite time limit, the quality of the marksmanship and the accuracy of the rifles can be more fully appreciated.

Targets were varied in the early shooting matches. Most often they were circular, with a bull's-eye in the center, similar to the modern form. Spotters with sticks and discs signaled the location of hits from bulletproof observation posts and scores were kept by the officials. Sometimes the target was a flat wooden bird set on a tall pole. Each joint that was shot off counted points, and all splinters over a minimum size could be weighed and counted toward the prizes. But there were more elaborate targets, also: human figures cut in silhouette from wood, fanciful forms, and even moving targets in the shape of warriors on horseback.

A whole slate of officials and judges presided at the contests. All arms had to be checked to see that they were of the specified calibers and that they were or were not rifled, depending upon the type of competition. Sights had to meet specifications and there were regulations about straps, handles, bizarre designs, and the like. Then it was necessary to see that each con-

testant fired in the proper manner without a rest or support, that he stood in the proper place, fired the correct number of shots in the prescribed length of time, and complied with all the other rules. Besides the judges and scorekeepers there was a special official called the *pritschmeister,* or prize master, who kept the contest moving, served as master of ceremonies, and acted the fool at the same time. As with all jesters, he was granted wide license to lampoon contestants regardless of rank. A poor shot drew certain ridicule and the unfortunate Sixteenth Century shooter who scored the contemporary equivalent of "Maggy's drawers" brought forth a spectacular performance. Poor marksmen were well advised to stay home. These were serious contests.

The use of the rifle was not confined to the target range. The deer, boar, and chamois of Central Europe offered wider scope for the new gun. Foresters and hunters—*jaeger,* as they were called in German — quickly adopted the new weapon, and the short European rifle is still known to modern collectors as a *jaeger* because of this association.

The military potential of the rifle was also recognized. Christian IV of Denmark (1588-1648) is generally considered to have been the first European monarch to equip troops with the new gun, and he took that step early in the Seventeenth Century. Before long the French Royal Horse Guards boasted eight rifled carbines per troop and within the next century the military use of the rifle had spread widely on the Continent, especially in Germany and Scandinavia. The Swedish model of 1761 even had a bayonet, signifying an arm designed especially for military purposes and not just an adapted sporting piece.

By this time the European rifle had evolved its standard form. The wheel lock had remained popular for rifles throughout the 1600's, and in certain areas of Germany it continued in use even into the Eighteenth Century. By then, however, the flintlock was also widely used for rifles and gradually the older system disappeared. These were short guns as a rule, averaging between three and four feet in length. Bores were large, with calibers of .75 not unusual. The rifling was deep and multigrooved. The barrels were octagonal, with a slight flare at the muzzle, an open rear sight, and a blade front sight. Usually there were set or hair triggers housed in a long, deep trigger guard. Most characteristic was a box carved in the right side of the stock with a sliding cover. Here the shooter carried his small tools, extra flints, or possibly his greased patches. Such boxes are usually called patch boxes today, but since almost none of those on early rifles show traces of grease, many students believe that the early riflemen carried their patches elsewhere.

This was the standard rifle of Central and Northern Europe at the time when religious, economic, and political disturbances led many to seek greater peace and freedom in new lands. William Penn's colony in America seemed to offer the opportunities they sought and large numbers of German and Swiss families picked up and moved to Pennsylvania. From Philadelphia they pushed inland to the frontier to establish new communities in the wilderness. With them went their rifles, and gunsmiths skilled in making them.

Life on the American frontier was considerably different from that in Central Europe. The rifle was far more important here as a tool of survival than it had ever been as a sporting arm at home. There was a wider variety of game, and shooting conditions in the wilderness were quite unlike those in the civilized areas of the Continent.

These conditions led to changes in the rifle to make it more useful in its new environment. Calibers were reduced to conserve powder and shot. Barrels were lengthened, both for greater accuracy at long ranges and to assure that all of the powder burned in the barrel. To make certain that he was not wasting precious powder by using more than would burn completely in the bore, the frontiersman frequently tested his charge by firing over an expanse of clean snow. If telltale grains of unburned black powder showed on the surface, he knew that the charge was too great, and he reduced it until the snow beneath the muzzle remained clean after a discharge.

There were stylistic changes in the rifle, too, which were less directly related to improving its function on the frontier. The sliding wooden cover on the patch box gave way to a hinged metal cover. Brass was the usual material, but once in a great while an iron cover is encountered. And there is no doubt that these boxes were now used primarily for the greased patches universally employed by American riflemen. American woods also were used for the stock, and gradually the hard curly maple with its intricate grain pattern became standard. The sling swivels and studs of the German rifle also disappeared, for few Americans carried their *137*

Below: A plainsman and his rifle in "Conference in the Stockade," a contemporary painting by W. M. Carey. Brass tacks, used by white man as well as Indian, ornament Hawken plains rifle (right).

home. During the second quarter of the Eighteenth Century, however, the evolution became more and more noticeable. By 1750, the true American rifle had developed. Still, its caliber was relatively large, ranging from .45 to .60, and its stock was straight and thick in the butt. Better specimens were carved with designs in relief, especially on the left side of the butt stock and around the lock and barrel-tang mortises. The next sixty years saw the rifle reach its highest peak, both in performance and design. The caliber continued to decrease to an average of .40 to .45. The stock became lighter and much more graceful as it developed a sweeping drop in the butt, a curving "Roman nose" comb, and a sharply crescentic butt plate designed to fit around the upper arm at the shoulder. Inlays began to appear—brass, pewter, silver— and frequently they were engraved. After 1810, however, a decline set in. Lines became more angular. Decoration tended toward the gaudy. Efficiency and accuracy remained, but the artistry was gone.

Many names have been applied to this graceful rifle of the frontier, and the arguments in favor of one or another as the only right and proper appellation have been long and loud. In the beginning it seems to have been called simply the "American rifle" and later the "long rifle." Then, after the exploits of the backwoodsmen in Kentucky and Tennessee and at the Battle of New Orleans, it became known as the "Kentucky rifle," and this name has stuck for over a century. More recently, a strong group has raised its voice in favor of naming the gun the "Pennsylvania rifle," after the state of its birth and greatest flowering. And there are other names as well, each with enough validity to keep the specialists arguing for at least another century.

No matter what it is called, it was a fine gun in a society that treasured both accuracy and reliability. Because firearms were so important on the frontier, every man became proficient in their use. Boys learned to shoot as soon as they

arms by such a strap or used it in shooting. Otherwise, it retained the multigrooved octagonal barrel, browned to eliminate glare, the same sights, and often the same set triggers.

Nevertheless, the changes had made it an entirely new arm, a long, graceful weapon, light but sturdy, and supremely accurate. No other rifle could outshoot it. It was America's first original contribution to the development of firearms. All other American advances had resulted from the colonists' insistence upon using the best of the European systems available, regardless of cost, so that the colonies were consistently ahead of Europe in adopting each improved arm as it appeared for standard use. Here, at last, was an actual improvement on a European arm, a truly American gun.

These changes in the rifle did not take place all at once. Rather they were strung out over a long period of years. The first rifles made by the German gunsmiths in Pennsylvania were exactly the same as those they had made at

were big enough to hold a long rifle steady. By the time they were twelve they could be expected to supply some of the meat for the family table and to take their place alongside the men in time of Indian troubles.

With such an excellent rifle and such constant practice, fine marksmanship became commonplace. Yet it remained a greatly admired skill. The German and Swiss colonists brought with them their love of shooting matches, and all along the frontier such contests flourished as one of the chief forms of recreation. There were turkey shoots with a live bird tethered behind a log as the target. The trick was to induce the turkey to show its head and then hit it. The first man to do so won the bird as prize. There were also beef shoots. Here each contestant brought his own target, a board or shingle about five by seven inches with an X marked in the center. The man to score the closest shot to the center of his mark won the choicest cut of beef, and so on for each round until the carcass was completely disposed of. The ranges varied. Much depended upon the size of the target. A small one, such as the head of a turkey, might call for distances of two hundred and fifty feet offhand, or three hundred and fifty feet with a rest.

Thus, a whole population grew up in the school of marksmanship. Proved in formal contest, in the hunt, and in the deadlier business of home defense against raiding parties, the true rifleman was ready for all emergencies.

And now the gun itself was ready to make its presence felt on the stage of world history. The trial ground was the eastern seaboard of the United States; the time the American Revolution. This would not be the first appearance of the rifle as a military arm. There had been regular riflemen in several European military establishments for more than a century. A few American riflemen also had participated in the French and Indian Wars, and British soldiers, impressed with what they saw, had issued American rifles to picked marksmen in their

flank companies as they battled the French or pushed through the wilderness after the wily Pontiac a few years later. But as yet the rifle had made no real impact on warfare.

The change began June 14, 1775, when the Continental Congress authorized ten companies of riflemen as a first step toward creating a new national army. The next day it appointed George Washington as commander in chief. The United States Army had been born and in the beginning it was all riflemen. Within weeks the paper organization was a reality. Daniel Morgan's company was first. Raised in Virginia, the backwoodsmen of Morgan's command marched six hundred miles in twenty-one days to join the local forces penning the British in Boston. Other companies from Pennsylvania and Maryland soon followed.

They were a rough-and-ready lot, these first Continental riflemen. Morgan, their captain, had been a teamster with Braddock as a youth twenty years before, and all of the men had grown up along the frontier with a rifle in their hands. All wore fringed hunting shirts, with a long scalping knife and a tomahawk thrust through the belt. Their favorite occupation was demonstrating their skill with their long rifles. One Virginian is said to have left the urbanites goggle-eyed by putting eight consecutive shots through a five-by-seven-inch target at a distance of sixty yards, and a whole company is supposed to have placed shots, one after the other, through a seven-inch target at a distance of two hundred yards.

This is almost unbelievable shooting with simple open sights, but it is confirmed by the testimony of an impartial observer at the time. Major George Hanger of the British Army was an excellent marksman himself, and he had the dubious pleasure of being shot at by an American rifleman. He recounted his experience with some awe:

Colonel, now General Tarleton, and myself, were standing a few yards out of a wood, observing the situation of a part of the enemy

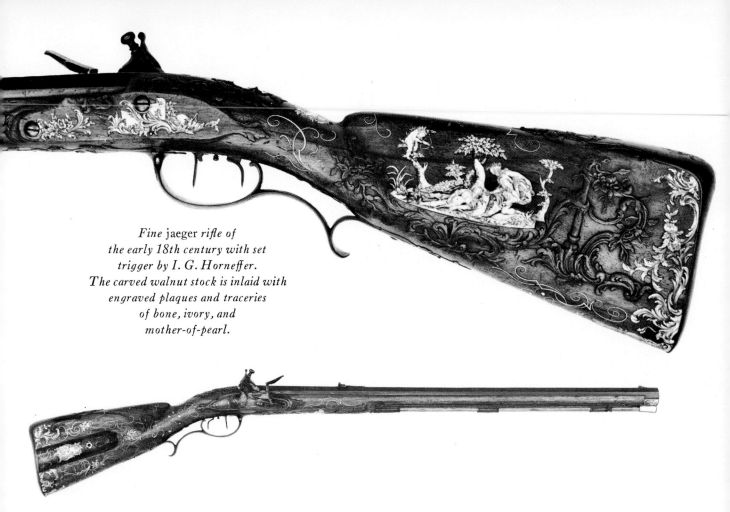

*Fine jaeger rifle of
the early 18th century with set
trigger by I. G. Horneffer.
The carved walnut stock is inlaid with
engraved plaques and traceries
of bone, ivory, and
mother-of-pearl.*

which we intended to attack. There was a rivulet in the enemy's front, and a mill on it, to which we stood directly with our horses' heads fronting, observing their motions. It was absolutely a plain field between us and the mill; not so much as a single bush on it. Our orderly-bugler stood behind us about three yards, but with his horse's side to our horses' tails. A rifleman passed over the milldam, evidently observing two officers, and laid himself down on his belly; for in such positions, they always lie, to take a good shot at a long distance. He took deliberate and cool shot at my friend, at me, and at the bugle-horn man. Now observe how well this fellow shot. It was in the month of August, and not a breath of wind was stirring. Colonel Tarleton's horse and mine, I am certain, were not anything like two feet apart; for we were in close consultation, how we should attack with our troops which laid 300 yards in the wood, and could not be perceived by the enemy. A rifleball passed between him and me; looking directly to the mill I evidently observed the flash of the powder. I directly said to my friend, "I think we had better move, or we shall have two or three of these gentlemen shortly amusing themselves at our expense." The words were hardly out of my mouth when the bugle-horn man behind me, and directly ·central, jumped off his horse and said, "Sir, my horse is shot." The horse staggered, fell down, and died....Now speaking of the rifleman's shooting, nothing could be better....I have passed several times over this ground and ever observed it with the greatest attention; and I can positively assert that the distance he fired from at us was full 400 yards.

Further, Hanger declared that he had examined hundreds and hundreds of American rifles and talked with many American marksmen. It would be average, he said, for an expert shot to hit the head of a man at two hundred yards, and "provided an American rifleman were to get a perfect aim at 300 yards at me, standing still, he most undoubtedly would hit me, unless it was a very windy day...." As a student of rifles, Hanger was familiar with all of the usual European types, and it was his con-

141

sidered opinion that the American rifle was the best in the world and the American marksman the best shot.

For all their auspicious beginning, however, the riflemen did not long retain their exalted position. For one thing, the backwoodsmen were too independent to accept the necessary discipline of an army without rebelling. More important, the rifle, despite its magnificent accuracy, still lacked many of the features necessary for an all-round military arm. It was slow to load and it required a skilled shooter to use it effectively. It also lacked a bayonet.

These were serious defects in a day of single-shot weapons. Firepower was as important then as it is now to hurl back an attacking enemy, or to weaken him sufficiently so that his assault could be beaten back with the bayonet. The linear tactics were the standard of the day and the rifle could not compete with the musket when it came to speed. A regular infantryman could get off three shots, each containing a ball and three buckshot, in the time it took a rifleman to load and fire once, and he had his bayonet for defense in hand-to-hand combat. The single rifle shot might be infinitely more accurate, but it was not enough, especially when it was considered that the rifleman would then have to flee because he had no bayonet to oppose his charging foe. Several American survivors of Bunker Hill had caustic comments about the barbarity of trying to stand up to a bayonet with a bare gun barrel. At one time Washington ordered all his riflemen to carry folding spears for just such emergencies. But he still cautioned Morgan never to let his riflemen be caught in a place where they could not run to safety.

Yet there were times when the rifle performed spectacularly. If trained marksmen were backed up by regulars with the bayonet, they could take a fearsome toll of attacking troops, striking them well beyond musket range. At Saratoga and again at Cowpens and Guilford Courthouse, riflemen operated in advance of the main lines to soften the enemy before hand-to-hand combat began. In fortifications they were magnificent, and for sniping, scouting, and general light infantry work they had no superior.

There was even one battle, at Kings Mountain, that the rifle won all by itself. It was a very special situation, true, with a British force surrounded in a wooded country without hope of aid from outside. But it dramatized the rifle's capabilities, nonetheless.

On the British side there were rifles also—the short German models of the "Hessian" mercenaries and a very few British-made arms. They shot well, and Americans were sometimes surprised at the distances from which they felt their sting. But all of them suffered from the same weaknesses as the American ones.

144

The musket was the work horse of the Revolution. It was the standard arm, bore the brunt of the fighting, and won most of the battles. But the rifle made a tremendous impression. Military men the world over heard of its performance and capabilities. European nations that did not have regular riflemen now began to add them to their armies; those that had them added more.

Great Britain lagged behind some of the continental nations in adopting an official rifle and organizing a special corps to use it, but this was only a temporary delay caused by the usual retrenchment following a major war and the eternal hopes for a lasting peace. When it became apparent that peace was not to be long enjoyed, the British government began to purchase rifles from the Continent. This led to a great confusion of sizes and designs, and it soon became evident that an official British rifle would be needed. Extensive tests were conducted by the Ordnance board at Woolwich in 1800. English, continental, and American types were fired and examined for accuracy, durability, and ease of loading. In the end, the board selected an English gun made by Ezekiel Baker, of Whitechapel, London.

This was the Baker rifle, soon to win fame with Wellington's army in the Peninsula. It had not been the most accurate rifle in the tests, but it had shot excellently at ranges up to two hundred yards and beyond. This was judged sufficient for most military uses, and it did have other features which impressed the judges. Its seven-grooved rifling made only a quarter of a turn in the length of the bore. This reduced friction and made the ball easier to ram home; it also tended to collect less fouling. In some rifles with a sharper twist, a soldier had to push so hard on his rammer that his hand became shaky and interfered with his aim. In addition, the slower twist resulted in a much flatter trajectory for the bullet, and this in turn required less skill on the part of the shooter in estimating distances and compensating for the expected drop. He could aim more directly at what he wanted to hit, a big advantage in training recruits. The Baker ball also was designed so that it was just loose enough to drop down the bore of its own weight if loaded without the greased patch. With the patch, it would take the rifling. Without it, accuracy was sacrificed, but the rifle could be loaded as fast as a musket and fired effectively in the closing moments of an engagement, when the enemy was close at hand and the smoke of battle all but obscured vision, anyway. In the beginning, Baker provided light wooden mallets as an aid in seating the patched ball, but these were soon found to be a nuisance and were discarded. To all intents and purposes, the Baker was a short German rifle with a slower twist, a ball better designed for military purposes, and—very important—a bayonet.

Once it had a rifle, the British government set about establishing a unit to use it. Volunteers were recruited from the regular regiments to form a Corps of Riflemen, then one battalion of the new 95th Regiment, which promptly became known as the Rifle Brigade. A second battalion was added in 1805. To distinguish this elite organization from the rest of the army, it was given green uniforms with black facings. It was a handsome distinction and brought pride to the unit.

With high esprit, the Rifle Brigade sailed off to the Peninsula to draw its first blood from the armies of Napoleon at Obidos, on August 17, 1808. And it gave a good account of itself and its weapons throughout the war. Tales of group and individual exploits are legion.

When the war in Spain ended, six companies of the Rifle Brigade shipped quickly to America where England and the United States were once more at war. They arrived just in time for the Battle of New Orleans, the only instance where the Baker and the American rifle opposed each other on the same field. And it was a needless battle at that, for the treaty of peace had already been signed in far-off Ghent, officially ending the War of 1812.

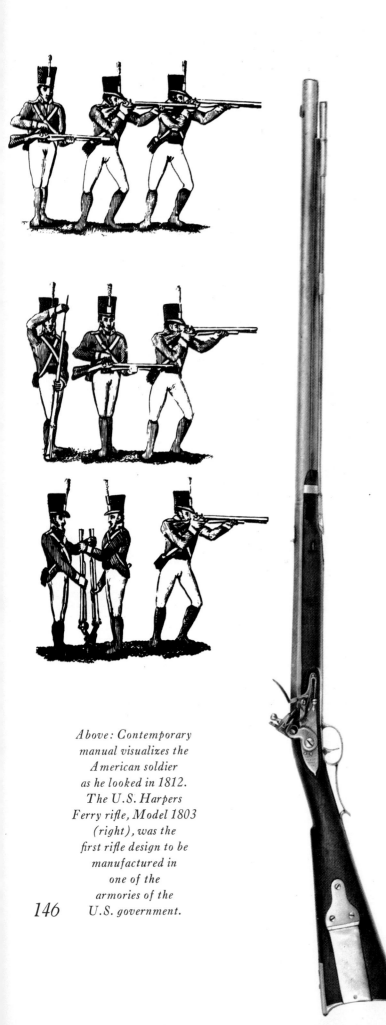

Above: Contemporary manual visualizes the American soldier as he looked in 1812. The U.S. Harpers Ferry rifle, Model 1803 (right), was the first rifle design to be manufactured in one of the armories of the U.S. government.

News traveled slowly in that era, however, and so the two rifles faced each other in a bloody and unequal battle. From the rifleman's standpoint, the Americans had all the best of it. They were entrenched behind an abandoned canal which provided a ready-made moat. For support they had regular infantry and superb artillery all along their lines. The British had to attack across open fields in the face of fierce fire from all of the American guns. Only the staunchest of veterans could have stood in the face of such unequal odds. The British not only stood, but continued to press forward until a few even succeeded in entering the American lines before they were driven back.

In two hours it was all over. The attacking forces had suffered terribly. Estimates of the British dead and wounded ranged from two to three thousand, while the Americans lost six or seven men. There are many accounts of red-coated bodies pierced with a single hole through the center of the breastplate or the forehead.

In this conflict the Baker rifle never had a chance. It found itself in a position where the rifle was at a disadvantage. All its weaknesses were emphasized and its special abilities could not be used. New Orleans is the prime illustration of the proper—and improper—use of the muzzle-loading, round-ball rifle. There were good rifles on both sides—but the Americans were in a better position to function effectively.

Still, the musket remained the standard American infantry weapon. At the close of the Revolutionary War, the army had all but disappeared; there were no regular riflemen whatsoever. In 1792, three hundred and ninety-nine riflemen were authorized and rifles for them were purchased from various Pennsylvania gunsmiths. But it was not until 1803 that an official U.S. rifle model was adopted and put into production at a national armory.

This new Model 1803 rifle was interesting in many ways. It marked a departure from the American tradition of the long barrel and small caliber, for this was a short rifle with a half-stock and a caliber of .54. Henry Dearborn, then Secretary of War, believed that these modifications would make the gun easier to load and less susceptible to powder fouling. He also stressed that the new rifle should be light and easy to carry. This was the reason for the half-stock and for the fact that the forward two-thirds of the barrel were turned round instead of left octagonal. Only the brass patch box and mountings indicated the heritage of the American long rifle. For the rest, it seemed more European in inspiration. But still this new rifle had no bayonet. American riflemen might carry scalping knives and tomahawks for self-defense and general utility, but their prime function was to shoot at long range, with regular infantry to support them if the enemy got close.

In performing this function, the Model 1803 carved a significant notch in American history. In 1803, just as the new rifle was being developed, Meriwether Lewis and William Clark were gathering arms and equipment for their trek through the uncharted wilderness from St. Louis to the Pacific Coast and back again. By the time the expedition set out in 1804, it seems certain that the twenty-six enlisted men who went along had some of the very first specimens of the new arm. They practiced with them, firing offhand at a range of fifty yards until they got the feel of the arm, and then tried them on all kinds of game, including huge, half-ton grizzly bears. After a number of experiences in riddling charging grizzlies with rifle bullets, however, Lewis remarked, "These bear being so hard to die rather intimidates us all; I must confess that I do not like the gentlemen and had rather fight two Indians than one bear."

With the coming of the War of 1812, the Model 1803 saw active service, but most of the militia riflemen continued to use the older Kentucky rifle, and it was this long rifle which performed at New Orleans, not the new arm.

There were other American military muzzle-loading rifles during the next fifty years. In 1814, the Model 1803 was altered slightly by lengthening the barrel three inches. In 1817 another rifle with iron mounts and a full stock was adopted, and promptly named the "common rifle" to distinguish it from the Hall breech-loading rifle of the Model 1819, which was manufactured and issued simultaneously with the muzzle-loading Model 1817. Then, in 1841, a percussion model was adopted.

Except for the Hall, all of these rifles were essentially the same. They were short. They had seven-groove rifling and they fired a round ball. They contributed nothing to the development of the rifle as a specific arm, or toward overcoming its military weaknesses.

It is necessary to turn to Europe to find active experimentation in this field. Perhaps Americans were too complacent about the quality of their rifles, or perhaps they failed to visualize the rifle as more than a supplementary arm. At any rate, they did nothing to try to increase its speed of loading, which was its main defect militarily, and they consistently failed to provide a bayonet, which was its second serious shortcoming. In Europe, the Swedes had added a bayonet to their rifles as early as 1761. Great Britain's Baker rifle of 1800 had one, and so did some others on the Continent. Bayonets were not provided for American rifles until the middle 1840's, when some were adapted for the Model 1841.

But it was the matter of quick loading that attracted most attention abroad. Many fearful and wonderful shapes and systems were devised and tested. A Captain Berner in Brunswick developed a gun with a slightly oval bore and two deep rifling grooves opposite each other. He reasoned that the fewer grooves would reduce friction and speed loading, and that less powder fouling would collect. As a further aid he devised two kinds of cartridges for issue to the troops, one with a patched ball to fit tightly and one with a smaller ball to be loaded naked, as with a smoothbore. At first these balls were cast oval, but soon simple spheres were substituted. Tests were generally favorable and in a short

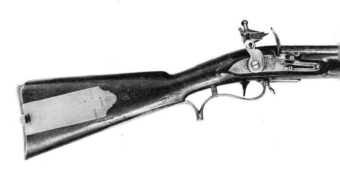

time other governments, such as Oldenberg, Hanover, and Russia, adopted or tested it.

England, too, was favorably impressed with the Brunswick system and adopted it in 1836. George Lovell, Inspector of Small Arms, however, had made significant changes in the original design and not all of them were beneficial. In place of the simple spherical patched ball, the British substituted a ball with a raised belt around its equator. The shooter placed the ball in the muzzle, with the opposite sides of its belt fitted into the two grooves, and then rammed it home. After a few shots the powder fouling accumulated sufficiently to make this a fairly hard task. Also there were ballistic problems. The fit of the belt in the grooves increased friction in the bore, thus using up much of the force of the charge before the ball even emerged, and at the same time creating a fearsome kick against the shooter's shoulder. When the ball did come out, the relation of the spin to the grooves set up a completely false equilibrium from which the projectile was always trying to escape. The result was a wobbling flight. After fifteen years of use, the Select Committee on Small Arms reported succinctly in 1852:

148

At all distances above four hundred yards the shooting was so wild as to be unrecorded. The Brunswick rifle has shown itself to be much inferior in point of range to every other arm hitherto noticed. The loading of this rifle is so difficult that it is a wonder how the Rifle regiments have continued to use it so long—the force required to ram down the ball being so great as to render any man's hand unsteady for accurate shooting. Comment is unnecessary.

But comment was made anyway by those who had to use it. They dubbed it the worst military rifle in Europe.

In France, quite a different approach to the problem was tried. As early as 1828, Captain Gustave Delvigne had decided that the loading of a rifle could never be speeded up sufficiently if the use of a tight-fitting ball was continued. He thought the projectile should be dropped loosely down the barrel in the manner of a musket ball, and then made to fit tightly after it was in position. To accomplish this he designed a rifle with a narrow chamber at the breech, large enough to contain the powder charge with just a little space left over. When the ball was dropped down the barrel, it came to rest against the opening of this chamber. Three light blows with the ramrod then flattened it sufficiently to make it fit tightly.

There was no question that Delvigne's system would work, that it was fast, or that it was easy. The difficulty was that his rifle was inaccurate. The squeezing of the ball between the ramrod and the mouth of the chamber gave it an irregular shape, and it wobbled and drifted in flight. Delvigne cupped the bottom of his

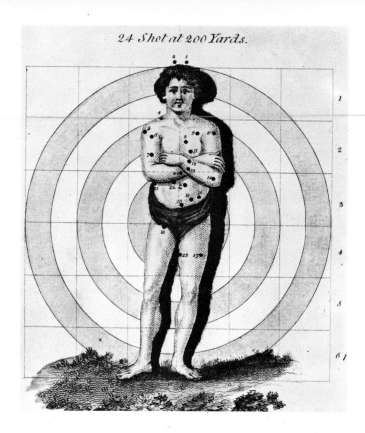

*Far left: A gentleman firing his Baker rifle
—much like the model above—from the frontispiece
of Ezekiel Baker's book on rifles, 1804. Another
panel from the book (right) shows a target
shot at by Baker. Left: An early 19th century powder
flask of tortoise shell and silver.*

ramrod to lessen this effect. His friend Colonel Pontchara added a wooden disc, or sabot, to prevent the bottom of the ball from being severely disfigured by the mouth of the chamber, and placed a greased patch under the lower half of the ball to help reduce fouling. Still, the problems were not entirely solved. Ten battalions of the French army were armed with the Delvigne-Pontchara rifles in 1840, and both Belgium and Austria also adopted the arm, but it never proved really satisfactory.

Nevertheless, the French seemed fascinated with the idea of loading a loose-fitting bullet and expanding it with rammer blows. Colonel Thouvenin of the artillery produced a rifle with a stout pin, half the diameter of the bore, projecting from the bottom of the breech. The powder charge filled the space around this pin, which then served as an anvil for flattening the bullet. In French this pin was called a *tige,* and the Thouvenin system is usually known today as a pillar breech, or a tige rifle. Once again the end of the ramrod was cupped so that the bullet was not badly distorted, but the pillars tended to bend after a time, and powder fouling became a real problem. Thouvenin switched from a spherical ball to an elongated projectile of cylindro-conical form. This did not solve the breech problems, but the projectile did perform better. Thouvenin rifles were issued to the *Chasseurs d'Afrique* in 1846, and extensively tested in America and elsewhere.

In Denmark, N. S. Jessen devised an oval bore that twisted about its axis to impart a spin to a cylindro-conical bullet. Charles W. Lancaster of England followed suit, while another

Englishman, Sir Joseph Whitworth, patented a rifle with a spiraling hexagonal bore and an elongated projectile shaped to fit. The Jessen, Lancaster, and Whitworth rifles were fine, accurate arms, the Whitworth spectacularly so; but it was none of these that brought the muzzle-loading rifle to the peak of its development.

The major breakthrough stemmed from an entirely different theory. Once again it was the expansion of an elongated projectile, but this time the force was supplied by the explosion of the charge, not by blows of the ramrod. Captain John Norton of England is often credited with having experimented with such an expanding bullet in 1823. According to tradition, this bullet was tested by the British Army but rejected with a righteous statement that a spherical ball was the only suitable projectile for military purposes. The celebrated English gunsmith William Greener also attempted an expanding bullet in 1836, but it was egg-shaped and functioned erratically. Then, in France, Captain Delvigne noted that when he tried cylindro-conical projectiles with hollow bases in his rifles, the lead was forced outward and into the rifling grooves by the force of the explosion. **149**

The loose-fitting projectile had expanded to fit the bore tightly. Here was the answer.

It was another French army captain, however, who gave his name to the system of gas-expanding projectiles. Claude Étienne Minié, who had seen service with a rifle regiment in Algeria and later became an instructor at the School of Vincennes, was also intensely interested in rifle projectiles. He refined the shape of Delvigne's hollow-based bullet and in 1849 he added a small iron cup. This cup was designed to be driven forward into the hollow base of the projectile by the force of the explosion, thus assuring a uniform expansion on all sides. Four regiments promptly were equipped with rifles firing the Minié bullet for experimentation, and other countries quickly seized upon the idea.

They soon found that the Minié system had decided drawbacks. The iron cup was a distinct hazard. It was likely to separate from the bullet proper as it left the muzzle and endanger other soldiers in the vicinity. It was expensive. Sometimes it drove the solid end of the bullet out of the gun, while leaving the thin, expanded sides still in the bore.

It also was found to be unnecessary. The British determined that a slightly redesigned bullet expanded and performed very well without a cup of any kind, although they rapidly reverted from this discovery and added a box-wood plug anyway. It did have the advantage of making the bullets less susceptible to damage in packing. At almost the same time the Americans, experimenting at Harpers Ferry, reached the same conclusions. James Henry Burton, Assistant Master Armorer, designed an excellent variant that needed no plug of any kind, and it was promptly adopted by the United States. It was Burton's bullet, but Americans insisted on calling it a "minie ball" just the same.

Such are the quirks of popular recognition. Delvigne, who first noted the possibilities of an expanding hollow-based bullet, received no credit in the popular mind for originating the system. Burton and the British designer who produced the projectiles which actually saw widespread use are seldom mentioned. But the name of Minié, whose system was defective and saw largely experimental use, became a familiar word, at least in the United States.

These new bullets were small, unimpressive pieces of lead, cast one by one in an individual mold or swedged in huge quantities by machines in government factories. But their importance bore no relation to their size or simplicity. The era of the smoothbore was over. Now a rifle could be loaded as fast and as easily as the quickest musket. Accuracy was available for every single soldier. It was no longer necessary to put up with wildly straying bullets for the sake of speed. The smoothbored musket vanished from the military scene almost overnight, and a new day dawned in firearms history. The rifle was supreme at last.

But there was still the problem of designing these supreme arms. In Great Britain, the first rifles of the new system were little more than rifled versions of the percussion smoothbore muskets of 1842. The .75 caliber proved too large, however, for elongated projectiles weighed much more than spherical ones of the same diameter. Lighter versions were tested in 1852, and a new Enfield rifle of .577 caliber was adopted the next year. A new Royal Small Arms Factory at Enfield was quickly equipped with American-made machinery for manufacturing the new gun, and who should turn up as chief engineer but James Henry Burton, late of the Harpers Ferry Armory and designer of the American bullet.

These newly designed guns were called rifle-muskets, a unique name in arms history, albeit a slightly improbable one. Tradition has it that the term derived from the fact that, while the bore was rifled, the exterior resembled the earlier smoothbore musket more than it did the shorter rifle, and that these new guns were designed for issue to all foot soldiers, not just to the Rifle Brigade or other select units.

Be that as it may, the Enfield rifle-musket

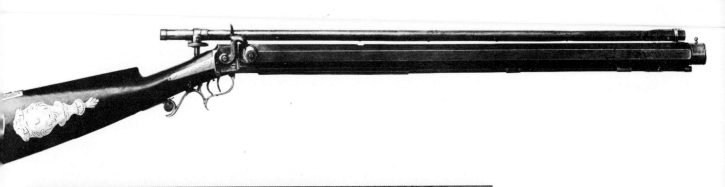

Left: This Union Army sharpshooter in a tree was drawn for Harper's Weekly, *by war correspondent Winslow Homer, during the Peninsular Campaign in Virginia in 1862. The Bench rifle (above), by Edwin Wesson, was used by a Civil War sniper. Its telescopic sights made accuracy possible, even at tremendous ranges.*

and short Enfield rifle were both excellent arms. The Crimean War was well along before production could get under way. But before peace was signed in 1856, some of the new arms appeared on far-off battlefields to replace the earlier Minié rifles of 1851 and to perform very well indeed. A few years later, many more were purchased by both the Union and Confederate governments for service in the American Civil War, where they were highly regarded by the troops on both sides.

The United States was a little slower than Great Britain in adopting arms for its new bul-let. It was 1855 before such guns were approved. There were three of them: a rifle-musket, a short rifle, and a long pistol with a detachable shoulder stock, known as a pistol carbine. The optimum caliber decided upon here was almost the same as that selected in England. Only three thousandths of an inch separated the American .58 from the British .577. It was found during the Civil War that English and American bullets could be used interchangeably, for a few shots at least, until fouling made the Enfield bores too tight for Burton's bullets.

A special characteristic of the American arm *151*

of the Model 1855 was a patented tape primer. This device had been developed by Edward Maynard, an internationally known dentist who practiced in Washington, D. C., but was intensely interested in military matters as a hobby. His device worked much like the roll of caps in a modern toy pistol. He enclosed small dabs of percussion compound in a long strip of tape which was then coiled and placed in a receptacle on the lock plate. When the gun was cocked, an arm automatically moved the tape forward and pushed a new dab of primer over the nipple. At least it was supposed to. Jefferson Davis, then Secretary of War, was greatly interested in this primer. It seemed to offer a way to speed the loading of a percussion arm by eliminating the need for fumbling in the pouch after a separate cap and placing it on the nipple for each shot. In practice, however, the device left much to be desired, and later models of the rifle-musket omitted it in favor of the conventional percussion cap.

With the rifle-musket, the muzzle-loading military rifle reached its high point. It was a magnificent arm. Its forty-inch barrel had only three grooves, but it was accurate. Up to two hundred yards, a good marksman could do precision shooting. Beyond that he could be expected to hit a target six feet by six feet at five hundred yards, and a target eight feet square about half the time at one thousand yards. And he could hit it hard. At a distance of one thousand yards, the standard five-hundred-grain minie ball, driven by sixty grains of black powder, would penetrate four inches of soft pine. Like any other percussion arm, the rifle-musket was a trifle slower than the flintlock. Still, a skilled soldier could fire three shots a minute under good conditions, and a sustained rate of two shots a minute was hoped for in combat.

Every infantryman now had accuracy at his command, not just the elite rifleman. And this made a difference in the way warfare was conducted. Opposing armies did well to remain farther apart than they had formerly. It was no longer wise for artillery to operate in advance of the infantry, as it had during the Mexican War. The dashing batteries that once delighted in galloping to within three or four hundred yards of the enemy and raking his lines with charges of canister now found that their cannoneers suffered a discouragingly high mortality rate. It was far safer to drop back to seven hundred or a thousand yards, where the new rifle-muskets were not quite so effective.

But tactics change slowly. It is experience that counts and that sort of learning is costly. The United States, with thirty-two million people, suffered casualties of 714,245 killed and wounded in the bloodiest war in its history, and the new rifle-musket was responsible for many of them. It was by far the most common arm on both sides of the battlefield.

As a special arm, the American rifle-musket lasted just ten years. During its brief history it passed through three definite models: 1855, 1861, and 1863. Some two million of them were made in the North, and a great many were produced in the South as well, although the records there are far less complete. Then the breechloader replaced it and the muzzle-loading rifle was discarded as a military arm.

While these major developments were taking place in the field of military rifle bullets, there was also a most interesting offshoot. This was the explosive bullet, or musket shell, as it was sometimes called. Exploding artillery shells had been made for years and it was, perhaps, only

British Whitworth hexagonal-bored rifle (upper) is a fine example with its checkered wrist and engraved lock. It probably was made for an officer of an elite unit. Lower: British Enfield rifle-musket, imported and used by both North and South in the Civil War.

natural that someone should think of attempting the same thing with rifle bullets.

One of the first to do so was Captain John Norton, whose expanding rifle projectile of 1823 had been turned down by the British government because only spherical balls were suitable for military purposes. This time his bullet was egg-shaped, with studs cast on its sides to fit the grooves of the Baker rifle. A cavity in its nose contained a heavy charge of fulminate and was closed with a boxwood plug. When the bullet struck its target, the plug was driven back against the fulminate and exploded it, rupturing the projectile and spurting flame. Norton argued that this bullet had extensive military possibilities. He envisioned troops specially armed with it who could hit and blow up enemy ammunition chests on caissons or limbers from distances at which it would be impossible to pick off individual cannoneers.

According to standard procedure, the new bullet was submitted to the usual testing committee. Almost always these groups seemed to contain a majority of artillery officers with a natural prejudice against any device that might weaken the importance of their own branch of service. Certainly it appears to have been so in this case. The idea of infantry blowing up caissons from long range was especially repugnant, and this particular committee lost no time in rendering a firm and unfavorable opinion.

For the next twenty or thirty years, Norton continued to devise plans for improving the ammunition used in British small arms, and each idea was rejected as fast as it was submitted. Across the world in India, however, there lived a kindred soul with a higher military position and a personal fortune large enough to permit him to carry on extensive experiments of his own. This was Colonel (later General) John Jacob of the Scinde Irregular Horse. Jacob refined Norton's projectile, achieving a form with an ogival point similar to a modern artillery shell. It was more streamlined and created less air resistance than Norton's egg-shaped bullet. He also used a bursting charge of gunpowder, with the fulminate serving only as a detonator, and thus achieved greater force for his explosion. With this bullet he succeeded in blowing up dummy caissons at distances of twelve hundred and two thousand yards. And the crowning achievement came when a party of riflemen firing his rifle shells actually exploded an enemy caisson during the bloody Indian Mutiny of 1857-1859.

These exploits were noted in America with considerable interest, and there were many who remembered them a few years later when pent-up sectional tensions burst forth in violent civil war. By this time, however, there was a definite fear of public reaction against such a weapon. The designers and sponsors of explosive bullets still spoke of blowing up caissons and other inanimate objects, but they knew full well that human flesh and bone were bound to be the victims of these fiendish explosions, as well. Those

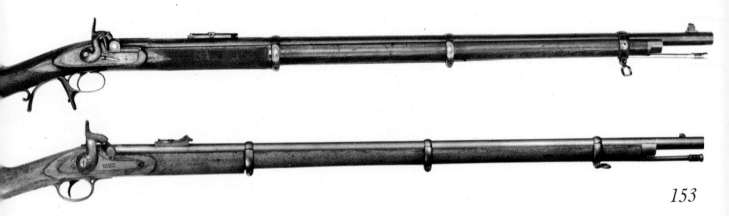

who advocated their use did so in secret. Military contracts were not publicized. Both sides manufactured and used them, but so great was the secrecy that the few reports of their use were treated as atrocity stories invented by overactive imaginations. After the war, a congressional investigating committee dismissed as wartime propaganda charges that the Confederates had used such musket shells, never realizing that both the Union and Confederate armies had fired them in some quantity.

The explosive bullets used in America were of two types. The first was a standard cylindro-conical bullet with a cavity in its nose containing fulminate and a bursting charge. It operated on the same principle as Norton's and Jacob's earlier versions. Then, in 1863, Samuel Gardiner, Jr., of New York City, patented an entirely different sort of shell. In this one there was an acorn-shaped cavity filled with powder, and a tube packed with a quick-burning fuze composition which opened into the hollow base of the bullet. When the rifle was fired, the flash from the charge ignited the fuze, which burned for about one and one-quarter seconds and then exploded the projectile wherever it might be—in the air or already within its target. There was an interesting side effect of such fuzed bullets. The burning of the fuze allowed the flight of the projectile to be followed by eye and thus provided the first tracer ammunition in military history. But the value of this seems to have been overlooked, even by those who took the trouble to mention having seen it. Almost another half century had to elapse before there

was a deliberate effort to achieve this same performance.

Of the two shells, the fuzed type was perhaps the most cruel. General U. S. Grant noted their use by the Confederates at Vicksburg. Most of them exploded harmlessly in the air, well over the heads of the besieging troops. Some, however, found a living target, and Grant summed up the general reaction of thoughtful military men on such bullets: "Where they hit and the ball exploded, the wound was terrible. In these cases a solid ball would have hit as well. Their use is barbarous because they produce increased suffering without any increased advantage to those using them."

The civilized world agreed. At a conference in St. Petersburg, Russia, shortly after the war, European nations solemnly agreed to outlaw the use of such small, explosive missiles among civilized countries. The United States did not sign the agreement, but never again were such projectiles used in any major conflict.

Sportsmen also took an interest in these devices. Untroubled by the sensibilities of those who scrupled to use them against fellow humans, the hunters felt that explosive bullets might be very effective in dropping big game. They were fairly popular until more powerful cartridges were developed late in the century.

But the round-ball rifle had by no means disappeared. The elongated bullet was fine for the military, who needed speed, and for other special purposes, but the great majority of civilian rifle shooters still used the round ball. Hunting and target rifles continued to be made for such

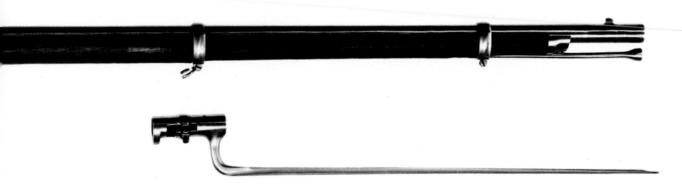

balls as long as the muzzle-loader was actively used in any part of the world. Specialized forms appeared, too.

One of these was the so-called plains rifle. It had developed from the graceful American long rifle of the eastern states, but all of the beauty had gone. Its barrel was heavy and its bore large. Its stock was thick and chunky, and there was little or no carving or decoration. It had nothing to recommend it except performance.

And performance was what trappers and frontiersmen needed out beyond the Mississippi in the vast new Louisiana Territory. They stalked bison and elk instead of deer, and the fierce grizzly rather than the eastern black bear. Small balls and light charges were worse than useless against such big game.

The gunsmiths who moved west from Pennsylvania into Ohio, Illinois, and especially to St. Louis, altered old guns and made new ones to meet the changing demands of their customers. Long guns were a nuisance on horseback, so barrels were shortened. Most ranged between twenty-eight and thirty-eight inches in length. Calibers were made larger to stop big game, mostly .45 to .55, and the barrels were built heavy enough for a minimum charge of one hundred grains of powder. Stocks were sometimes full length to the muzzle and sometimes short half-stocks. Either way, they were sturdy, thick in the wrist and wide in the butt. This destroyed all grace of design, but it created a stock that would not snap at the first fall from a horse's back. The guns could have been decorated with carving and inlay, and a few ac-

U.S. Model 1863 rifle-musket (top) no longer has tape primer used in Model 1855. The primer was abandoned in 1861. Above: Julian Scott's "Behind the Earthworks" shows Union soldier firing rifle-musket from his entrenched position.

tually were. But usually, the plainsman avoided any ornamentation that might catch the sunlight and either spoil his aim or attract an enemy's attention.

The barrel was soft iron and the rifling grooves were cut in a slow spiral. Balls pushed by a hundred grains or more of powder would not take rifling with a rapid twist. They would skip and fly wild unless charged exactly right. The slow twist with soft iron permitted a wide variety of loads, even up to two hundred and 155 fifteen grains, with equal accuracy. Such huge powder charges could only be handled by a heavy gun, however, and many a plains rifle weighed fifteen pounds or more. Almost all of them, too, were percussion. Some of the first ones were flint, but by the time the rifle had reached its full development, the older lock had become obsolete.

This was the rifle of Jim Bridger, Kit Carson, Joe Meek, and their brethren of the High Plains and the Rockies. With it they slaughtered buffalo for food and fur, brought down the mighty grizzly, and fought the Sioux and Blackfoot. With its almost foolproof reliability, no matter how rapidly and carelessly charged, its excellent accuracy and long range, it was their constant delight. Henry Chatillion showed the astonished historian Francis Parkman that he could regularly drop buffalo with a clean shot through the lungs at distances beyond three hundred yards. And Lieutenant George Brewerton was amazed when an old hunter named Lewis winged a Digger Indian on the dead run at more than two hundred yards.

The heyday of the plains rifle lasted from 1820 until almost 1870. The minie ball was never any threat to these work horses of the far reaches. Word of the minie's success did not reach the mountain men until late, and no one seems to have got around to designing proper bullets in the various plains-rifle calibers before the end of the Civil War, which brought new breechloaders to the West in ever increasing quantities to push all the older rifles to one side.

There also were specialized target rifles. Guns for such use became precision instruments, capable of magnificent accuracy, but impractical because of size or fragility for any other type of shooting. At one extreme of such arms were the *schuetzen* rifles developed in Central Europe and highly popular in America from the mid-Nineteenth Century until World War I. In *schuetzen* competition all firing was done offhand. Rifles made for such use had exaggerated stocks with long projections at the top and bottom of their butt plates which crossed over the shoulder and under the arm and helped steady the piece. Often there was a folding hand rest attached to the forestock for better support with the left hand as well. It wasn't a gun anyone would take into the woods, but it was an excellent target arm.

Heavy as it was, the *schuetzen* was among the lightest of the regular outdoor target rifles. At the other end of the scale were the ponderous bench rifles, weighing thirty or forty pounds, or perhaps even more. With such arms the shooter either lay prone or sat alongside a special bench which supported his gun. It was a slow procedure to load these behemoths. The marksman measured the charge carefully, trimmed the ball, and centered it exactly in its patch. Often he used a false muzzle and starter to be sure of this. Painstakingly he adjusted the long telescopic sight for vertical and lateral deviation as he judged the wind, temperature, and other atmospheric factors which might possibly affect his shot. Having satisfied himself that all was in order, he cocked the hammer and placed a cap on the nipple. Peering intently through the sight, he pulled the first of his set triggers. Another pause followed as he rechecked his aim to make sure he was dead center. Then, and only then, he touched the hair trigger to fire the piece.

Artificial as such shooting may seem, it should be noted that target rifles, even including some of the lighter bench rifles, saw some use during the Civil War. Picked marksmen welcomed precision arms for sniping duties and many an officer, including generals on both sides, fell victim to the bullet of just such a target arm.

Round-ball or minie, military or civilian, the rifle had risen to dominance. It had acquired the necessary accuracy, power, speed, and strength. New machines reduced the cost of cutting the spiral grooves into the barrels. There was no longer an economic reason for a man to choose a smoothbore. Increased accuracy and range were available to everyone. Fowling pieces and a few special-purpose arms might retain their unblemished bores because of their particular functions, but the great majority of all guns—even pistols—now boasted the magical grooves. The day of the smoothbore was done. The rifle was supreme.

In the turkey shoot (left), painted by John Ehninger in 1879, contestants were allowed to rest percussion target rifles on planks, saw horses. Schuetzen rifle (below), made by John Meunier of Milwaukee about 1876, has carved stock, gold and silver inlay. Below left: Early 19th century French powder flask.

157

LOADING
AT
THE BREECH

*It soon became clear that it was easier and faster to load a gun from the breech
than from the muzzle. Putting a charge of powder, a ball, and wadding down a
barrel from the forward end and ramming each element home was time-consuming business and nearly impossible to execute lying down or crouching in cover.
Soldiers in action usually had to load while standing exposed to enemy fire. In the
heat of battle, misfires often went unnoticed and soldiers loaded a second or third
charge on top of the first—with a real chance of bursting their guns when and if the
original load was ignited. In the excitement, paper cartridges might be loaded ball
end first, rendering the gun useless until the reversed load was removed. Breech-*

loading would solve these problems, but there were dangers to overcome.

ecognizing the need was one thing, finding a solution another. If a gun was to be loaded at the breech there would have to be another opening in the barrel. This opening would have to close tightly to prevent flame and gases from escaping, with loss of power for the shot and possible injury to the shooter. At the same time, it would have to open and shut quickly and easily, without jamming or breaking. This was difficult. The search for a satisfactory breech seal would continue for many centuries.

It is certain that breech-loading cannon were used early in the 1400's, but they may have appeared much earlier, perhaps within a few years after de Milemete's drawings of 1326. Normally, these primitive breechloaders consisted of a simple tube with a separate chamber or breech piece. These chambers were themselves short tubes closed at one end and just long enough to contain a charge of powder. Usually they necked in slightly at the mouth, so that they could be inserted for a short distance into the breech end of the barrel before being locked in place with a wedge or key. Often there were a number of such chambers for each gun, which could be loaded in advance and stand ready for rapid insertion and firing.

Other early cannon, including such huge ones as the Dardanelles Gun, had breeches which were threaded and could be unscrewed. The smaller cannon may have been loaded through such screw breeches, but it is doubtful that the great monsters ever were. It would not take many trials to prove it easier to load through the muzzle, rather than to organize a crew of men with levers, ropes, and pulleys to unscrew, lift off, load, and replace a breech section weighing hundreds of pounds. In these cases the removable breech was undoubtedly designed for ease of transportation, allowing the great piece to be moved in sections. Still, the screw-breech principle had appeared.

Breech-loading small arms came much later than cannon, but even in this field there is respectable antiquity. Henry VIII of England, for instance, had at least two breech-loading long guns, one of them dated 1537, and a considerable number of circular shields, each mounting a breech-loading pistol in its center. All of these guns used a separate iron tube remarkably similar in appearance to the modern cartridge case to hold its charge. The long guns had hinged trap doors on the tops of their barrels at the breech which could be lifted to permit the insertion of the tube, then closed and latched. Neither piece has its original lock today and there is some dispute among students as to whether they were originally matchlocks or wheel locks. Both are handsome specimens, however, befitting a royal owner who was greatly interested in arms of all sorts, and they are the earliest datable breech-loading small arms to survive.

Yet the pistol shields are perhaps even more interesting. Their number and workmanship indicate that they were probably intended to arm special troops, such as a royal guard, although they are not handsomely decorated weapons. They are matchlocks, and this is also significant, for only one other matchlock pistol of European origin is known. The basic concept of such an arm is intriguing in itself. Here was a circular wooden shield protected on the outside with steel plates and covered with leather inside. In the center was the pistol and above it a small, barred peephole for sighting. It would seem to be an ideal device for shooting from cover, completely masking the user's head as he peered over a wall or around a corner. No one knows for certain who made these pistol shields or when. But it is believed that at least some were made by an Italian gunsmith from Ravenna named Giovan Battista, since there is still preserved a letter he wrote in 1544 offering to make such a shield for King Henry. Actually, the shields may have been made by several different persons, for they exhibit a number of minor variations in design and construction. All *161*

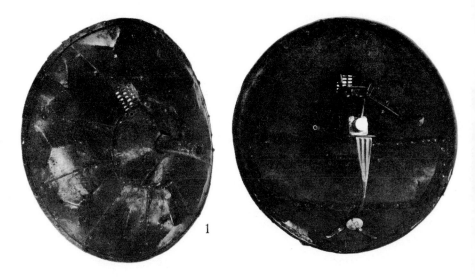

1

of them, however, have a pivoted breech which swings up so that an iron tube can be inserted into the barrel, then dropped back in place and fastened with a spring catch. The serpentine holding the match is pivoted on the shield itself and moved by a small lever at the side, where it can be conveniently seized by the right hand.

Clever as these shields were, there must have been a number of very real drawbacks in actual use. For one thing, they were heavy. It was necessary to pass the left arm through leather or iron loops to support one. The act of fastening the lighted match into the serpentine with only one hand must have required considerable practice to avoid burned fingers and singed clothing. In aiming the piece, the shooter had to hold the little opening directly before his eyes. Accordingly, the breech of the pistol would be directly in front of his face and the smoldering match only inches away. The ignition flash in such a situation could have been highly damaging to eyebrows, and a leaky breech seal might remove beard and mustache as well. All of these circumstances must have been highly discouraging to potential users of the piece, and thus it is not surprising that most of the wear exhibited by the remaining specimens in the Tower of London seems to have been caused by the ravages of time, not by active use.

It was almost two centuries after Henry VIII

before real interest was once again displayed in arming soldiers with a breech-loading weapon. This time it was a variant of the screw breech which made the breakthrough. The idea of a threaded plug on the top, bottom, or side of the breech, which could be unscrewed for loading, had appeared early among the various screw-breech devices, but there were serious drawbacks which had prevented it from becoming popular. It was difficult to screw the plug back in again, especially when the shooter was excited. A small, loose plug could easily be lost. A plug fouled by powder was likely to stick fast and become almost impossible to remove without a wrench.

In 1704, a French engineer named Isaac de la Chaumette overcame most of these difficulties and attracted the attention of military theorists to his device. In Chaumette's gun, the plug passed all the way through the barrel. The lower end was attached to the trigger guard, which acted as a handle and provided leverage for turning the plug when it became stuck. It no longer was necessary to remove the plug completely, for when it was depressed an aperture appeared in the top of the barrel. A ball and powder could be dropped into this and the plug turned up again to form a combination seal and breech plug.

As a Huguenot, Chaumette left his native

2

3

1. *Breech-loading pistol shields made for King Henry VIII of England.*

2. *This breechloader also belonged to Henry VIII. Originally, it was probably a wheel lock. Its present lock is a modern replacement.*

3. *German breech-loading wheel lock is similar to those used by Henry VIII, but this piece is later and more highly decorated.*

land and fled to England in 1721. Nevertheless, it is believed that France armed at least one regiment of dragoons and perhaps some sailors with his gun in 1723. And the great French soldier and military writer, Marshal Saxe, advocated use of the Chaumette breech for both carbines and wall guns. In England, Chaumette obtained a royal patent and earned the jealousy of the native English gunsmiths who tried unsuccessfully to break his control of the device. One of his licensees, a fellow Huguenot with the intriguing name of Bidet, manufactured an improved version of the gun with a quick-acting thread that dropped the plug to the loading position with only one turn of the guard, rather than several. A beautifully decorated specimen with this improved thread was made for George I. It survives with the inventor's own modest appraisal of the importance of his work engraved in French verse on the barrel:

New Carbine
La Chaumette has made this terrible gun.
All its patrons will be blessed.
For it is the means of ending war
And establishing the Golden Age.

Unfortunately, it had no such effect, nor did the further improved versions which followed.

It remained for a Scotsman to bring the Chaumette system to its fullest development, as well as to its greatest prominence, as an official arm for a small unit of the British Army during the American Revolution. Patrick Ferguson was a soldier almost from the cradle. Born in 1744, the second son of James Ferguson of Pitfour, a laird of Aberdeenshire, he was serving in Germany as a cornet in the Scot's Greys by the time he was fourteen. Ill health brought him home in 1762, but by 1768 he was back in service, this time campaigning against the Caribs in the West Indies with the 70th Regiment of foot. Again illness forced him back to Scotland in 1774. There, at the ripe age of thirty, he began serious work with firearms.

Always a gun enthusiast, Ferguson was also an excellent marksman. Chaumette's breech-loading system was well known at the time and the young Scot was undoubtedly thoroughly familiar with it. He was also familiar with its drawbacks and these he set out to correct. The biggest problem had always been fouling. So Ferguson designed his breech plug with a smooth surface which formed the end of the bore when the plug was closed. This, he reasoned, would not collect fouling when the piece was fired and then transmit it to the grooves in the barrel wall as the continuous threads had done. Next he cut a series of channels in the threads of the plug to reduce fouling still further and provided a small space in back of the plug in which smoke and residue could collect. These alterations, he believed, would practically eliminate the fouling problem and he was right. At the same time he thickened the bottom of the barrel so that the top of the plug could be dropped entirely below the bore for more thorough cleaning. And he also developed an adjustable rear sight and a system of four-groove rifling.

By 1776, Ferguson was back with his regiment. His new rifle was ready. On April 27, he conducted one test before the master general of the Ordnance which clearly proved his gun's superiority to the common musket. But this was not enough. The next demonstration on the marshes at Woolwich gave every indication that he could claim to have developed the finest military firearm in existence. The day selected was certainly inauspicious. There was a high wind and it rained hard throughout the demonstration. Ordinary flintlocks would not have functioned at all under such conditions, but Ferguson's performed marvels. Setting up a target some two hundred yards off, he fired for four or five minutes at a steady rate of four shots per minute. In one minute of extra rapid shooting, he fired six shots. As if this were not enough, he walked rapidly toward the target firing at the rate of four shots a minute. Then, as if to prove the impossible, he poured a bottle of water into the pan and down the barrel of

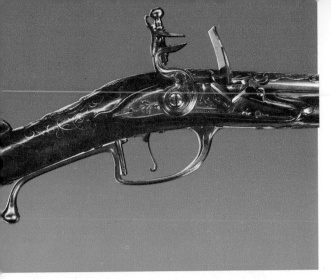

This breech-loading flintlock, invented by Isaac de la Chaumette in 1704, was made for King George I of England (1714-1727).

the loaded piece so that all the powder was wet. Within half a minute he had the piece firing again as well as ever. Finally, he lay on his back on the wet ground and hit the target one hundred yards away. In the entire demonstration, despite the varying winds and rains, he missed the target only three times.

It was a performance to make the assembled officers forget that they were soaked to the skin, and it produced results. Within weeks the master general of Ordnance stopped the manufacture of all muzzle-loading rifles for the army, ordered the production of one hundred rifles of Ferguson's pattern, and authorized the inventor himself to supervise their manufacture. By September they were finished. On October 1, Captain Ferguson and a detachment from Lord George Lennox's regiment demonstrated them to the royal family at Windsor. There the young officer told the wondering king that he could fire as fast as seven shots a minute with his fine rifle, but modestly admitted he probably would not be able to "knock down above five of His Majesty's enemies" each sixty seconds at that rate of fire.

He was soon to have his chance to test this estimate. Now that the rifles had been completed, the master general of Ordnance stepped aside and Viscount Barrington, Secretary for War, took charge. He detached Ferguson from his regiment and ordered the recruiting of a corps of one hundred men, mostly from the 6th and 14th Regiments. By the end of March, 1777, the new unit was ready to sail for America and the war. When it arrived, General Sir William Howe welcomed Ferguson. The general looked forward to great things from this corps commanded by "so intelligent an officer" as they set sail for Chesapeake Bay and a campaign against Philadelphia from the south.

It was not to be. The first big engagement of the rifle corps was also its last. Attached to Hessian General Knyphausen's column, Ferguson's corps led the van down Polly Buckwalter's Lane toward Brandywine Creek on September 11. This was to be a diversionary attack on the Americans at Chadd's Ford while the main British column slipped around to cross upstream and take the rebels on their flank. At the start the deception was successful, and the Americans gave their primary attention to the feint. Action was hot and the young British officer acquitted himself so well that Knyphausen sent a commendation to Howe. Then an American bullet struck. It shattered Ferguson's right elbow and crippled his arm. With its commander disabled and facing a possible amputation, the rifle corps was disbanded, the men returning to the light companies of their original regiments, never again to serve as a unit.

The fate of Ferguson is well known. By sheer determination he continued his career in the army. His right arm was saved, but it remained stiff. He had to teach himself to write, fence, and shoot left-handed. This he managed to do, and many other things as well. He was a daring and resourceful commander, used principally with Tory troops. In 1780, he was made inspector general of militia in Georgia and the Carolinas, and there he died at the Battle of Kings Mountain, October 7, 1780, victim of an American rifle ball fired from a muzzle-loader.

The fate of the original hundred Ferguson rifles, however, remains a mystery. There are rumors and theories, but no definite facts. The men of the corps may have taken their arms

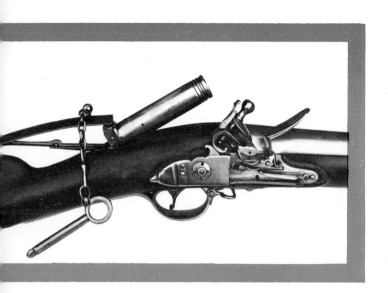

with them when they returned to their original regiments, or they may have turned them in to be placed in a warehouse. There is no evidence that any of Ferguson's later commands had them, although this is often claimed. One surviving specimen of the original group exists today in the museum at Morristown National Historical Park, New Jersey. But except for the fact that it evidently was found in a New England attic, its provenance is unknown and it offers no clue to the fate of the others. Thus the finest weapon of the American Revolution vanished almost without a trace.

There were, of course, other Ferguson rifles besides the original one hundred. The East Indian Company bought some for its troops. A few volunteer companies apparently purchased them, and some were made as personal arms and sporting weapons. Nonetheless, the gun today is a great rarity.

British Ordnance still was interested in breechloaders, but it began to follow new lines. It wanted an arm that would fire the standard paper cartridge, rather than use loose powder and ball as the Ferguson had. Thus, Ordnance commissioned the celebrated London gunsmith,

Durs Egg, to make a number of carbines with a tip-up breech. In this system the rear portion of the barrel was pivoted. A spring release allowed it to be tipped up so that a cartridge could be inserted and then secured in place once more. The Austrians had tried just such a gun, invented by Giuseppe Crespi of Milan, from 1770 to 1779 and had abandoned it because it leaked gas. The reports of the British trials in 1788 indicate the same difficulty, and testing was postponed until more information could be got from Vienna. The tests were never resumed.

In all of these instances, from Henry VIII's gun shields to Durs Egg's tip-up models, breechloaders had been used in small quantities by picked troops. It remained for the United States to take the next step by adopting a breechloader as a standard military arm for use by large numbers of soldiers. This it did in the year 1819.

The gun it chose was the invention of a Yankee from Maine named John H. Hall. Surprisingly enough, there were three John H. Halls, all contemporary and all from the same Maine locality. Two were named John Hancock and one John Harris. One was a jeweler, one a shipbuilder, and one a gunsmith. Records for the period are scanty and for more than seventy years historians have had a dreadful time straightening out the three namesakes. Most often it has been thought that John Harris Hall was both a shipbuilder and a gunsmith. But documents discovered within the last year have finally established that it was the younger John Hancock Hall, born January 21, 1778, who invented a new breech-loading rifle and developed into a mechanical genius.

Very little is known about the origin of the Hall rifle. The inventor himself asserted that at the time he was "but little acquainted with rifles and . . . perfectly ignorant of any method whatever of loading guns at the breech." Thus he tackled the problem fresh and developed a tip-up breech with no knowledge of the work of Crespi or of the experiences of the Austrians and British with somewhat similar mechanisms. But Hall was not entirely alone. A young Washington architect named William Thornton was working on a similar device. They got together and combined their ideas. Hall contributed the major design elements, Thornton made minor suggestions, and they obtained a joint patent in 1811. The finished rifle differed from the Crespi pattern mainly in that the whole breech-block, including the lock, tipped up to load, and that there was a simpler spring catch to hold it in position when closed.

The eve of the War of 1812 would seem to have been a fine time to develop a new gun, but it was not until after the war was over that young Hall was able to interest ordnance officers in his invention. Then extensive tests were held. The new rifle performed admirably. In 1819 it was adopted as an official arm and production began at the Harpers Ferry Armory with John Hall himself to supervise proceedings.

Hall's presence at the armory was significant in more ways than one. Not only had he invented the rifle itself, but he had also devised the machinery to manufacture it on an assembly line basis with completely interchangeable parts. Such a system had been tried in France late in the Eighteenth Century. Eli Whitney, inventor of the cotton gin, had attempted it in the United States some twenty years before Hall, but mechanization was limited and tolerances were too great. Hall's were the first completely interchangeable arms in America and quite possibly the first in the world. His contributions to arms manufacturing technique far exceeded his breech design and his work became a milestone in all industrial history.

But what of the rifle itself? The breech system was simple and safe, but it was by no means perfect. It had a tendency to leak gas after it became worn, just as the British and Austrian arms had done. The little lever for the spring catch was a liability. It stuck out beneath the stock and often became entangled with belts and

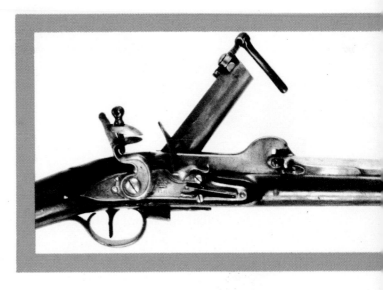

Durs Egg breechloader, based on the Crespi tip-up breech system, was tested by British Ordnance in 1788.

other bits of equipment. Soldiers also complained that it galled their shoulders. Nevertheless, the Hall was made in both rifle and carbine lengths for some twenty-five years. A percussion version of the Hall carbine was the first official arm of that ignition system made for the United States service. Halls were used all along the frontier, in minor wars with the Indians, in the Mexican War, and even in the Civil War.

And the soldiers soon noticed an interesting thing about the percussion models. They could take out the breechblock and carry it as a pistol in case of emergency, when they did not want to take the whole gun along. This was a happy discovery. As a pistol it was difficult to hold. The flash from the cap might singe the shooter's hand, and since the ball of the cartridge would be right at the muzzle with no "barrel" to guide its flight, it wouldn't shoot accurately across the room. It was very effective at close ranges, however, and many a dragoon on leave in a captured city during the Mexican War was happy to feel the angular lines of a Hall breech in his pocket. Sam Chamberlain of the 1st U.S. Dragoons tells of one such instance in *My Confession,* a recollection of his fantastic personal

169

adventures. Caught in a dance hall by guerrillas late one night, Sam reported:

I thought my time had come, but resolved not to be rubed out without a struggle. With a bound I sprang behind a large table used for a bar, drew the chamber of my 'Halls Carbine' (that I always carried in my pocket), said a short prayer, and stood cool and collected, at bay before those human Tigers, guerrillars. There was one grizzly old fellow who seemd more ferocious than the others, he had but one eye that glared on me with the fierceness of a wild beast. He rushed for the table as if he would spring over, when the sight of the little iron tube pointing straight for his solitary optic, caused him to pause. A few tallow dips cast a feable light on the savage faces in my front, cries of 'murte! murte! los Americano ladron que meueren los Yanque burro' came from all parts of the room, but none offered to strike, twenty brigands were held at bay by the strange weapon I held, they seemed to know it was sure death to one, and none seemd willing to be that one.

With his usual luck, Sam escaped. He carried his Hall breech into many more scrapes before settling down as a retired Civil War general to write of his escapades for the edification of his grandchildren.

While the Hall was the first breechloader to be adopted as a standard arm, and the United States was the first country to issue such an arm in quantity, other nations were by no means idle in this field. Throughout Europe there were

tests and experiments with breech-loading arms and a host of gunsmiths and inventors directed their attention to the subject.

One of the first and foremost was Samuel Johannes Pauly, a Swiss inventor and balloon enthusiast, whose travels during the Napoleonic Wars took him first to Paris and then to England. Along the way he changed his given names to Jean Samuel and Samuel John and then back again, thus creating some confusion as to how many Paulys there were. But whatever name he used, he was responsible for producing some very advanced designs for breech-loading arms.

The year 1612 found Pauly in Paris. His attempts to design and construct a dirigible under the patronage of one of Napoleon's marshals had ended in frustration. So, he had entered the gun business in association with the patent plagiarist, Prélat, who took advantage of the current French regulations to obtain French patents on every new foreign firearm which came to his attention. In this stimulating atmosphere, Pauly observed the efforts of many gunsmiths throughout the world to develop a breech-loading arm and to find some way of utilizing the new percussion compounds which exploded when struck. And here he created his own design, patented on September 29.

Pauly was an independent thinker and innovator, and his gun boasted a radically different approach from those being tried elsewhere. Among its features were an internal firing pin with a cocking lever on the outside, a break-open breech closed with a lever on long guns and a

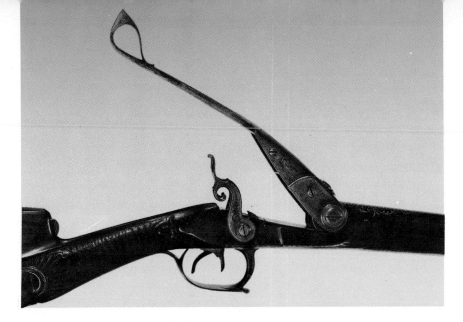

tip-down barrel for pistols, and, perhaps most important, a center-fire cartridge with a brass head and a paper body. As with all new inventions, there were imperfections and these prevented Pauly from ever achieving widespread commercial success with his gun. Nevertheless, his inventions represented a major advance in firearms design and an excellent case can be made for Pauly as the father of the modern single-loading shotgun in both its action and the ammunition it uses.

Pauly's real contribution lay in the concept of the ammunition as the key to breech-loading design. Here was the first use of a cartridge with a rimmed head of soft metal, designed to expand and form a seal against the escape of flame and gases. This is the theory on which all firearms operate today. The percussion cap had not yet been invented; Pauly's cartridge had a tiny pan to hold a small charge of percussion powder on its outside surface, with a narrow channel leading to the main charge inside. Otherwise it was in all respects a metallic, center-fire cartridge, detonated by a firing pin in the modern method. Pauly's most effective cartridges had paper bodies with brass heads, like present-day shotgun shells, but he also offered reloadable cases made entirely of brass.

In the hands of experts, Pauly's guns worked magnificently. A committee of five tested the invention for the Society for the Encouragement of National Industry, in Paris, and reported enthusiastically on the speed, safety, and reliability of the arm. Pauly himself fired twenty-two shots in two minutes and felt that any competent huntsman could manage ten a minute with a double-barreled gun. The Emperor of Russia ordered tests and so did Napoleon, but Bonaparte was not convinced of the immediate practicability of the new weapon. He thought it needed improvement and he was right. It was not yet rugged enough or foolproof enough to stand the treatment of awkward recruits.

Meanwhile, Pauly had moved to England where more disappointments followed. His later inventions—among them cannon shells which exploded on impact, breech-loading cannon, locks for firing cannon, and ignition of powder charges through the heat of compressed air—were received indifferently. Perhaps worst of all was the failure to complete another attempt at a huge fish-shaped dirigible in partnership with Durs Egg. Yet even here he pioneered in the rigid frame and movable ballast later used successfully by Count von Zeppelin.

The date of Pauly's death is unknown, but his influence spread far and wide. Guns on his principle were made in France, England, Denmark, and perhaps elsewhere as well. The principles were studied by gunsmiths throughout the world. Improvements were stimulated and one of his workmen, Johann Nickolaus von Dreyse, became a leading figure in the development of breechloaders as the inventor of the bolt action and the famous needle gun.

As a young man, von Dreyse had worked as a lockmaker for Pauly in Paris from 1809 until 1814. In that year Pauly moved to England

171

American troops (left), storming Chapultepec on September 13, 1847, charge up the slope to the Mexican citadel. Sam Chamberlain's painting of himself (below) shows him holding a band of Mexican guerrillas at bay with the chamber from his Hall carbine.

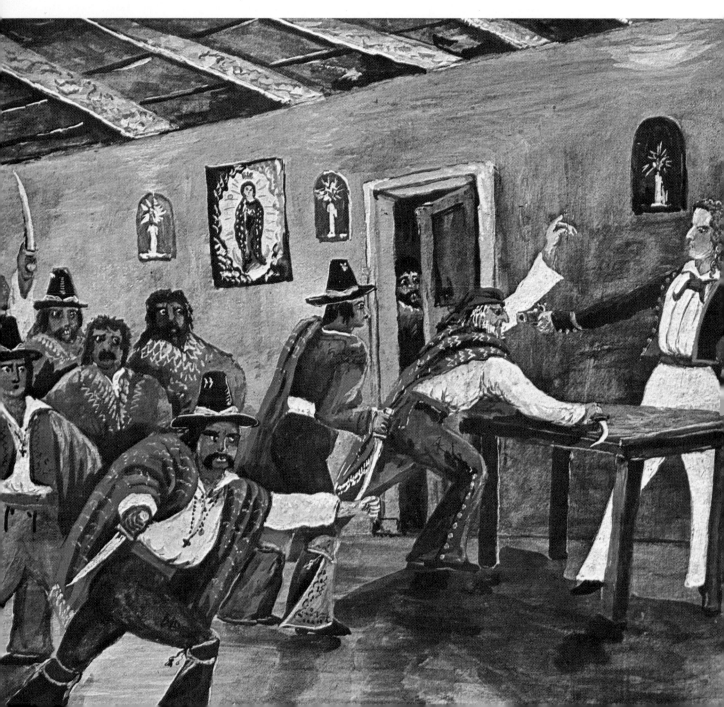

and von Dreyse returned to his native Söm-merda, in Prussia. There, in 1824, he operated a percussion-cap factory under the name of Dreyse & Collenbusch. It was this business which, according to fable, led directly to the invention of the needle gun. As the standard story goes, von Dreyse was using a needle to scrape the priming out of a foreign percussion cap when it exploded in his fingers. This would seem a strange procedure for a cap manufac-turer to attempt, but it conveniently and dra-matically explains how he came to begin work on a firearm in which the priming compound was exploded by a long, slender firing pin. The fact that he had seen firing pins used in Pauly's arms, and that he merely lengthened his pin so that the percussion compound could be lodged at the base of the bullet instead of being left ex-posed in an open pan in the head of the cartridge, was far too prosaic an explanation for Nine-teenth Century romanticists.

However it may have been inspired, von Dreyse's first needle gun appeared as a muzzle-loader between 1827 and 1829, and as a breech-loader in 1837. The basic idea comprised a lead bullet with a percussion compound in a hollow at its base. This was detonated by a long, slen-der firing pin with a sharp point, which passed through the powder charge and struck the priming in its protective nest. The shape of this pin gave rise to the name needle gun. In the first muzzle-loading versions, loose powder and ball were used, but soon a combustible cartridge was devised and this continued to be used when the breech-loading action was invented. It was in every sense a self-contained, fixed round, just as a modern cartridge is, and the breech system that von Dreyse developed was in all essentials the bolt action as it is employed today in rifles throughout the world.

The effect of the needle gun on the rest of Europe was spectacular. Prussia adopted the arm officially in 1848 and thought so highly of it that construction details were kept secret. In the Danish War of 1864, the new gun helped the Prussians triumph quickly, and with it the Austrian war of 1866 lasted only seven weeks. It became a factor in the unification of Germany as a nation.

In France in 1866, Antoine Alphonse Chasse-pot developed an improved bolt-action rifle that was promptly adopted by the French Army. It improved upon the Dreyse by having a shorter firing pin which struck an inverted percussion cap in the head of the cartridge. Thus, it was not so susceptible to the main disadvantages of the Dreyse: the fragility of the long pin and its tendency to corrode, bend, and break, a prob-lem aggravated by its being in the center of the burning powder charge each time a shot was fired. The Chassepot was a fine rifle. It was adopted for musketoon and carbine use as well, and following the Franco-Prussian War the Saxon army adopted it, using captured French guns which they altered to take their own car-tridge—the sincerest form of tribute.

Probably the last of the important breech-loaders made without a self-sealing cartridge was an American invention, the famed Sharps rifle and carbine. Christian Sharps had worked at Harpers Ferry under the tutelage of John Hall and had learned from him much of the technique of gunsmithing and assembly line pro-duction. Hall left Harpers Ferry in 1840, and soon thereafter young Sharps moved to Cincin-nati, Ohio. Here he began active work on a breechloader of his own which he believed would overcome the faults he had noted in the Hall. A patent was granted in 1848, and the Sharps action appeared to take its place among the world's great firearms.

It was a simple but strong mechanism. A breechblock slid vertically in a mortise cut in the receiver. The trigger guard acted as a lever, and when this was pulled down the block was low-ered, exposing the chamber for the insertion of a cartridge. When the guard was returned to its normal position, the breechblock was raised and a knife edge cut open the base of the cartridge, thus exposing the powder within to the flame

173

from the primer. This primer was separate, and Sharps tried several systems before deciding upon a disc which was fed automatically over the nipple as the hammer fell. So sturdy and fool-proof was this action that it continued to be used for later single-shot rifles firing self-sealing metallic cartridges, such as the Winchester, Stevens, and Farquharson. And it is still used today for some antitank rifles and other arms requiring exceptional strength.

The Sharps appeared upon the scene just in time to take part in some of the dramatic events of American history. The country was deeply troubled over the slavery issue and there was open fighting in the area of Kansas and Missouri between slave- and free-state forces. The New England Emigrant Aid Company and other antislavery groups throughout the Northeast sent Sharps rifles and carbines to the free-state settlers for their defense, and the new gun became a decisive factor in keeping the territory free. It became a symbol of freedom, in fact, and the noted Brooklyn minister, Henry Ward Beecher, declared that he believed the Sharps rifle to be a truly moral agency. There was, he said, "more moral power in one of those instruments so far as the slave-holders were concerned than in a hundred Bibles." Thus, a name was coined. The Sharps were "Beecher's Bibles" until the eve of the Civil War turned people's minds from "bleeding Kansas."

Once more it was a Kansas free-stater who brought the Sharps prominently to the public attention as the war clouds thickened. John Brown of Osawatomie used a consignment of Sharps carbines that had been destined for Kansas in his wild raid on the Federal armory at Harpers Ferry, Virginia, in 1859. There he hoped to obtain more guns to arm slaves and lead them in an armed rebellion against their owners throughout the South. The plot failed. The raiders were captured and Brown was hanged at nearby Charlestown to become a symbol in the war that was soon to follow. His Sharps carbines were seized, and ever since then the models of 1852 and 1853 with the slanted breech and brass mountings have been known to collectors as the "John Brown Sharps."

Military attention also had been attracted to the Sharps. Both the United States and British governments had conducted tests and armed some troops with the new gun on a trial basis. But it was the great Civil War that really brought the new gun to the fore. Here it performed prodigious feats in the hands of the marksmen of Colonel Hiram Berdan's famed regiment of Sharpshooters. Indeed, the name was sometimes spelled "Sharps Shooters" in contemporary accounts.

Time and again these marksmen dramatically demonstrated their shooting ability. One of their noted exploits occurred at Malvern Hill

during the historic Seven Days before Richmond in 1862. Posted in front of the Union line as skirmishers, the green-clad Sharpshooters saw a dashing battery of the elite Richmond Howitzers whirl into position opposite them at full gallop. As the battery unlimbered it came within range of their Sharps rifles. Instantly, there was a staccato greeting. Horses went down on all the teams. Artillerymen strove to cut the beasts free and manhandle the pieces into position only to be cut down in turn by the murderous fire. Soon the guns and limbers stood silent. "We went in a battery and came out a wreck," marveled one of the surviving officers after the war.

Lesser marksmen also recognized the gun's excellence. Union soldiers generally thought it the finest single-shot breechloader of the war. The Federal government purchased 9,141 of the rifles and 80,512 of the shorter carbines for cavalry use. States and individual units purchased still more, and the Confederates manufactured their own copy of it. There was even one model with a coffee mill in its butt stock. The theory was that the mill would be useful for grinding corn and other grain that the troopers might forage from the countryside, as well as the issue coffee. Very few were ever made, however, and the coffee-mill Sharps is today one of the rare American military arms.

In the West, the Sharps also played an impor-tant role as a buffalo gun. Market hunters sought the valuable buffalo hides for the carriage robes so prized in the East. The builders of the great transcontinental railroads needed to feed their construction gangs, and professional hunters were hired to bring in buffalo meat. And then there were the sportsmen who wished to test their skill and marksmanship against the huge beasts. The Sharps was ideally suited for these purposes. Its strong breech permitted extra heavy powder charges for long-range shooting and its large bullets hit hard. Buffalo hunters of all types quickly adopted and used it, sometimes the regular carbine, sometimes a special long-range model with heavy octagon barrel that has since come to be known as the Sharps buffalo gun. Under this onslaught, the great herds of bison that once roamed the American plains all but disappeared.

In less sanguinary activities the Sharps also made its mark. The same breech strength that made it popular with the buffalo hunters also suited it ideally for long-range target shooting. Special target rifles were made with precision

French troops equipped with
Chassepot rifles battle the Prussians at Bapaume
(left) on January 3, 1871. Despite
the fact that the Chassepot was a fine arm, the
French were quickly defeated in the
Franco-Prussian War by troops armed with the
Dreyse needle gun seen below.

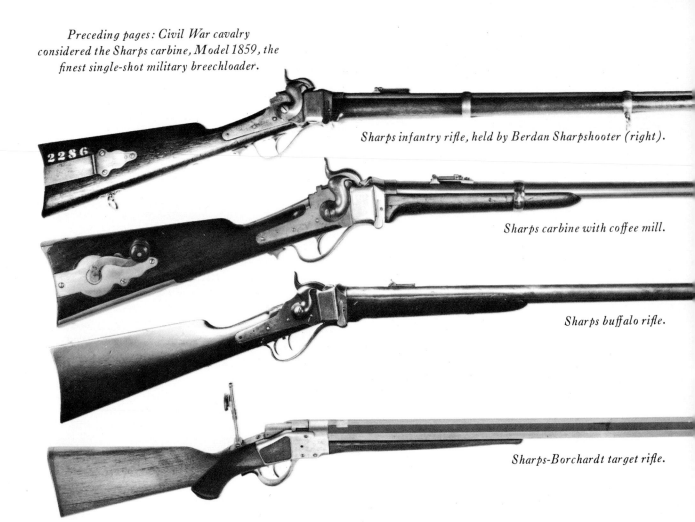

Preceding pages: Civil War cavalry considered the Sharps carbine, Model 1859, the finest single-shot military breechloader.

Sharps infantry rifle, held by Berdan Sharpshooter (right).

Sharps carbine with coffee mill.

Sharps buffalo rifle.

Sharps-Borchardt target rifle.

sights, and on September 13 and 14, 1877, an American team armed with brand-new Sharps-Borchardt rifles won the International Match at Creedmoor, Long Island. The victory was unexpected since the sport was new in this country. The *London Sporting Gazette* expressed surprise, but added, ". . . in the Sharps Rifle the Americans seem to have at last secured a match rifle which, for accuracy at long ranges, is unsurpassed, perhaps unequalled."

The Sharps-Borchardt rifle was a vastly different gun from those used by John Brown or Hiram Berdan. At the close of the Civil War many Sharps arms were converted to take the new self-contained metallic cartridges which had everywhere demonstrated their superiority to the old paper or linen cartridges with separate priming. Except for the change in ammunition, however, the rifle remained almost unaltered. Then, in late 1877, the Borchardt improvement

permitted a new hammerless line with an enclosed firing pin in the breech. It was a smooth and efficient action, but it never seemed to catch the popular fancy. The Sharps Rifle Company suspended operations in 1881. By then, however, Christian Sharps himself was long since dead and buried in Vernon, Connecticut, where he had retired to experiment with the artificial breeding of trout.

The Civil War also produced a host of other breech-loading systems as separately primed ammunition died out. Literally dozens of different actions were patented and sold to a people desperately in need of arms. Some were good, some mediocre, and some so downright undependable and dangerous that not even a wartime economy could make a success of them. There were arms with top levers, tilting barrels, sliding breech bolts, sliding barrels, dropping, rotating, or tilting breechblocks, and even an

ways in its base. A pin poised above it and protruding through the case gave the type its name of pin-fire. A blow from the hammer drove this pin into the cap and exploded it, setting off the charge. It worked well, but it was fragile and the exposed pin could be struck accidentally and either break off or explode the cartridge at an inconvenient time. Then there were teat fires, with the primer in a little projection at the head of the cartridge; lip fires with the primer in a protuberance on the rim; enclosed pin-fires with the pin covered by the case, and a number of other attempts to find a truly successful form.

In addition to these short-lived varieties, however, there also appeared the direct ancestor of the modern rim-fire cartridge. Here the percussion compound was spread in a cavity which encircled the rim of the base. In the first of these cartridges the percussion compound also supplied the propellent force, for they were used mostly for indoor target guns—saloon or gallery guns, as they were called. Thus, only a weak charge was desired. Then two Americans, Horace Smith and Daniel B. Wesson, whose fame popularly rests with their revolver, improved upon this and in 1858 produced a rim-fire cartridge with a suitable charge of black powder, plus the priming compound.

The Smith and Wesson cartridge won quick favor and soon was used in a variety of firearms. Nevertheless, its possibilities also were restricted. It was impossible to produce a metal case strong enough to withstand the explosion of a heavy charge and still soft enough to be indented easily by the hammer of the gun. Thus the rim-fire was limited to cartridges with fairly weak loads.

The center-fire cartridge removed this limitation. Many inventors in England, France, and the United States contributed to its development. In the center-fire cartridge, a small primer in the base is crushed by the hammer against a rigid anvil with a hole (or holes) leading to the powder charge. This was essentially Pauly's system, although he had used a loose

underhammer bolt action. Cartridges were made of paper, linen, rubber, metal foil, and sheet metal. The study of these arms is a delight for the mechanically minded collector. In no other contemporary group of weapons is there such diversity of approaches to the basic problem of all breechloaders: obtaining a quick-acting, gas-tight seal for that second opening. But here the interest and significance of such guns are ended. None performed as well as the Sharps and none had any lasting effect on the development of firearms.

Pauly's idea of the expanding metallic cartridge which formed its own seal and contained its own primer had at last caught on. The path had been devious and pioneered primarily by French gunsmiths and inventors such as Pottet, Flobert, Le Faucheux, and Houillier.

After Pauly, the first successful self-contained cartridge held a percussion cap mounted side-

priming compound with the head of the cartridge itself as the anvil. Practical center-fire cartridges with inside primers were made in England as early as 1852, but were ultimately perfected by Colonel Hiram Berdan, of Civil War Sharpshooter fame, and by Colonel Edward M. Boxer of the British Royal Laboratory in 1866. There have been no major changes since. The metallic cartridge had reached its fully developed state and the day of separate primed guns had passed.

Breechloaders could now be made as foolproof and as tight as muzzle-loaders. Any number of systems were possible with the problem of the gas seal solved and a host of different actions poured from the inventors' benches. Several of them had their start during the American Civil War, and most of the breechloaders adopted by military establishments throughout the world in the years immediately after the war were the products of American ingenuity.

In the United States itself, the decision to adopt a breechloader was reached during the late years of the war. The excellent performances of the better breech actions made the defects of the muzzle-loading Springfields so glaringly obvious that even the most conservative and hidebound ordnance officer could not ignore them. But at the end of the conflict the arsenals were full of perfectly good Springfield rifle muskets. The usual postwar retrenchment had set in. Funds were scarce and the vast quantity of muzzle-loaders in excellent condition could not be scrapped. Thus, a means of converting these arms to breechloaders was sought, rather than a radically new arm, although this might have been better in the long run. Erskine S. Allin, Master Armorer at the Springfield Armory, devised such an alteration, and conversions began in 1865. With minor improvements, the Allin system eventually became the well-known .45-70 Springfield adopted in 1873.

The new Springfield was a simple and sturdy arm. A movable breechblock, including a firing pin, was hinged at the forward end so that it could be flipped up, trap-door fashion, exposing the chamber and ejecting the spent cartridge case if a shot had been fired. In a few quick motions, a fresh cartridge could then be slipped into the chamber, the block snapped shut, and the side hammer cocked, ready for firing. The ammunition fired by the fully developed Model 1873 was a center-fire cartridge with a .45-caliber bullet and seventy grains of black pow-

U. S. soldier in the West (above) with a .45-70 trap-door Springfield was drawn by Frederic Remington. Below: Allin alteration of 1865.

der for a propelling charge. This cartridge not only gave the arm its designation of .45-70, but also provided a hard-hitting bullet with a flat trajectory that made it especially useful for firing at the long ranges commonly encountered in the American West.

The board of officers that selected the Allin action felt that it was the best of a host of models studied. Many American experts and most foreign ordnance officers disagreed, believing that the Remington and Peabody, among others, were superior. Nevertheless, the Allin served well, with few complaints from the field except for occasional difficulty in extracting empty cartridge cases after prolonged firing.

This fault received considerable attention in the press following the disastrous Battle of the Little Big Horn in 1876. The annihilation of George Armstrong Custer and five troops of the famed Seventh Cavalry by Sitting Bull and his band of Sioux and Cheyennes shocked the nation, while the aura of mystery and drama surrounding "Custer's Last Stand" attracted interest throughout Europe. Scapegoats were needed and many were found, including the .45-70 Springfield carbine which the troopers had carried in addition to their Colt revolvers. Cartridge cases with their heads torn off were picked up on the battlefield, indicating that at least some of the soldiers had had their rifles jam in the crucial test, and this fact was magnified. Actually, the frequency of such failures seems to have been relatively low and unimportant, and the trap-door Springfield served, with minor alterations and model designations, as the principal United States service rifle and carbine throughout the entire period of the Plains Indian Wars. Volunteer units carried it in the Spanish-American War, and some state troops were still armed with it at the beginning of World War I.

In Great Britain, the change-over from muzzle-loaders to breechloaders came at almost the same time and in the same way. Once again there were large stocks of good muzzle-loading rifle-muskets on hand which a wise government did not wish to waste. Thus, in 1865, it selected a conversion system designed by Jacob Snider of New York. Once again the system consisted of a hinged breechblock, but this time the pivot was along the side and the trap door swung open to the right for loading. Again there were extraction difficulties; the gun had to be turned upside down to eject the spent cartridge case completely. The Snider-Enfield was a good arm, however. Colonel Boxer's improved center-fire cartridge of 1867 made it shoot even better than the original muzzle-loading version. It hit hard, too, as Rudyard Kipling noted in his description of an incident in Burma when:

A snider squibbed in the jungle—
Somebody laughed and fled,
And the men of the first Shikaris
Picked up their Subaltern dead,
With a big blue mark in his forehead
And the back blown out of his head.

The difference between the American and British experience lay in what followed these early similarities. The Snider conversion was only a stopgap. A board of officers was promptly convened to study all available breech-loading systems and find the best arm to replace the Snider conversions as soon as possible. There was a host of new guns to choose from. Some

one hundred and twenty different actions and forty-nine different cartridges were tested before the final decision was made and a new arm adopted in 1871.

Once again the new rifle had an American ancestor. This time, however, it had passed through the hands of a master Swiss mechanic and been vastly improved. As far back as 1862, Henry O. Peabody of Boston had patented a breech system known as the falling block. In this action the breechblock was hinged at the back. Pulling outward on a lever—usually the trigger guard—tilted this block downward in front and exposed the chamber at the foot of an inclined plane formed by the top of the block itself. The United States did not get around to testing the Peabody until 1865. The trial reports were glowing, but by then the Civil War was over and the decision was made to convert the rifle-muskets on hand rather than adopt a new arm. Canada bought a large number of Peabodys, however, and so did a number of European countries.

In Switzerland the Peabody came under the influence of Frederich von Martini, and a good gun was made even better. Peabody had retained the traditional, outside, separate-cocked hammer. Martini discarded this and substituted an internal self-cocking striker, thus protecting the mechanism and increasing its speed of action. This Peabody-Martini was the breech system the British board selected for its new service arms. It was coupled with a barrel designed by Alexander Henry of Edinburgh and the new gun was called the Martini-Henry. Poor old Peabody who had invented the basic action was completely forgotten. This apparently was to be his destiny, for the Austrians modified his breech and called it a Werder, while later arms —some still in use today—are known as Francotte-Martinis, Swinburns, Stahls, or other names with never a reference to the man whose falling-block design they employ.

From 1871 until after the adoption of smokeless powder, the Martini served as the principal British single-shot weapon. With different barrels it provided the teeth in the "thin red line" that maintained order throughout the British Empire, from Burma, Malaya, and India to Africa, South America, and the West Indies. It beat back Fuzzy-Wuzzys and Boers, Afghans and Zulus in minor wars and unnamed engagements. Kipling, who understood the soldier and his weapons, noted its role in the preservation of the Empire in countless references —especially in his advice to "The Young British Soldier" on his relationship to his rifle:

When 'arf of your bullets fly wide in the ditch,
Don't call your Martini a cross-eyed old bitch;
She's human as you are—you treat her as sich,
—An' she'll fight for the young British soldier.

There was one other breech system developed at the close of the Civil War that in its day was the most widely used of all. This was the Remington rolling block. Leonard Geiger and Joseph Rider developed the system in the Remington Arms Company plant at Ilion, New York, and brought it to completion in April, 1865, just as Lee was surrendering the Army of Northern Virginia to Ulysses S. Grant at Appomattox Court House. Perfection was achieved the following winter, well after the Civil War was over and the best chance for an American market had vanished.

The rolling-block breech was as simple and as strong and as nearly foolproof as a gun could be. The breech was opened by cocking the hammer and rolling the solid breechblock straight back with the thumb. A cartridge could then be inserted and the block rolled back up, while a locking lever held the hammer cocked, then locked the breech closed. When the piece was fired, the hammer struck the firing pin mounted in the breechblock and added its weight to the breech at the moment of explosion. In addition, these parts were so designed that pressure from the chamber forced them more tightly together. The greater the recoil, the more closely the pieces interlocked.

With the ammunition available it was liter-

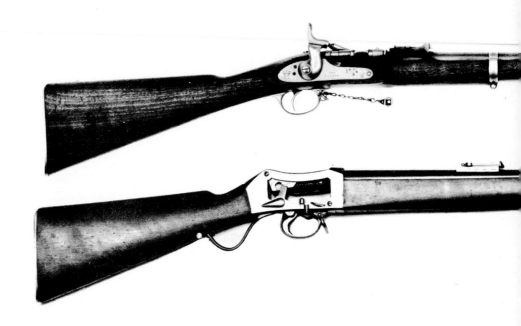

Upper right: Snider conversion of the Enfield rifle was adopted by Great Britain in 1865. Lower right: A cutaway view of the British Martini-Henry rifle, 1871. British troops (below) battle fiercely at Tell el-Kebir, Egypt, 1882. In such engagements, British troops carried Sniders and Martini-Henrys.

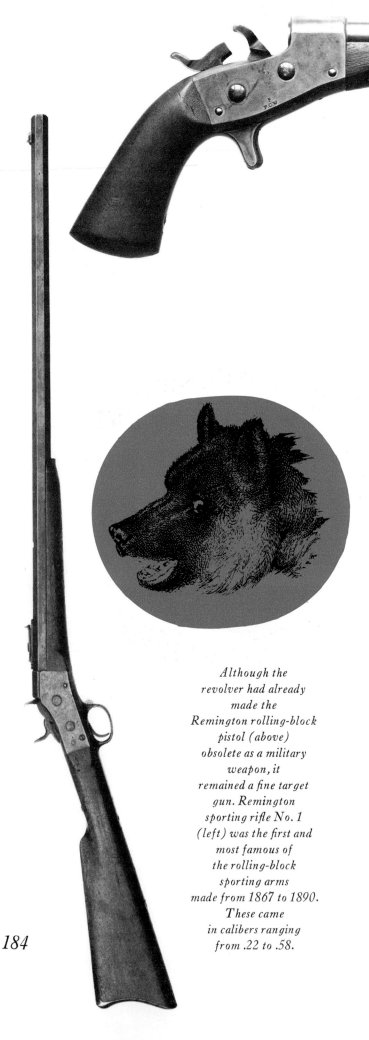

Although the revolver had already made the Remington rolling-block pistol (above) obsolete as a military weapon, it remained a fine target gun. Remington sporting rifle No. 1 (left) was the first and most famous of the rolling-block sporting arms made from 1867 to 1890. These came in calibers ranging from .22 to .58.

ally impossible to blow out a Remington breech. Certainly the Belgians tried. In the world-renowned proving house at Liége, Belgium, a .50-caliber Remington was loaded with seven hundred and fifty grains of black powder, forty balls, and two wads so that the barrel was completely full and would hold no more—a charge more than thirty-six inches long. It was fired, and the director of proof noted laconically that "nothing extraordinary occurred."

And the Remington performed just as well in the field as it did in the proof houses. One of the very first shipments of rolling-block rifles to the West found its way into the hands of Nelson Story and his group of thirty determined cowboys. Story and his band were driving three thousand head of cattle from Texas to Montana. At Fort Leavenworth they got word that Red Cloud and the entire Sioux nation were on the warpath. To reach their goal they would have to shepherd the slow-moving herd along the Bozeman Trail in the heart of Red Cloud's territory. Undaunted by the news, Story bought thirty of the brand-new Remington rolling blocks and issued them to his men.

The huge herd and its wagon train moved north and west. They reached Fort Laramie without incident, then Fort Reno on the edge of the Wyoming Badlands after a minor skirmish with perhaps two hundred braves. The unexpected firepower of rifles that could be fired seventeen times a minute so startled the braves, who had been used to facing muzzle-loaders, that they withdrew to think things over and let the caravan proceed—for the time being. But one cowboy was dead and two were wounded. Story had only twenty-seven men left when he reached Fort Kearney, the army's farthest outpost. Colonel Henry Carrington forbade him to go on. Three thousand Sioux, Cheyennes, and Arapahoes blocked the trail, he said. His three hundred soldiers, armed with the best Springfield rifle-muskets made during the war, did not dare venture far from the fort. It would be suicide for twenty-seven men to attempt to get through, especially with several thousand cattle to look after. Story pushed on anyway, slipping away from Fort Kearney one night. He knew Carrington would not pursue him.

Then one brilliant autumn afternoon the test came. Crazy Horse and his warriors, reportedly some five hundred strong, swept down upon the little band. Letting the cattle fend for themselves, the cowboys drew their wagons into a circle, just as the Hussites had done against the cavalry charges of the imperial armies centuries before. The Indians were used to this tactic. They dashed up close enough to draw the defenders' fire, then waited for the lull that would indicate the cowboys were reloading, so that they could make their real onslaught. The lull never came. A steady galling fire from the rifles first drove the attackers back, then broke and dispersed them completely. Story had not lost a man. Twice again during the trek the Indians attacked the dauntless cowboys only to be driven back with more braves dead and never a coup counted. It was bad medicine and the warriors gave up. Story reached Montana safely to found the cattle industry there, and the Remington rolling block had proved its worth.

The first spectacular success for the Remington had come in the American West. Different but even more spectacular triumphs quickly followed abroad. In 1867, the Imperial Exposition was held in Paris with new achievements and inventions from all over the world displayed to show the wonders of the modern world and proclaim man's scientific advances. Products were examined and tested by boards of specialists in each field, and it was here that the High Commission on Firearms unanimously selected the Remington rolling block as the finest rifle in the world, commemorating the event with the Silver Medal of the Exposition, the highest award for military and sporting arms.

Obviously, here was a gun to interest all nations. Denmark adopted it that very year. Norway and Sweden followed in 1868, Spain in 1869, Egypt in 1870, and Argentina in 1879.

China, Austria, Italy, and several South American countries purchased and used the Remington in some numbers and almost every nation experimented with it. In all, more than a million rolling-block rifles and carbines were sold.

In its own country the Remington's reception was mixed. Test reports were full of praise, but official orders were few. The navy purchased rolling-block pistols in 1866 and 1867, and the army bought some in 1871. They were excellent pistols and target shooters still like both the action and balance. But the revolver had superseded all single-shot handguns for military purposes and the Remingtons were soon abandoned. Some thirty-three thousand rifles also were manufactured for army and navy use, but their impact was small. The trap-door Springfield remained standard for the American soldier. Among sporting arms, however, the rolling-block breech was quickly adopted for many target guns and it remained popular well into the present century.

By 1870, all of the principal breech-loading systems had been invented. The bolt action, trap door, falling block, rolling block, dropping block, and tip-down barrel were widely used. The muzzle-loader was obsolete, used only by primitive peoples and an occasional die-hard sportsman who scorned new-fangled ways. Ironically, the single-shot breechloader, too, was obsolete. It had been outmoded before it was perfected. The self-contained, metal-cased cartridge which made the breechloader practical also made the repeater possible. And who would want a single-shot weapon when he could command a magazine of bullets? Only a marksman to whom time meant nothing, a boy who could afford no more, or an ordnance officer who worried about the reliability of the new systems, the cost of replacing existing arms, and the possible waste of ammunition if soldiers could shoot faster. It was these three groups, primarily, who provided the later history of the single-shot breechloader. The rest of the world wanted rapid-firing weapons.

185

CHAPTER *9*

*Preceding pages: Seven-barrel′d
naval volley gun, invented by James Wilson
and manufactured by Henry Nock.*

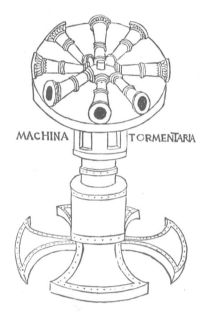

MACHINA TORMENTARIA

TO LOAD BUT ONCE AND FIRE OFTEN

One shot is seldom enough. Even a superb marksman misses occasionally; often there are many targets to hit. The moments lost in reloading can be critical if the target is moving away—or if it is shooting back. There also are circumstances in which it is difficult or impossible to reload—while riding a galloping horse or when boarding a ship. Almost from the beginning, therefore, the ability to shoot several times after each loading and the increased firepower available in a repeating arm were viewed as both desirable and necessary.

One way to obtain several shots was to carry several guns, and this frequently was done. Pistols often were made in pairs so that the owner might have two shots at his command. The pirates of the late Seventeenth and early Eighteenth Centuries went even further. Unable to reload once an action had commenced, they carried as many as eight pistols in their pockets or attached to belts or ribbons. Usually, these were small pistols, but even so they were a cumbersome burden.

Interestingly enough, multishot weapons had been designed long before the era of the buccaneers, and some had proved quite successful. Some fired all their shots at once in a volley, others ticked them off, one after another, in true repeater fashion. But well before 1700 all of the basic types of multishot and repeating firearms had been invented and tried. These included multiple barrels, revolving cylinders, magazines, and superposed loads. The basic principles were discovered early. Refinement and perfection took centuries.

The most obvious approach and also the earliest was the use of multiple barrels. The great ribauldequins, which probably came before the first handgun was invented, already have been mentioned. These could be mounted in tiers, like the huge Italian towers of the Duke of Verona, with a hundred and forty-four barrels in each, or they might be a single line of ten, twenty, or thirty barrels fastened to a beam or a platform. In such a position, the individual tubes reminded viewers of the pipes of an organ, and they came to be called organ batteries, organ guns, or in German a *Totenorgel*—death organ. Some of the more ingenious of these organ batteries used a triangular block, instead of a flat platform, with a row of barrels fastened to each face. After firing one volley, the block could be rotated for a second and then a third. In all forms of the organ battery, the touchholes of each row of barrels were aligned and all set off together.

The principal drawback of the organ-battery system was its weight and awkwardness. It had to be mounted on wheels and pulled either by draft animals or several men, depending on its size. In certain situations it was useful, and the same form has come down to modern times in the Billinghurst Requa Battery and the Vandenburg Volley Gun of the American Civil War, the mitrailleuse, and the homemade batteries of the market hunters of half a century ago which almost destroyed the flocks of waterfowl along the eastern seaboard. In these last devices, old gun barrels, or sometimes just lengths of iron pipe, were fastened to a frame which could be set up to command a flyway or feeding area and fired just the way the Fourteenth Century batteries were. The Duke of Verona would have been perfectly at home assisting one of these market fowlers of 1900 in his operations in the field.

The average individual, however, did not want to be bothered with a gun that had to be hauled on a cart or fired from a fixed position. Fewer and smaller barrels were one obvious answer to his desires. Guns and pistols with two, three, four, or even more barrels were developed soon after hand firearms appeared. One of the more primitive, although certainly not the oldest, is the three-barreled hand cannon of the Chinese, made of wrought iron and so closely resembling early European arms in workmanship that it is frequently identified as such. The Europeans had multibarreled hand cannon, too. A seven-barreled specimen is listed in a 1435 inventory of the Bastille, but it is only the Oriental variety that seems to have survived in quantity. Then the practice became popular and there are matchlocks, wheel locks, and flint and percussion arms with a bewildering profusion of barrels.

Many of these multibarreled weapons were volley guns that fired all their charges at once. In one imaginative design, four barrels were splayed out from a common center so that the shots would spread and cover a wide arc. These pistols, made toward the end of the Eighteenth Century, are known to collectors as duckfoot pistols because of their shape. Supposedly they were favored by prison guards, tough sea captains, and other individuals who might be faced by a threatening mob. Indeed, they must have been impressive weapons to confront. They would almost certainly hit someone in a group, but almost certainly fail to pick out a single individual. Several people obviously would be endangered and this could dampen the enthusiasm of any mutinous mob. A pair of such guns would have been truly imposing, and one can only wonder at the recoil as all four charges exploded simultaneously. It might have been possible for a tough captain to hold both guns on the mutineers, but a weak-armed mate might well have found himself perforating the sails.

Other volley-type guns had even more barrels. Usually they were clustered in a circle, however, and so did not spread their shot over so wide an area. Thus, they were more useful for self-defense, or even for hunting or military purposes. Seven seems to have been a popular number of barrels for such weapons. The first European reference—1435—mentions a gun with seven barrels. The earliest dated example of a multibarreled handgun is a sporting gun in the Tower of London. It has seven barrels and was made in 1612. During the late Eighteenth Century and the first half of the Nineteenth, literally hundreds of such arms were made. There may have been some magical or superstitious reason for this particular number. Seven has long been considered to be lucky. But it should also be noted that if six barrels of equal diameter are clustered around a central barrel of like size, the seven group themselves nicely.

Undoubtedly the most famous of all the seven-barreled volley guns were those made by Henry Nock for the British Navy in the 1780's. Their origin has long been obscured by a romantic Nineteenth Century legend that they were invented as a result of the death of Lord

Nelson at Trafalgar in 1805. As his flagship

1

the *Victory* drifted slowly toward the *Redoubtable* in that battle on the October seas, its decks were raked by the fire of snipers in the tops of the French ships. It was almost inevitable that a bullet from one should eventually strike down the heroic, one-armed, one-eyed admiral on the quarter-deck. News of his death brought sorrow to all Britain and, the story goes, the seven-barreled volley gun was developed to clear enemy tops and decks and give greater protection to other admirals in the future.

Unfortunately, there are several things wrong with this tale. For one thing, Nelson and his successors abhorred the idea of placing snipers in the tops. Such marksmen were a fire hazard, the admirals believed, and sometimes they did succeed in setting their own vessels afire by igniting the canvas around them. Thus, the practice of manning the tops of English ships in action had all but ceased by the time of Trafalgar. Most damning of all, however, is the fact that the seven-barreled guns actually had been made for the British Navy almost a quarter

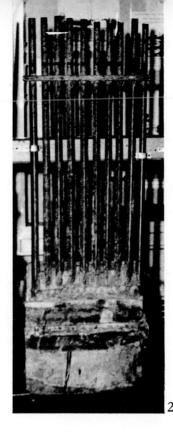

1. *Billinghurst &
Requa "Eureka" Battery
gun of 1862.*

2. *Wildfowler's
organ battery of about
1900. Bulky structure
and weight made these
weapons difficult
to maneuver.*

century before Nelson's death and, far from being invented, were apparently abandoned at just about that time.

In reality, the inventor was one James Wilson, and he had presented his "new Invented Gun with seven barrels to fire at one time" to the Board of Ordnance for trial on July 29, 1779. The board was very favorably impressed with the gun, but felt it was more appropriate for use aboard ship than in the field. Thus they referred it to the Lords Commissioners of the Admiralty. Henry Nock, the London gunsmith, made sample pieces with rifled barrels and in October of that year orders for the volley guns began to be placed with him in quantity, although the rifling was abandoned in favor of smoothbores. For the next several years Nock reigned supreme as the sole maker of these arms for His Majesty's Navy, and he produced over five hundred before the orders ceased.

Making volley guns was a very complicated process and they cost the navy £13 apiece. All seven barrels were made separately and then brazed together. There were special breech plugs to be fitted, firing channels to be drilled, a chamber and screw spindle to be made, as well as the usual flintlock, stock, and furniture found on all guns. The rifled versions had cost £15 apiece, and since they would have been little more effective than smoothbores, the navy was well-advised to save the money. Two pounds sterling would more than pay for an extra sea-service musket.

The theory of the gun's operation was simple. The fire from the pan was communicated to the chamber which fired the central barrel. Six channels radiated out from this barrel to carry the fire from its explosion to the other charges. Thus, the center shot fired before the other six, but the time difference was only momentary, hardly noticeable in the general roar of the discharge. The recoil was considerable, but after lengthy experimentation a satisfactory charge was developed that kept recoil within reasonable limits. The main difficulty with the arm seems to have been in the care required for

*Above: Colonel Thomas Thornton shown
with his celebrated twelve-barreled volley gun. Right:
Three-barreled percussion gun was made by
M. L. Rudd, owned by Indian fighter Bill Hamilton.*

after that system came into vogue, they must have been prized arms.

One of the great champions of the seven-barreled gun among sportsmen was Colonel Thomas Thornton, who also had a twelve-barreled gun and one monster double seven-barrel. Both sets of seven barrels could be mounted together on the same stock or each could be mounted on a single stock. The complete gun with all fourteen barrels weighed eleven pounds, eight ounces, and it needed a special fore-end handle to help support the weight.

The seven-barreled volley gun hung on much longer than one would expect. A percussion model was displayed at the Great Exhibition of 1851 in London with the note that it was particularly useful for shooting wildfowl. But probably the final version was developed by the Belgian gunsmith, Henri Pieper, who produced one that fired .22 rim-fire cartridges with a Remington rolling-block breech!

One of the more intriguing of all these many-barreled arms was a military belt bristling with a total of fifteen pistol barrels. The inventor, who bore the delightful name of J. Lillycrap, presented this device to the Select Committee on Ordnance at Woolwich in 1842. It was the inventor's belief that each British soldier sent against the foe with such a belt and a six-barreled pistol in each hand would be a veritable army in himself. "A touch on a waistcoat button and bang goes five of the barrels," cried Mr. Lillycrap, obviously thrilled at the thought. But the Select Committee had distressing visions of the poor soldier getting up off his back, clutching a badly bruised stomach, both handguns probably having been fired involuntarily as he fell. They rejected the offer.

Most multibarreled firearms were more modest, however. Two- and three-barrel combinations were usual, with four-barreled specimens slightly less popular. Among these arms the barrels generally were fired separately, rather than as a volley. Many devices were developed to accomplish this. Sometimes there were separate

proper charging and the tendency of the firing channels to foul and clog. Hang fires and misfires often occurred in one or more of the barrels without the shooter realizing it, so that he would continue to pile loads into the malfunctioning tubes.

The navy experimented with the volley gun for less than ten years, but there was a civilian market as well. Nock continued to make seven-barreled arms for sportsmen, and other gunmakers joined him. There were rifles, smoothbores, and even pistols, and if one may judge by the number that was converted to percussion

192

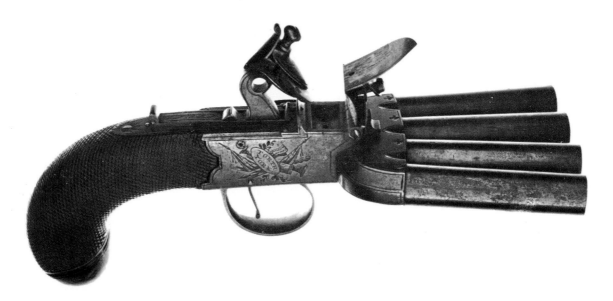

English duckfoot flintlock pistol—so called because of its splayed shape—was made by Forth of York in late 1800's. Hook at side permitted gun to be hung from the belt. Sliding safety latch is behind center cock. Duckfoots might have been used to advantage during actions such as the sea battle shown at right.

locks for each barrel. Sometimes the barrels rotated and sometimes, in the case of flintlocks, there were valves in the pans which directed the fire to the selected barrel. Some of these combinations have remained popular to the present day. The double-barreled shotgun and the shotgun-rifle combinations, often with three barrels, are still common.

The multibarreled pistol has all but disappeared, but even that weapon continued in widespread use until quite recently. The advent of the metallic cartridge, in fact, revived a flagging interest in such arms. Guns using the new ignition system were less bulky than percussion-cap pistols and a whole new line of pocket models followed this discovery. Many of them boasted two or more barrels.

One of the more popular of these was a four-barreled pistol patented by Christian Sharps in 1859. Already famous for his breech-loading long arms, Sharps scored once again with his pistol, an estimated 148,000 of them being manufactured and presumably sold. In this tiny

weapon the four barrels were bored from a rectangular block. The firing pin revolved each time the hammer was cocked, so that it discharged one barrel after the other. The .22-caliber model, which was the most popular, seems to be a completely inoffensive weapon to the modern eye, but the .30- and .32-caliber pistols were highly respectable. Even so, with their extremely short barrels, they were meant for close work. A man thirty feet away stood a reasonably good chance of escaping at least the first shot. The three additional barrels lessened his chances considerably.

Another popular type of pistol had the barrels arranged in a straight line, either vertically or horizontally. The idea was to produce a gun that would lie flat in the pocket. In one version, patented by William W. Marston of New York City, in 1857, there were three barrels, one above the other. The firing pin moved up after each shot and a circular dial on the outside indicated how many shots had been fired. A quite modern model known as the Reform Pistol has four barrels which move up and down in front of a stationary firing pin.

An example of the horizontal barrel arrangement is found in the so-called harmonica pistol patented by A. E. and P. H. Jarre of Paris in 1873. Here a series of barrels (the inventors considered ten to be the maximum desirable) were fashioned in a horizontal block. The handle with the hammer and mechanism could be slid along from one to the next, much in the

fashion of a virtuoso playing the scale on a harmonica. Hence the name. For carrying, the handle was moved to the end of the block and twisted so that it was in line with the barrel block instead of perpendicular to it. In this position it fitted as smoothly in the pocket as the Marston or Reform, and far less noticeably than the revolver, with its conspicuous bulge around the cylinder.

But the biggest seller of all the multibarreled pocket pistols was undoubtedly the Remington Double Deringer. It was a deadly little weapon. Its two barrels, one above the other, were only three inches long. It could fit into a stocking top, a lady's bosom, a muff, or a gentleman's pocket, with hardly a wrinkle. But its .41-caliber bullets were more than enough for almost any job. The Remington armory had pioneered in the tiny cartridge pistol, presumably for the protection of ladies against Evil as personified in the mustachioed villain of the day. In actuality, it mattered not that many of the feminine purchasers were far more interested in defending their property than a virtue that might be dimly remembered at best. The gun was just as effective for them, too, and they were more likely to be interested in the special models with pearl grips and engraved gold-plated barrels.

For some sixty years this deadly little gun proved an excellent seller. Between 1866 when production began and 1935 when it halted, more than 150,000 were sold. Now it is being manufactured once again, but primarily as a curiosity for the historically minded shooter of today.

These were but a few of the multibarreled cartridge pistols. Adding extra barrels was such an obvious device for gaining extra shots that the total number of different combinations, types, and models has never even been estimated.

Not nearly so obvious a method of increasing firepower was the technique of loading a number of charges, one on top of another, in the same barrel. Yet here again the idea appeared very early. The first definite reference to the practice so far discovered occurs in England in 1580 when John the Almain, or John the German, recommended one of his countrymen who could make an arquebus "that shall containe ten balls or pellets of lead, all the which shall goe off, one after another, haveinge once given fire." But perhaps the system was known even earlier, for the next century finds it being tested repeatedly throughout England and Western Europe.

John the Almain's system apparently was the simplest form of such a gun. In it each of the bullets was pierced and the hole filled with a fuze compound. A number of charges separated by these bullets would then be placed in the barrel and the foremost one fired either by a lock or with a match or powder train. If the bullets fit the bore tightly and if the fuze holes were properly aligned, the flash from the first charge would ignite the fuze in the hole of the ball immediately behind it. This would burn through and ignite the second charge, and so on to the last load. The effect was very much like that of

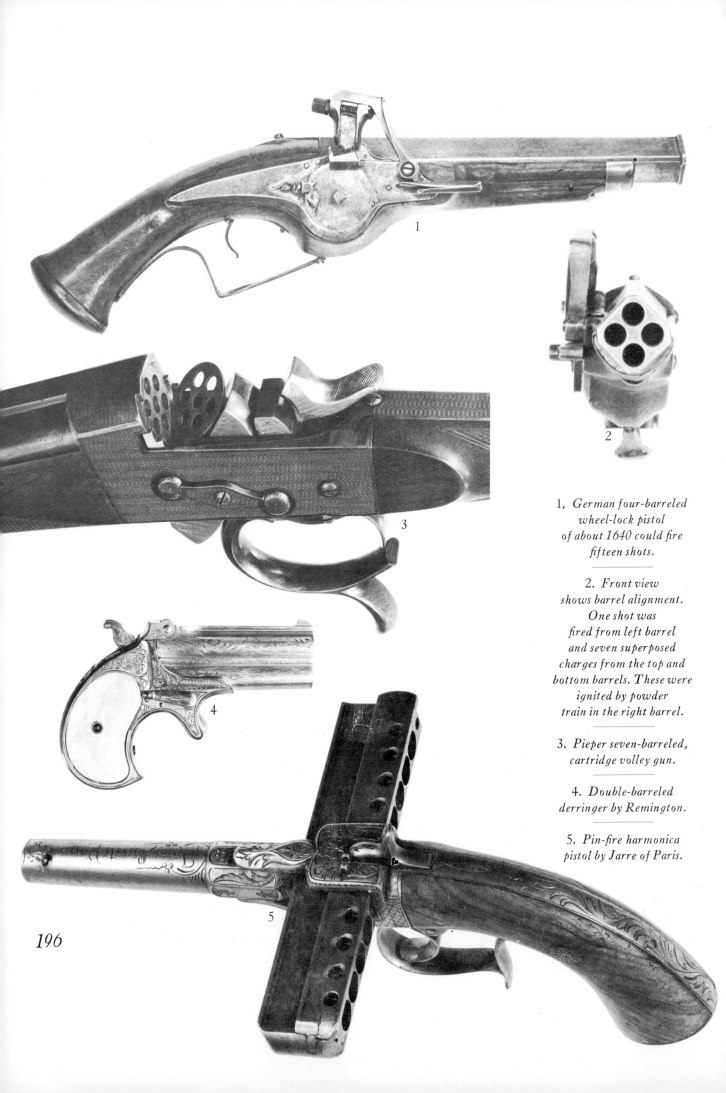

1. *German four-barreled wheel-lock pistol of about 1640 could fire fifteen shots.*

2. *Front view shows barrel alignment. One shot was fired from left barrel and seven superposed charges from the top and bottom barrels. These were ignited by powder train in the right barrel.*

3. *Pieper seven-barreled, cartridge volley gun.*

4. *Double-barreled derringer by Remington.*

5. *Pin-fire harmonica pistol by Jarre of Paris.*

a Roman candle in a fireworks display, and this is the name by which such guns usually are known today.

Refinements were quickly added. One of the first was the placing of a second lock in the normal position, so that once the initial load of six, eight, ten, or more shots had been fired, Roman-candle fashion, the gun could be loaded and fired as a single-shot weapon, just like any other firearm of the era. This was an important improvement, for the proper charging of a gun with superposed loads was a time-consuming operation, almost impossible to achieve under battle conditions. Were it not for this second lock, the gun would be useless once it had been fired as a repeater. Perhaps John the Almain's friend had thought of this refinement. If so, John did not mention it, but a wheel-lock arquebus with such an arrangement has survived. Charles Cardiffe of England mentioned it in his patent of 1682, and throughout the Eighteenth Century dozens of other inventors in Europe and America claimed to have invented both the system itself and the advantage of the second lock. Interestingly, almost no one seems to have disputed them and each claim was dutifully tested anew by the government to which it was offered as the ultimate in secret weapons.

One such inventor was Joseph Belton of Philadelphia, who wrote to the Continental Congress in April, 1777:

I would just inform this Honorable Assembly, that I have discovered an improvement, in the use of Small Armes, wherein a common small arm, may be maid to discharge eight balls one after another, in eight, five or three seconds of time, & each one to do execution five & twenty, or thirty yards, and after so discharg'd to be loaded and fir'd with cartrage as useal, which I am ready to prove by experimental proof, and can with eaquel ease fix them so as to discharge sixteen or twenty, in sixteen, ten or five seconds of time, which I have kept as yet a secret, thinking that in two or three Months we might have an armey thus equipt, which our enemy should know nothing of, till they should be maid to know it in the field, to their immortal sorrow.

Actually, the British had tested similar guns many years before and rejected them. Congress, nevertheless, promptly authorized Belton to make a hundred guns of his design for test purposes and directed that he receive a reasonable compensation for his trouble, plus all just and necessary expenses. By then it was early May. In June, Sir William Howe sailed from New York with a British army, and on September 25 he occupied Philadelphia. Congress had fled and there is no further word of Belton until he turns up in England at the end of the war to attempt to sell an improved repeating gun to the British government.

It was another American, however, who achieved perhaps the greatest success with a Roman-candle firearm. Joseph G. Chambers, also a Pennsylvanian, was granted a patent in repeating gunnery on March 23, 1813. All details of the patent are lost, but from other descriptions and two surviving guns it seems obvious that it covered the standard system with two locks. Chambers was more fortunate than most of his fellow gunsmiths who had professed to invent that type of arm. The United States Navy and the Commonwealth of Pennsylvania actually ordered eight hundred and fifty of his muskets, rifles, and pistols, plus a number of seven-barreled swivel guns which would fire an impressive two hundred and twenty-four shots each. At least six hundred and probably more of the small arms were completed, inspected, and accepted, and in 1814 fifty muskets, fifty pistols, and fifteen swivels were sent to Commodore Chauncey to test in active service against the British flotilla on the Great Lakes. From all indications other Chambers guns saw service in the War of 1812 as well. Then they disappeared.

Today one swivel gun survives in Liége, Belgium, and one musket in the Rotunda at Woolwich. The swivel was given by an American a

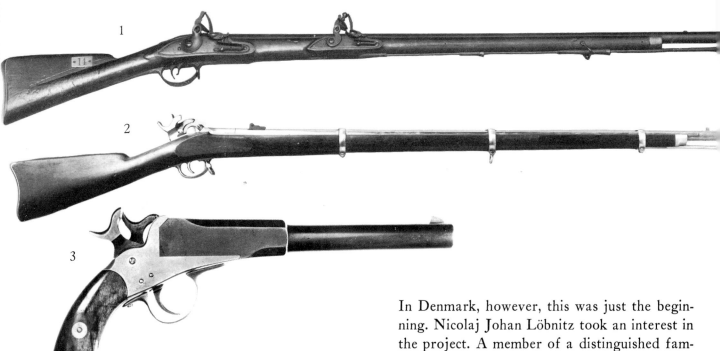

1. *Chambers repeating musket,*
the only existing model of its kind.
2. *American double musket by*
John P. Lindsay was patented in 1860.
3. *Lindsay's .44-caliber army*
pistol, which was patented in the same year.
4. *Isaiah Jennings' rifle*
with a sliding lock, patented in 1821.

century ago. The story of the musket is much more interesting. In 1815, one John Bland, who listed himself as a "Black and White Smith" from Philadelphia and who claimed to have helped in the manufacture of the Chambers guns, came to London and offered to sell the secret to British Ordnance. A pistol, a musket, and a swivel were submitted for inspection, but the British already were familiar with this sort of weapon. They rejected it once again, but the specimen musket survived, the only Chambers gun of its kind still in existence.

There were still Roman-candle guns in active use, however. The Danes had developed their version, which they called an *espingole*, during the Napoleonic Wars. Typically for the period, it was considered a highly important secret weapon and all details were kept hidden until 1844. By that time Great Britain and the United States had long since abandoned the principle.

In Denmark, however, this was just the beginning. Nicolaj Johan Löbnitz took an interest in the project. A member of a distinguished family of gunsmiths and himself the inventor of a breechloader and a military air gun, he concentrated all of his considerable talent on improving the weapon. He developed new ammunition, increased the number of barrels, and arranged them in two parallel tiers so that their pattern of fire would be more effective in battle than the circular clusters of the Chambers system. With its rows of barrels it was a direct descendant of the ancient organ batteries and from them took its name of *orgelespingole*. In October, 1850, Löbnitz demonstrated a twenty-barrel model, firing some three hundred shots at a time and requiring three-quarters of an hour to reload. Officials were enthusiastic and the *orgelespingole* became an official arm for the Danish Army and Navy for more than twenty years. By the time it was abandoned it had become an anachronistic contemporary of the Gatling gun.

The Chambers, the *orgelespingole*, and other Roman-candle guns fell from favor for several reasons. For one thing, they were difficult to load. The bullets had to fit tightly or flame would leak around them and all charges would go off almost simultaneously, with considerable damage to both gun and shooter. Even the fusillade of shots, which was their most impressive feature, also had its disadvantages. Once the shooting started, there was no way to stop it until all the charges had been fired. The gun

4

of a soldier shot dead after pulling the trigger, or dropped by a wounded or frightened man, was a menace to everyone in the vicinity.

There was one way to overcome the difficulty of controlling guns firing superposed loads. A separate lock could be used for each charge or, a more practical approach for large numbers of shots, a single movable lock could be used and its position shifted after each shot. Pierre Bergier, who made the waterproof wheel-lock pistols for Louis XIII, used superposed loads and separate locks on his firearms. Some of them carried as many as four shots. In 1780, John Aitken patented in England a gun with superposed loads and a sliding lock. The improved system that Joseph Belton took to London at the close of the American Revolution boasted both a separate chamber and a sliding lock. Belton did not succeed in interesting the British Ordnance, but some muskets, pistols, and carbines on his system were made, and a few were purchased by the East India Company. Some authorities believe that Chambers also experimented with a sliding lock, but the evidence is not definite. In America, Isaiah Jennings patented a rifle with a sliding flintlock in 1821, and Reuben Ellis obtained a contract to make five hundred and twenty of them for the New York militia. Jacob Mould patented a similar gun in England in 1825, which was manufactured with percussion locks as well as flint. And there were countless others.

With guns firing only two or three shots, the problems were simpler. Separate locks or hammers, or adjustments in pan, hammer nose, or firing channels were possible. All of these were tried with some degree of success, but none achieved real popularity. The difficulty of loading properly was always a disadvantage, even when a given device functioned well. And a single careless mistake could cause trouble.

Nevertheless, the idea died hard. A firearm with double hammers firing two superposed loads was invented by John P. Lindsay of New York and it was patented in 1860. After having tried the Belton, Chambers, and Jennings guns, the United States should have been thoroughly familiar with the theory and its drawbacks. Even so, it ordered one thousand rifle-muskets of Lindsay's pattern and accepted delivery in 1864. Pistols also were made, but these were for private sale only. When it came to handguns the government at last seemed to have overcome its fascination with the system.

It was the self-contained metallic cartridge that finally brought an end to this enticing line of endeavor. As long as firearms were loaded with separate primed ammunition, someone somewhere was sure to discover the superposed load system all over again and bring it forth as dramatically new, at least in some detail. With the advent of metal rim-fire or center-fire cartridges, the idea became obviously impractical enough for everybody to realize it.

Besides, there were better ways to increase firepower other than adding extra barrels or piling one shot on top of another.

CHAPTER 10

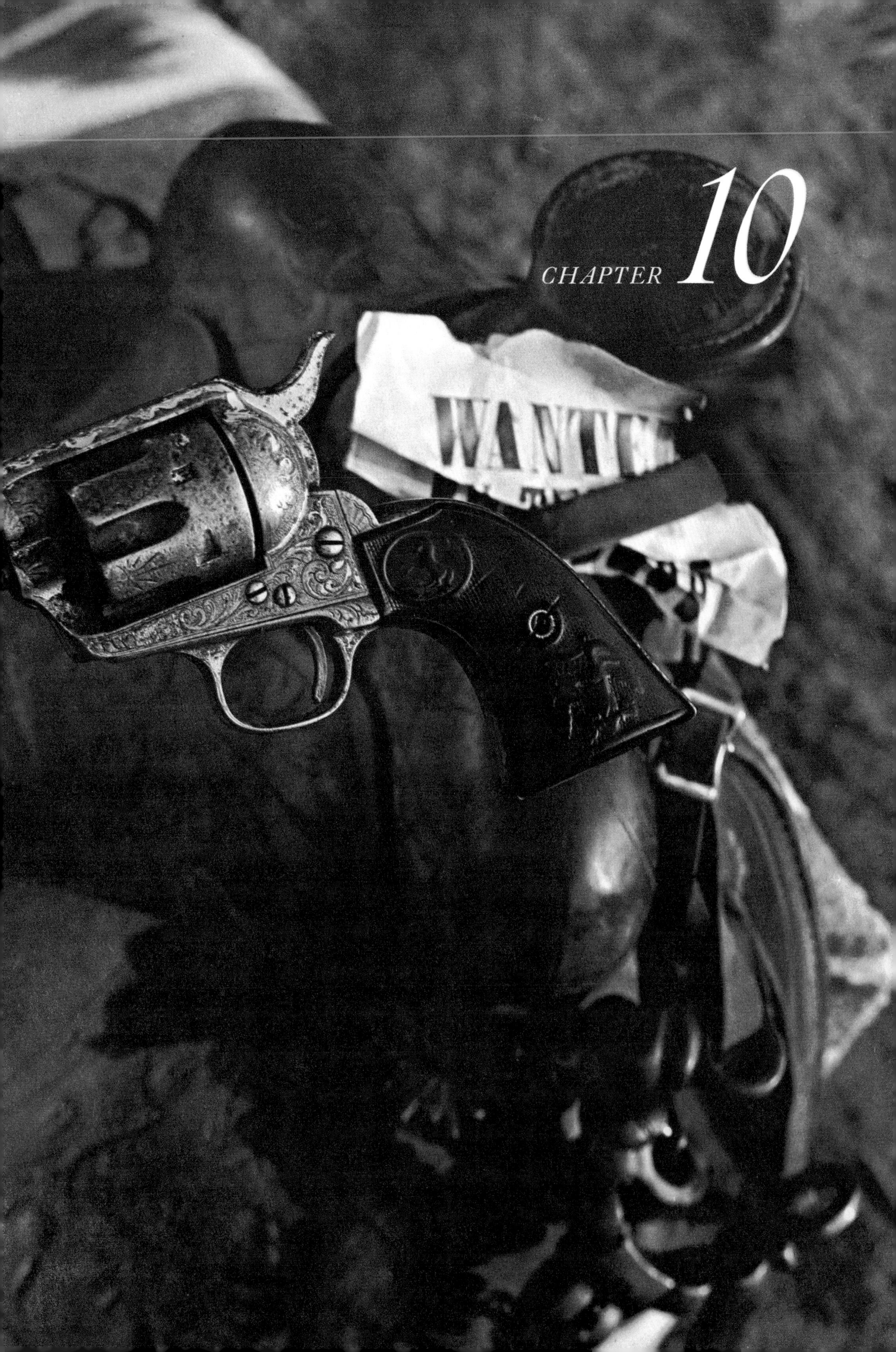

THE
REVOLVING
CYLINDER

A revolver is a firearm in which a series of barrels, or a cylinder with a series of chambers, revolves around a central axis. In this way each barrel or chamber comes before the firing mechanism in turn. The revolver can be a pistol, a long gun, or even a machine gun. The Sixteenth Century matchlock musket with a revolving cylinder, now in the Germanisches Museum, the famed Colt single-action of the American West, and the new, rapid-firing Vulcan cannon carry this basic principle across four centuries of firearms history. Through them and 202 *countless other examples, the multibarreled gun reached its highest development.*

Collectors today differentiate between guns with revolving barrels and those with revolving cylinders. They call the first pepperboxes and reserve the term revolver for a gun with a cylinder. The latter, using the term in this modern sense, represents the system at its most advanced stage. The pepperbox is obviously simpler and clumsier. Thus, there is a tendency to think of it as an earlier development and a precursor of the revolver. Actually, no one knows which came first. Both appeared at a very early date and continued in use until technical refinements finally made the cylinder as safe and efficient as the solid barrel.

Revolving firearms cannot claim a Fourteenth Century origin along with the simple multibarrel types, but they certainly had appeared on the scene before the close of the Sixteenth Century, a date of quite respectable antiquity. In Venice, for instance, there is preserved a matchlock pistol with three revolving barrels which is almost certainly the *"schioppo da serpa con tre cane"* listed in an inventory of that city in 1548. Several early wheel-lock pepperboxes and revolvers are known, and in the Tøjhusmuseet in Copenhagen are two snaphaunce revolving carbines believed to have been made by Hans Stopler of Nürnberg. One of them is dated 1597. Thereafter examples multiply rapidly.

Revolvers and pepperboxes had a problem in common: providing for the ignition of each barrel or chamber in turn. One part of the mechanism naturally would be stationary—the serpentine in a matchlock, doghead for a wheel lock, cock for one of the flint arms, or hammer for a percussion gun. It was still necessary to supply a priming pan for each barrel or chamber and sometimes, in the case of the flintlock, a frizzen as well. Pan covers had to fit tightly to keep powder from spilling and to prevent the flash of one pan from igniting others.

Revolvers had even more problems. The cylinder had to revolve easily, but it also had to line up directly with the breech of the barrel and lock securely in that position until it had been fired. Otherwise the force of the charge might drive the bullet against the frame or side of the barrel with disastrous results for both the gun and the shooter's hand. James Gorgo, an English gunsmith of the late 1600's, tried to avoid this problem completely. Instead of attempting to align chamber and breech, he used a funnel arrangement to catch the ball and deflect it into the barrel. It was simple and inexpensive, but not practical.

A neighbor and contemporary of Gorgo's solved the alignment problem more successfully and became one of the first men in history to attempt to market the revolver on a large scale. This was James Puckle, a notary public and a writer of highly moral tracts who had a weakness for extremely dubious financial operations. In 1718 he patented a large revolver, the size of a wall gun, mounted on a tripod. According to his own modest description, it was a "portable gun or machine called a defence, yet discharges so often and so many bullets and can be so quickly loaden as renders it next to impossible to carry any ship by boarding." And he recommended it especially

For Bridges, Breeches, Lines and Passes
Ships Boats Houses and other Places.

The weapon consisted of a barrel and interchangeable cylinders with varying numbers of charges. These cylinders were revolved by hand. There was a crank at the back by which they could be screwed up tightly against the barrel for each shot, while the coned mouth of each chamber fitted into the countersunk breech to form a reasonably gas-tight joint and assure proper alignment. It could be fired either by a match or a flintlock. A feature of the gun was its adaptability. Puckle announced that it could fire round bullets against Christians or square ones against Turks, which may have seemed an advantage to those who believed, like Puckle, that infidels could be killed more readily with extraordinary shot. Special cylinders were provided for either contingency. *203*

*Above: 78th Highlanders at the Siege of Lucknow, in
water color by Orlando Norie. Indian Mutiny of 1857 taught British
to prefer large-caliber, double-action revolvers for fighting
at close range. Below: Hunting buffalo
with a Colt revolver, from a painting by George Catlin.*

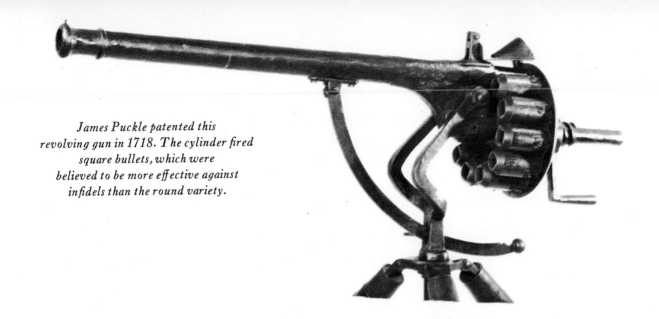

The inventor exhorted prospective buyers that "Defending King George your country and lawes Is defending yourselves and Protestant cause." But marketing the gun was not so easy as he might have hoped. He demonstrated it at Woolwich in November, 1717, but Ordnance disapproved. That meant private sales were his only chance. A stock company was formed, public demonstrations were held, and shares were offered for sale. A few buyers were found, but skeptics, remembering Puckle's other financial ventures, warned that his contraptions were:

*A rare invention to Destroy the Crowd
Of Fools at Home instead of Foes Abroad.
Fear not my Friends, this Terrible Machine.
They're only Wounded that have Shares therein.*

Nevertheless, the guns were produced. Some were of iron and some of brass. In one demonstration reported by the *London Journal* in 1722, a Puckle gun was fired sixty-three times in seven minutes during a rainstorm. Two of Puckle's guns actually were taken on an expedition to the Islands of St. Lucia and St. Vincent in 1727, but no mention was made of their performance in action, if, indeed, they were ever used. That was the last of the Puckle gun historically. The company failed. The shareholders presumably suffered, and the highly imaginative weapon is represented today by two specimens in the Tower of London and one in the Tøjhusmuseet.

Succeeding years of the Eighteenth Century saw other flintlock revolvers produced throughout England and Europe. Some were long arms, some handguns. Some had separate frizzens for each chamber, a thoroughly awkward arrangement, while some reverted to the snaphaunce system of one steel with separate sliding covers for each pan. A rare few even had a little priming mechanism which filled the pans just before they slid under the frizzen, and so avoided the hazard of numerous ready-primed loads all next to each other. All had difficulties.

It was almost exactly a century after Puckle's invention that the first really practical revolver was introduced. And the manner of its introduction was sufficiently peculiar to obscure its origin for another hundred and fifty years. Some details still are not clear and perhaps never will be. The actual inventor appears to have been Captain Artemus Wheeler of Concord, Massachusetts, who obtained a patent for a "Gun, to discharge 7 or more times" on June 10, 1818. This gun was a flintlock revolver with a priming magazine and probably a mechanism for automatically rotating the cylinder, although this device is missing on the two surviving specimens in the United States National Museum. Wheeler tried to interest the navy in his invention. He failed and apparently gave up all active interest in either manufacturing or marketing the gun shortly thereafter.

But the Wheeler revolver was far from dead. Within weeks after the patent was granted, Elisha Collier of Boston sailed for England with a sample of the revolver and obtained an English patent in November. A short

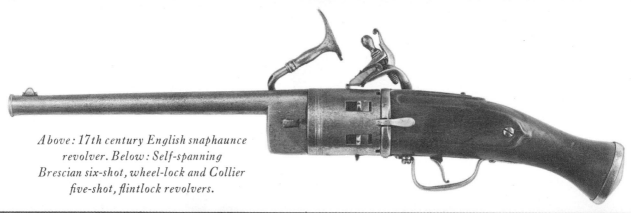

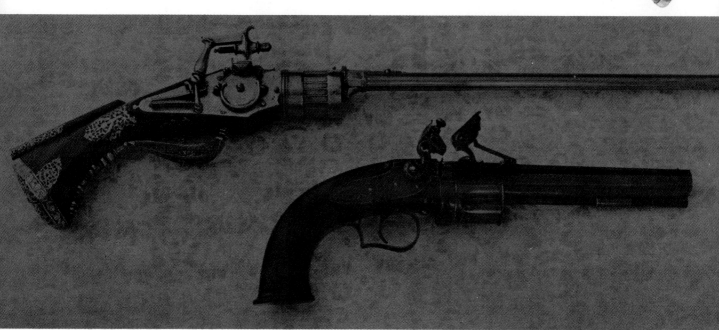

Above: 17th century English snaphaunce revolver. Below: Self-spanning Brescian six-shot, wheel-lock and Collier five-shot, flintlock revolvers.

time later Cornelius Coolidge, also of Boston, journeyed to France with another model and took out a patent there. It may have been a joint undertaking, with Collier and Coolidge acting for Wheeler, but this is dubious. (Testifying in court many years later, Collier professed to have difficulty even remembering Wheeler's name.) It could have been a sharp operation to capitalize on Wheeler's work in areas where his United States patent would not protect him. Or Collier and Coolidge may even have purchased some rights from Wheeler. No one knows for certain.

In any event, Collier made no claim to complete originality in his British patent application. He stated that it had been partly communicated to him by "a certain foreigner living abroad," but insisted that he had made improvements in the design. Possibly these included a different priming magazine and an

improved joint between the chambers and the barrel. Actually, Collier's joint was very similar to Puckle's, except that Collier coned the breech and countersank the chambers.

Collier was no more successful in interesting British Ordnance in the revolver than Wheeler had been with the United States Navy. The Select Committee at Woolwich admired the ingenuity of the weapon at a trial in 1819, but rejected it as too complicated. To simplify the gun, Collier eliminated the automatic rotating mechanism and in 1824 presented a percussion model with a hand-turned cylinder for another trial. With this one he fired one hundred shots in twenty-nine minutes, placing seventy-one of them in a target a hundred yards distant. This was little better than a common musket could do. The committee turned Collier down again.

Meanwhile, Collier succeeded in finding a civilian market of sorts. Both flint and percus-

Wheeler revolving carbine, patented in 1818.

sion models were manufactured and sold. Advertisements pointed out the advantages of the weapon to officers aboard ship, and especially recommended a rifle version to "Gentlemen who are in the habit of shooting Deer in their own Parks." Years later, in 1851, Collier asserted that he had sold £100,000 worth of rifles, shotguns, and pistols, mainly for use in India, but other testimony indicates his memory was inclined to optimism and this may well be a greatly exaggerated figure. Nevertheless, a large enough number of the guns was made to classify it as a successful revolver and to fix it firmly in the public mind as the Collier system, while Wheeler was almost forgotten.

Thus the Collier can be called the first "practical" revolver or the first "successful" revolver. It was indeed both, but with definite limitations. Greater practicality and success came with the percussion pepperbox pistols. In these weapons the caps could be placed on the nipples when the gun was loaded. There was no loose powder to fall out of a pan, no magazine of priming powder that might be exploded by a stray spark. The percussion hammer could be made smaller and more streamlined than the flintlock cock. It would fit in the pocket more neatly and could be drawn out without catching. Finally, since the motion of closing the frizzen before each shot was eliminated, the gun could shoot faster. With all these advantages, the percussion pepperbox quickly became a highly popular gun.

Development of the pepperbox to this stage, however, was not sudden. Pepperbox arms had been made for centuries, along with cylinder revolvers. It was only natural that the new ignition systems should be applied to them—the first such models probably appeared in the 1820's.

Initially, the barrels were revolved by hand. Then they were made to move automatically when the hammer was cocked, although there was nothing new in this either. The English gunsmith, John Dafte, for instance, had made flintlock revolvers which operated the same way as far back as the Seventeenth Century, and other gunsmiths in England and on the Continent had designed similar mechanisms. Thus, there was nothing to patent and no date can be ascribed to the first European pepperbox with automatically revolving barrels. In America, however, Benjamin and Barton Darling did succeed in obtaining a patent on such a mechanism on April 13, 1836. Theirs is the first American patent for a pepperbox, and it is believed that the same general system became popular in Europe at the same time.

All of these pistols were single-action. That is, it was necessary to pull the hammer back to cock the gun and rotate the barrels before each shot was fired.

The next advance eliminated this step and produced the so-called double-action, or self-cocking, gun. A single pull on the trigger cocked the hammer, rotated the barrels, and then fired the pistol. Again there is no English patent for a double-action pepperbox because the idea was already generally known.

In America, no early double-action lock had been patented, however, and so Ethan Allen—not the famous Revolutionary War hero—was able to claim its invention in 1837. Like Wheeler, Collier, and the Darlings, Allen, too, was from Massachusetts. In a series of partnerships with various relatives he became America's most important manufacturer of pepperbox pistols. His gun was the fastest-firing pistol of its day, and for over a decade it was far better known and more popular than Colt's.

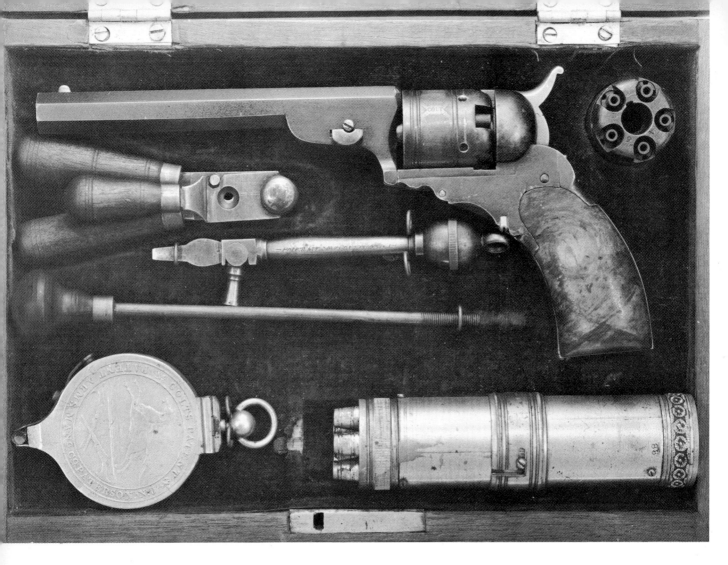

Indeed, the double-action pepperbox was a rapid-firing weapon. Ready loaded and primed in advance, the pistol could be pulled from the pocket and fired in one motion. Hammers were streamlined or even enclosed, so that there would be no rough contour to slow the draw. And there were enough barrels so that even a thoroughly frightened amateur had a good chance of hitting his enemy if he kept firing. The most common models had four or six barrels, but some had as many as eighteen.

Here was just the gun that many people had been waiting for. Shopkeepers, homeowners, and others not highly skilled in the use of firearms were attracted by its speed. No longer did the first shot have to count. The forty-niners who set out for California and the gold fields found the pepperbox a handy companion on the long trek across the continent and excellent protection against claim jumpers and gold thieves when they got there. Less savory individuals

also joined the ranks of pepperbox enthusiasts: gamblers, dance-hall girls, and the like. Some pepperboxes were even employed by the United States Army, and their use is recorded in a cavalry fight with the Cheyennes as late as 1857.

Despite their good qualities and popularity, the pepperboxes had serious defects. Worst of all was their inaccuracy. The hammer was usually right in the line of sight. The heavy trigger pull and the revolving of the barrels on the double-action models also prevented accurate aiming. Mark Twain, who was well acquainted with the pepperbox from his days in the gold camps of the West and on the river steamers, had several humorous comments on the Allen and its shortcomings. On the subject of accuracy, he told of a stagecoach passenger who attempted to demonstrate the effectiveness of his pepperbox by shooting out the coach window. "He aimed at the bole of a live oak," wrote Twain, "but fetched the nigh mule!"

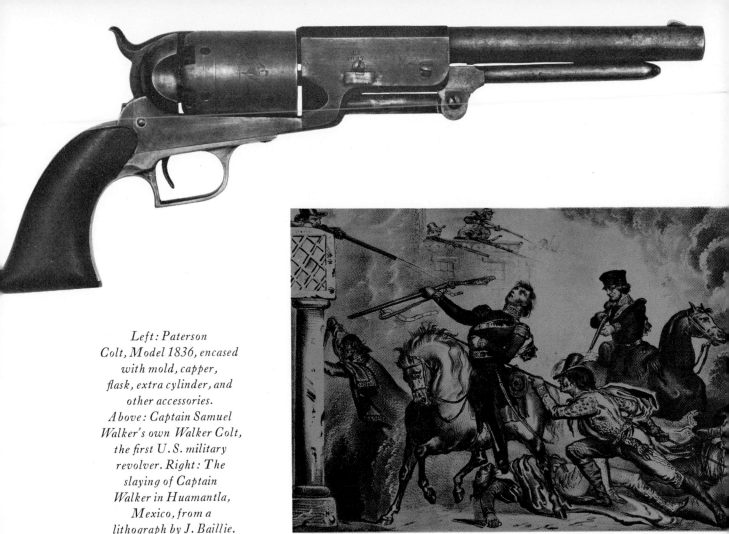

Left: Paterson Colt, Model 1836, encased with mold, capper, flask, extra cylinder, and other accessories. Above: Captain Samuel Walker's own Walker Colt, the first U.S. military revolver. Right: The slaying of Captain Walker in Huamantla, Mexico, from a lithograph by J. Baillie.

And there was another defect of the pepperbox which Twain also noted. In common with most revolving arms before the era of the metallic cartridge, it had a tendency to fire several barrels at once as the flash from one charge spread over and ignited others. This resulted in a rude jar to the shooter and a hail of bullets all over the landscape. In Twain's version, a storyteller, upset because his tale of shooting a tree-climbing buffalo with his pepperbox had been hooted at, complained, "I should have shot that long gangly lubber they called Hank if I could have done it without crippling six or seven other people—but of course I couldn't, the old Allen's so confounded comprehensive."

The final drawback of the pepperbox was one shared with all other multibarreled arms. It had a tendency to become clumsy and muzzle heavy in large calibers. This was particularly true of those versions with eight or more barrels. It took a strong wrist indeed to hold an eighteen-barreled model on target and pull the trigger at the same time.

The weapon that overcame these defects was the percussion revolver. All of the advantages of the pepperbox were shared by the revolver, while its single barrel reduced its weight and made accurate aiming possible. This was obvious to practically everyone. Gunsmiths all over the western world set to work promptly, and percussion revolvers began to appear at almost the same time as the pepperboxes. The percussion models of the Collier were probably the first. But there were others within a few years. Most of them were the products of unknown designers. But Peder Rasmussen of Denmark developed a series of revolvers in the 1830's, and Jonas Offrell, of Sweden, patented a highly original version in 1839.

The real father of the revolver in its modern sense, however, was Samuel Colt. As a very young man Colt decided to be an inventor, and

209

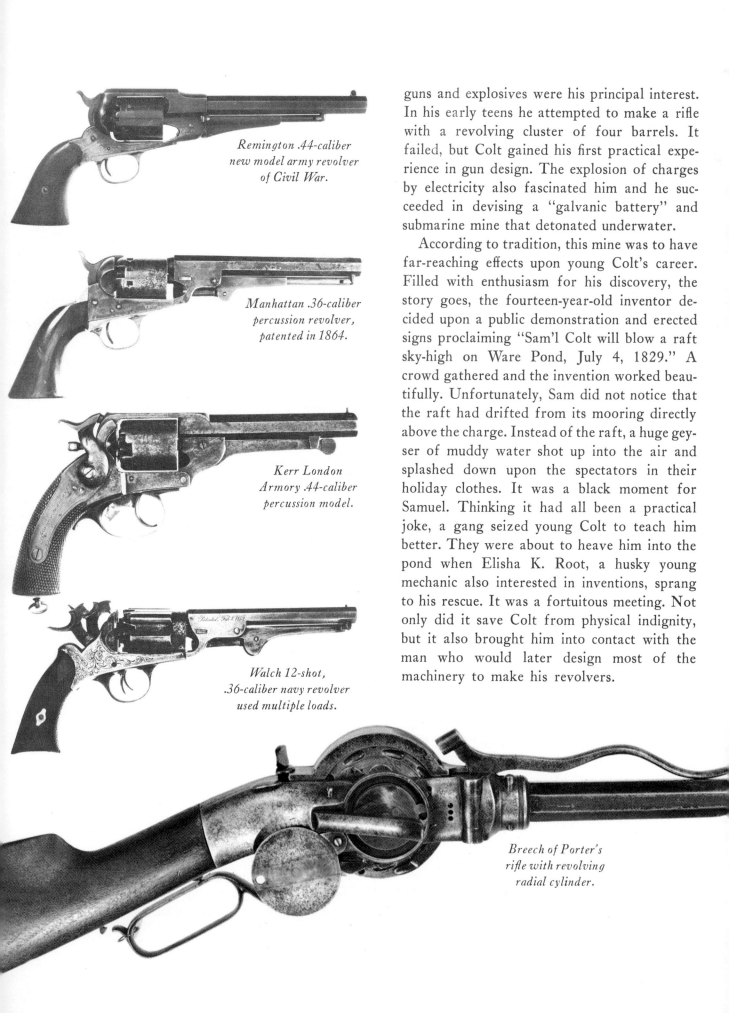

Remington .44-caliber new model army revolver of Civil War.

Manhattan .36-caliber percussion revolver, patented in 1864.

Kerr London Armory .44-caliber percussion model.

Walch 12-shot, .36-caliber navy revolver used multiple loads.

Breech of Porter's rifle with revolving radial cylinder.

guns and explosives were his principal interest. In his early teens he attempted to make a rifle with a revolving cluster of four barrels. It failed, but Colt gained his first practical experience in gun design. The explosion of charges by electricity also fascinated him and he succeeded in devising a "galvanic battery" and submarine mine that detonated underwater.

According to tradition, this mine was to have far-reaching effects upon young Colt's career. Filled with enthusiasm for his discovery, the story goes, the fourteen-year-old inventor decided upon a public demonstration and erected signs proclaiming "Sam'l Colt will blow a raft sky-high on Ware Pond, July 4, 1829." A crowd gathered and the invention worked beautifully. Unfortunately, Sam did not notice that the raft had drifted from its mooring directly above the charge. Instead of the raft, a huge geyser of muddy water shot up into the air and splashed down upon the spectators in their holiday clothes. It was a black moment for Samuel. Thinking it had all been a practical joke, a gang seized young Colt to teach him better. They were about to heave him into the pond when Elisha K. Root, a husky young mechanic also interested in inventions, sprang to his rescue. It was a fortuitous meeting. Not only did it save Colt from physical indignity, but it also brought him into contact with the man who would later design most of the machinery to make his revolvers.

Nevertheless, given the general climate of opinion it seemed to Colt a good time to leave town. At first he went to Amherst Academy to further his education, but the faculty there was no more entranced by his continued explosive experiments than the townspeople of Ware had been. Finally, after setting part of the school on fire, he was encouraged to give up academic pursuits altogether.

The sea seemed a safe place, completely cut off from supplies of gunpowder and other materials for experiment, so Christopher Colt packed his son off as an apprentice seaman on a voyage to India. It was on this trip that the Colt revolver was born. According to tradition, the inspiration came to young Samuel on the Indian Ocean as he idly watched the helmsman at his duty. No matter which way the great wheel turned, a spoke always lined up with a clutch that would lock it in position if the helmsman desired. It struck Colt that the same idea could be applied to a revolving firearm, and he began to whittle a wooden model. The year was 1830. Sam was then just sixteen years old.

It is a long journey from a crude wooden model to a finished firearm. Colt found it was an expensive one as well. To raise money he gave lectures on chemistry with practical demonstrations of nitrous oxide, or laughing gas, billing himself as "Dr. Coult, late of New York, London and Calcutta." He even contemplated smuggling. Finally the working models were perfected. British and French patents were granted in 1835 and an American patent followed in 1836. A manufacturing company was formed and production got underway at Paterson, New Jersey. After six years of waiting, the Colt revolver was a reality.

Samuel Colt believed in giving his customers what they wanted. He made three models of revolving pistols, as well as carbines, rifles, and shotguns. There were minor variations within these models, and he was always willing to make special adjustments if the buyer would pay extra. He had an accommodating nature and a fine product. Yet the company failed. The pepperbox still dominated the civilian market and the government refused to place a large order for the new arms. In addition there was a financial panic. It takes time and money to establish a new product and Sam did not have enough of either. The Paterson factory closed in 1843. All assets were liquidated and Colt turned to other things.

It was a period of disappointment for the young inventor. Then his luck changed. Some of his revolvers had found their way to the West and there they began to win friends. Men on the far frontier who worked and fought on horseback appreciated the new gun, even if easterners and ordnance officers didn't. There was nothing like it for a running fight with Indians or bandits. In one instance, Captain Jack Hays and fifteen of his Texas Rangers armed with Colt Paterson revolvers defeated seventy-five Comanches, reportedly killing thirty-five, although the numbers fluctuate in various accounts. The Texas Navy also had a supply of the revolvers which performed prodigious feats. And thus the new gun won fame all along the border.

Then came the Mexican War. The Texas Rangers were mustered into the United States service and the Colt enthusiasts among them at last convinced Ordnance of the revolver's value. Captain Samuel H. Walker, who had been with Jack Hays in the Comanche fight, was sent to find Colt and persuade him to go back into business. Walker did this and more; he helped redesign the revolver itself to make it a stronger and more powerful weapon. With the Walker Colt of 1847, the United States became the first nation in the world to issue revolvers to its troops. Colt was back in business and the revolver had arrived as a major firearm at last.

The years that followed were propitious for Colt. It was a turbulent era. The Mexican War was followed by the discovery of gold in California and the big migrations to the West

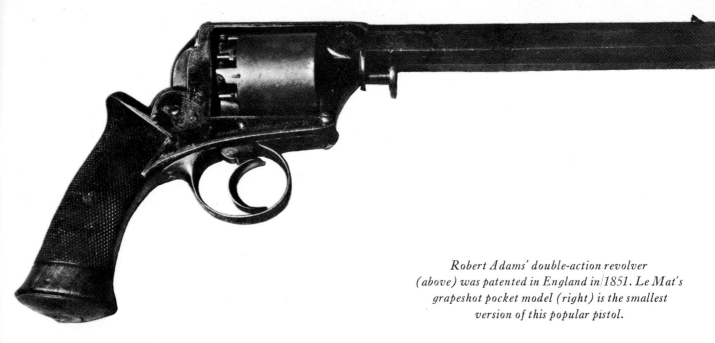

Robert Adams' double-action revolver (above) was patented in England in 1851. Le Mat's grapeshot pocket model (right) is the smallest version of this popular pistol.

where almost half a nation waited to be won. In Europe the Crimean War offered a market for revolvers, too. Orders came in rapidly and the number of different models multiplied to fit the needs of each group of customers.

Such success brought imitation. Some makers copied Colt products as exactly as they could. Others improved upon them or at least added variations. The Massachusetts Arms Company came too close and suffered suit. Remington brought out a revolver with a solid frame which many modern shooters feel was better than the Colt, although it was not so popular in its day. And there were dozens of others, especially after the Colt patent expired and the Civil War stimulated a demand for arms.

Some of the new revolving arms were wildly original. In an attempt to avoid Colt's patent, a whole series developed in America and Europe with wheel-shaped cylinders, the chambers radiating outward like spokes. Sometimes these wheels were mounted vertically, sometimes horizontally. Modern collectors frequently call the horizontal variety turret guns, but there is no evidence that this name was used at the time. All of these arms, however, suffered one serious drawback: one or more of the chambers would always be pointed back toward the shooter. A flashover from the charge being fired could very well set off a shot directly at the operator. According to one popular story, P. W. Porter, the inventor of one

of these arms, was killed in just this way while demonstrating his weapon to Colt. Apparently there is no foundation for this story in fact, but the possibility of such an accident was immediately apparent to men with practical experience in the field.

In England a serious rival for Colt appeared in the form of a double-action revolver patented by Robert Adams in February, 1851. Adams' guns boasted a solid frame, which he claimed made them stronger than the Colt, and bigger bores, ranging up to .50 caliber, which gave them greater stopping power. The double-action lock also made them faster firing than the Colt revolvers, all of which required the hammer to be cocked separately. Colt's pistols had the advantage of greater range and accuracy. Their mechanism was simpler and they were machine-made on a production line with complete interchangeability of parts. Adams' weapons still required much handwork for fitting. For the first few years Colt enjoyed supremacy in the English market and even established a flourishing factory in London. Colt revolvers were purchased for the British army and navy, and some were issued to special allied units such as Count Zamoyski's Cossacks of the Sultan. Then the tide began to turn. Adams improved his revolver by purchasing rights to Frederick Beaumont's patented mechanism of 1855, which allowed the gun to be fired either single- or double-action. And he

refined his manufacturing techniques.

Experiences in the field during the Crimean War and the Sepoy Mutiny also confirmed the superiority of the Adams revolvers for British military use. In the fighting which typified those wars, the long-range accuracy of the Colt was of little value. The enemy closed in and fought hand-to-hand, and they were not knocked down easily. Everything depended upon speed and stopping power. Two incidents illustrate the situation. From the Crimea, J. G. Crosse of the 88th Regiment wrote Adams:

I had one of your largest-sized Revolver Pistols at the bloody battle of Inkermann, and by some chance got surrounded by Russians. I then found the advantages of your pistol over that of Colonel Colt's, for had I to cock before each shot I should have lost my life. I should not have had time to cock, as they were too close to me, being only a few yards from me: so close that I was bayonetted through the thigh immediately after shooting the fourth man.

Speaking of the Sepoy Mutiny in India, Lieutenant Colonel G. V. Fosbery noted the need for stopping power:

An officer, who especially prided himself on his pistol-shooting, was attacked by a stalwart mutineer armed with a heavy sword. The officer, unfortunately for himself, carried a Colt's Navy pistol, which, as you may remember, was of small caliber [.36], and fired a sharp-pointed picket bullet of sixty to the pound and a heavy charge of powder, its range being at least 600 yards, as I have frequently proved. This he proceeded to empty into the sepoy as he advanced, but, having done so, he waited just one second too long to see the effect of his shooting, and was cloven to the teeth by his antagonist, who then dropped down and died beside him. My informant, who witnessed the affair, told me that five out of the six bullets had struck the sepoy close together in the chest, and had all passed through him and out at his back.

In view of these and similar experiences, the British government adopted the Beaumont-Adams as its official revolver. Colt closed his London Armoury, but continued to export and sell revolvers there to those customers who preferred the accuracy and range of his weapons.

Another imaginative and practical contemporary of the Colt was a ten-shot invention of Dr. Jean Alexandre François Le Mat of New Orleans, patented in 1856. Here was an impressive weapon, indeed. Its cylinder was bored for nine chambers fired in the normal fashion through a rifled barrel. Both .42 and .36 calibers were made. Immediately beneath this regular barrel was a large smoothbore barrel of .60 caliber which could be loaded with buckshot and discharged by turning down the nose of the hammer. It was this feature which gave the pistol its contemporary nickname of the "grapeshot revolver." At close range such a charge

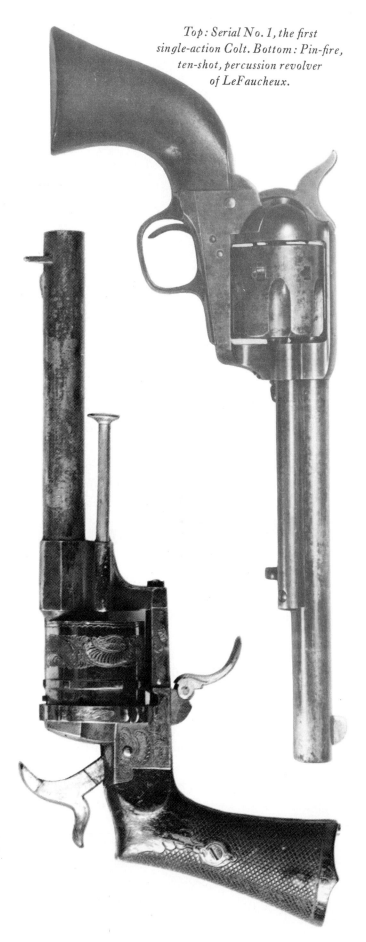

really must have been "formidable," as the good Dr. Le Mat claimed.

But the Le Mat was not only formidable. It was reliable as well. The officers who tested it for the United States Army before the Civil War recommended it highly, but Ordnance could not be interested. With the outbreak of war, the Confederacy was quick to place orders, and the worthy doctor journeyed to France to arrange for the production of his revolver. Soon fleet blockade runners were carrying cases of the new gun into southern ports. General Pierre G. T. Beauregard, who had at one time been a partner of Le Mat's, carried one. So did the dashing cavalry leader J. E. B. Stuart, and General Patton Anderson as well.

The grapeshot revolver survived the Civil War. Some models were even manufactured for the new metallic cartridges, but European markets were limited and the company eventually ceased operations.

By this time, the days of the percussion revolver were numbered. Like all other firearms, it, too, would succumb to the metallic cartridge. For years revolvers firing the new ammunition had developed quietly. Then, just as the percussion models reached their peak of profusion, they found themselves superseded.

It was inevitable that the revolver would be adapted for the new self-contained metallic cartridges just as the single-shot pistols had been. The French were probably the first to try such new weapons on a large scale with pin-fire cartridges—Lefaucheux's to start with, then Houllier's improved version. A Lefaucheux revolver was exhibited at the Great Crystal Palace Exhibition of 1851, in London. Big military models were imported and used by both sides during the American Civil War, and small, pocket versions remained popular in Europe at least through the 1870's. Elsewhere revolvers were developed to fire most of the other early cartridges. There were even Dreyse "needle-fire" revolvers, but not many.

Two Americans, however, made the cartridge

revolver a practical reality. Horace Smith and Daniel B. Wesson had both been gunsmiths from early youth. They had served apprenticeships and hired out to various gunmakers in the Connecticut Valley. Finally they met and worked together making gun barrels in the shop of Allen, Brown & Luther. Each recognized the other as a kindred spirit with an inquiring mind and an interest in firearms design. Neither was content to remain a journeyman gunsmith all his life. A friendship quickly developed and they pooled their skills and knowledge. In 1851, Smith patented a breech-loading rifle. Then together they perfected a repeating magazine rifle and pistol, and formed a partnership to manufacture the new guns even before they obtained a patent on them in 1854. In 1855, they sold out to the Volcanic Arms Company. Wesson remained as superintendent of the factory, and Smith retired to operate a livery stable with his brother-in-law.

But the association continued. The two men had another project in mind and the new situation gave them more freedom to work on it. They had developed an improved rim-fire cartridge, and they wanted to produce a revolver to fire it as soon as the Colt patent expired at the beginning of 1857. Their gun was soon designed, but one thing stood in their way. Someone else had patented a cylinder with the chambers bored all the way through so that a cartridge could be loaded from the breech.

This was an essential feature for any practical, well-designed cartridge revolver, and Smith and Wesson set out to obtain rights to use it. The patent itself had been obtained in 1855 by Rollin White of New Haven, Connecticut. It covered a thoroughly impractical revolver he had designed in an attempt to evade Colt's patent. The bored-through cylinder was just one part of it. Because the gun itself was so obviously unfeasible, there was some question whether the patent was valid. A court test might have thrown it out, but Smith and Wesson decided it would be better business to try to

The first Smith & Wesson revolver produced from the Rollin White patent.

Colt .45-caliber army model, a double-action revolver patented in 1878.

obtain exclusive rights to manufacture revolvers with this feature and hope that other gunmakers would be prevented from using it by the patent. In November, 1856, they succeeded in negotiating a royalty agreement with Rollin White which granted them this sole right—and left White himself with the task of defending the validity of his patent in the court cases which were sure to come. Their gamble paid off. The patent was attacked, but it held, once on a tie vote by the panel of judges. It was close and it was precarious, but the Smith and Wesson partnership held a virtual monopoly on practical cartridge-revolver design until 1869. It was a tremendous advantage.

215

*In the street fight (below), drawn
by Frederic Remington, the antagonists are
using single-action Colts.*

With the beginning of 1857, Colt's patent expired and Smith and Wesson were ready with a complete wooden model. A metal model was completed in January and used for promotion purposes. It aroused so much interest that the partners were deluged with requests for their new gun before they could get into production. It was October before the first regular production pistol appeared. Then business boomed at $12 per pistol and 75 cents for a hundred cartridges. A year later they were already planning a new and larger factory. The Smith & Wesson revolver was a huge success.

The early Smith & Wesson revolvers were fragile pistols of small caliber. The first model was a .22 and fired a cartridge with a light powder charge. It hardly seemed much of a weapon to attract so much interest. Nevertheless, many soldiers actually purchased and carried these little weapons during the Civil War. And so did the home folks. By 1864 the firm was two years behind in filling orders. In 1860, a larger, .32 caliber "model" was designed and this became even more popular. It was a tribute to the superiority of the cartridge revolver over its percussion rival that these small-caliber arms, without trigger guards and with a complicated mechanism, found such an enthusiastic market.

Then George Wheeler Schofield took a hand. An officer in the 10th Cavalry and a distinguished veteran of the Civil War, Schofield undoubtedly encountered the Smith & Wesson for the first time when a board of officers under the command of his brother was testing the .44 American Model in the spring of 1870. The army was not impressed, but Schofield was. He became an agent of the company and sold the revolver in Kansas and Colorado. Close association with the pistol led him to see ways in which it could be simplified, strengthened, and made more suitable for rugged use along the frontier. In June, 1871, he obtained his first patent for modifications, and as the years passed he eventually claimed improvements on thirteen different parts.

The Schofield-Smith & Wesson was indeed a rugged arm and a good one. The army was never particularly enthusiastic, purchasing a grand total of 8,285 between 1873 and 1879, but other agencies and individuals bought them in quantity. Wells Fargo & Company and the American Express Company armed their guards and agents with the Schofield. The valuable cargoes hauled by both outfits made them tempting targets for the lawless elements of the West, and such heavy, reliable weapons were needed for protection. Law men carried them also, and so did some outlaws. Jesse James, for instance, is supposed to have laid one aside just before he was treacherously shot by Bob Ford.

Sales were still smaller than its designer had hoped, however, and Schofield continued to work on improvements. But he was becoming noticeably unstable, and in December, 1882, he committed suicide with one of his guns in his quarters at Fort Apache. The newspapers noted that he had been "crazed for eight or ten days over some invention" and called it temporary insanity. With his death the heyday of the Schofield-Smith & Wesson ended.

Neither Smith nor Wesson had been complacent about their revolvers. They continually worked at improving them and the infinite variations which they produced make the classification of their arms one of the difficult tasks for students today. A complex scheme of model and issue designations has had to be devised to cover the arms made for the civilian market in the United States and for buyers as far away as Russia, Mexico, and Turkey. Horace Smith retired in 1873; Daniel Wesson continued alone until 1883, when he took his sons into partnership to help manage the firm and ensure its continuance in keeping with his own high standards as a family enterprise.

The big Smith & Wesson revolvers, especially the Schofield, sold widely in the West and some were purchased by the army. But there was another revolver that stood head and shoulders above all the rest with civilian and soldier alike. This was the Colt single-action revolver. As long as the Rollin White patent gave Smith & Wesson a virtual monopoly on practical cartridge revolvers, other makers were severely handicapped. True, there were attempts to evade the patent with cylinders that loaded from the front or the side, or which used teat-fire or lip-fire cartridges. Colt, too, tried a special cylinder to get around the patent and enter the cartridge field. None of these evasions was really successful, although some worked reasonably well. Then the patent expired and the field was free to all comers.

Strangely, Colt was not ready. It took four years before the new single-action revolver was perfected and in production. The Colt Company called it the Model P, and the first finished pistols began to appear in 1873. It was a sturdy gun with a solid frame, a cylinder bored for six cartridges, and usually an ejector on the right side. Calibers varied. The first ones were .45. In 1878, a second line was chambered

1

3

2

1. *Multibarreled flint pistols. The longer model was made by Probin of London, and has a valve which selects the barrels to be fired. The shorter pistol fires all barrels at the same time.*

2. *Knubley of London's three-barreled pistol with valve, or tap selector, produced about 1780-1800.*

3. *Double-action pepperbox revolver, patented by Ethan Allen in 1837.*

4. *Right: Robbins & Lawrence American pepperbox revolver. Left: Marston three-barreled cartridge pistol.*

5. *Top: Five-barreled Budding English pepperbox. Bottom: Bond's four-barreled English pepperbox*

6. *Head-on and profile views of cased set of four-barreled, Belgian Mariette pepperboxes.*

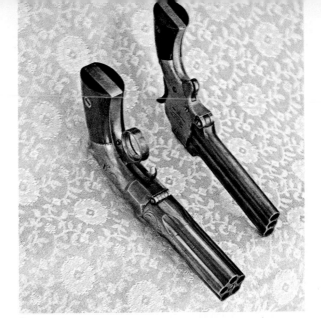

4

5

6

Colt Buntline Specials with sixteen-inch barrels
are shown (right) with an original holster and skeleton shoulder
stock. The Colt company called this model the pistol
with carbine barrel and attachable stock.

for the .44-40 Winchester cartridge so that a westerner who wanted to carry both a rifle and a revolver needed only one type of ammunition. Other calibers were added to these until there was a spread from .22 to .476. Barrel lengths ranged from three inches to seven and one-half inches in standard models, and even longer ones could be had on special order. And there were other variations. Some short-barreled versions known as "house" or "storekeeper" models were made without ejectors. Other models were fitted for shoulder stocks. There were standard and flat-topped frames, special sights, and always available were special finishing, plating, engraving, and custom grips of many materials.

With all the variations in design, there was also a myriad of names. The first trade name adopted by the Colt Company was the Peacemaker and this applied to those models made in .45 caliber. By the middle 1880's, the pistol became the standard army side arm and it was more often referred to as the Single-Action Army Revolver. The variant chambered for the .44-40 Winchester cartridge was known as the Frontier Six Shooter, or just Frontier Model. In 1896, a target version was produced and called the Bisley. And popularly there was a host of nicknames: "thumb-buster," "plow-handle," "hog leg," "equalizer," "single six," just plain Colt "sixgun," and many more.

One of the best-known variants today is the Buntline Special, but in its own time it meant little and few were made. It all began in 1876 when the Colt Company produced what it called "Colt's pistol with carbine barrel and attachable stock." The gun was displayed that year at the great Centennial Exposition in Philadelphia and it evidently caught the eye of Edward Z. C. Judson, the famous pulp writer who used the pen name Ned Buntline. A gifted promoter (Buffalo Bill was one of his "products"), Buntline bought five of these revolvers for about $26 each and presented them to five famous western · peace officers: Wyatt Earp, Neal Brown, Charley Bassett, Bat Masterson, and

Bill Tilghman. The presentation is supposed to have taken place in Dodge City, Kansas, late that year or early in 1877, and it is this event that has given the gun its collectors' name of Buntline Special. Buntline had no other connection with the arm whatsoever, although he undoubtedly fostered the popular story that he had designed it personally.

The Buntline Special differed from the standard single-action in several ways. The most noticeable difference was in the length of barrel. The longest of the standard models was seven and one-half inches, but Buntlines were made in both ten- and sixteen-inch lengths. There was also the screw for attaching the shoulder stock. This stock was a skeleton of cast brass with a nickel plating. It hooked under the screw on the frame and was tightened with a knurled nut against the base of the grips. There is some evidence that Wyatt Earp had a walnut shoulder stock for his Buntline, but this must have been a special product made outside the Colt factory. Colt manufactured only the skeleton type.

Despite its colorful appearance and its association with men like Ned Buntline and Wyatt Earp, the Buntline Special was never popular. Earp was fond of his and used it regularly in performing his duties as marshal. The other four peace officers apparently thanked Buntline for his present and then put the guns on the shelf or cut down the barrels to normal size as soon as they got home. The Buntlines were just too long and inconvenient. Factory records show that a total of thirty of these guns was made and it is not certain that even all of these were sold. The Buntline's latter-day fame rests solely on its appearance and on the exploits of Earp. Almost no one else was interested.

The regular models, however, were something quite different. Even if the single-action couldn't perform all of the feats attributed to it in modern movies, it was a magnificent arm. It was accurate for normal pistol ranges. It had the stopping power that was necessary to

220

drop an opponent or a wild animal with one shot, and it was ruggedly built. This strength of construction was important. Pistols might be dropped, stepped on by a horse, or suffer other harsh treatment. Then there was also the old western custom of pistol whipping in which the gun was held by the grips and the barrel used as a club. In this department the Colt far outdistanced its rivals, which tended to bend upon contact with a skull and required professional readjustment.

Also the Colt single-action was designed with tolerances that permitted it to operate even if dropped in the sand, and this again was important. There were many instances when a man might drop his gun or might fall and be dragged so that considerable dirt would find its way into his weapon. It would be small comfort in such circumstances to have a gun that had to be taken apart and thoroughly cleaned before it could be used. There might not be that much time.

As might be expected with all these advantages, the Colt single-action has been extremely popular. It was the standard side arm of the army throughout the major Indian campaigns after 1873. No other revolver was even a close competitor for civilian use in the West as sheriff and outlaw, cowboy and miner alike favored it above all others. Even after the army discontinued the single-action in favor of double-action revolvers and then automatic pistols, many officers continued to purchase the old Model P and carry it. General George S. Patton, Jr., with his fully engraved, silver-plated Peacemakers fitted with carved ivory grips, was but one notable example. He purchased his pair in 1916, wore them on the Mexican Border and during both World Wars. So did many others who did not attract so much attention. Production of this famous revolver was discontinued by the Colt Company in 1941, but the gun was too good to die. The demand for it kept on. Prices for antique or just plain "used" specimens soared. After World War II, copies were manufactured by other firms, and eventually the Colt Company itself decided to revive its most popular arm. Thus, almost ninety years after the first production model, it is still possible to buy a new Colt single-action revolver.

It is interesting that a single-action revolver has stayed popular so long, in view of the general swing to self-cocking pistols. In France, the trend had begun early. The Lefaucheux pin-fire had been double-action. So were the Perrin and Raphael revolvers which followed

Above: Jesse and Frank James (seated) pose with the Younger brothers.
Preceding pages: The James boys' revolvers, belts, and holsters. On the left,
Jesse's Schofield Smith & Wesson and, right, Frank's Remington.

it. In England, John Adams, brother of the inventor of the first successful British percussion revolver, developed a double-action cartridge model in 1867 that was adopted by the army. And there were Tranters and Webleys in a variety of models, as well as several lesser makes. The Colt Company itself had introduced a pair of double-action revolvers in 1877. One, in .38 caliber, was called the Lightning, while the other, a .41, was known as the Thunderer. Billy the Kid, who began his brief and notorious career as a gunman that same year, favored the Thunderer, but the United States Army preferred a larger size and adopted a .45-caliber model in 1878.

Even the rapid-firing double-action revolver did not offer enough protection in the minds of some, however. They wanted a weapon that would afford more choice, and so they devised ways of combining the revolver with all sorts of other weapons. Pistols had been built into swords at least since the Sixteenth Century, but the cartridge revolver seemed to bring the desire for combination weapons to its most exotic flower. Cavalry sabers, artillery short swords, large knives, and even lances afforded opportunities that could not be overlooked by such designers as they added revolver mechanisms in a host of ingenious ways. Most of them, however, were more ingenious than practical. A patent model and one or two samples usually represented their total production. But there were two outstanding exceptions to this rule: the French Apache pistol, and the American knuckle-duster of James Reid.

The Apache pistol was truly a curious and

possibly a versatile weapon. It took its name from the street gangs of the Paris slums with whom it was supposed to have been popular. Little is known of its origin. Most specimens are marked as being the invention of one L. Dolne, but exactly who he was and how he came to develop his unique arm remain mysteries.

Whoever he was, he designed his weapon for a street fighter who wanted to be prepared for any emergency. It consisted of a revolver mechanism with a six-shot cylinder, a folding dagger blade, and a set of brass knuckles. With the knuckles pulled out and locked in position, it became a pistol with a folding trigger and the knuckle loops for a grip. There was no barrel, so it could only have been used at point-blank range. When the knuckles were folded down, the cylinder formed a grip for the palm while the fingers were passed through the loops. It would deal a nasty blow, but if this were not enough, the dagger blade could be pulled out for extra help. The Apache pistol was made in both pin-fire and rim-fire models, and enough of them survive today to indicate a reasonably large production. Either that or they were such colorful weapons that almost all of them were saved as curiosities.

Much more is known about James Reid and his knuckle-duster. A native of Ireland, Reid patented his pistol in 1865 after he had moved to the United States. It was a much simpler weapon than the Apache. It, too, was a revolver fired through a hole in the frame without the benefit of a barrel to guide the bullet, but there was no dagger, and the knuckle device, which remained fixed, had only one loop. According to Reid's claim, this was "a bow through which the finger may be passed when the piece is grasped, so to be used in hitting a blow for self-protection before using the bullet or after the revolver has been fired." Reid named the weapon "My Friend," and this title appears on most specimens. About fourteen thousand of these weapons were manufactured, the great bulk of them in .22 caliber. A few

were made in larger calibers and a very few were fitted with barrels in an attempt to obtain a minimum of accuracy. The knuckle-duster was a popular gun during the 1870's, even being imitated in Belgium under the trade name of "The Fisticuff." But the market disappeared suddenly about 1880, and production ceased two or three years later.

Interesting as they may be from the standpoint of oddities, the Apache pistol, the knuckle-duster, and related combination weapons were sterile offshoots of the revolver. So were such other curious weapons as chain pistols, in which the cartridges were fed under the hammer on an endless belt instead of in a cylinder. They were of no real significance in the evolution of the weapon. The revolver had reached its highest development with the appearance of the double-action mechanism and the center-fire cartridge. Nothing was left then except refinements for specific jobs or tastes.

Apache pistol: revolver, dagger, brass knuckles.

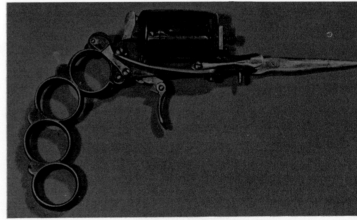

Reid's .32-caliber knuckle-duster.

225

"THE VERY PERFECTION OF FIREARMS"

The revolving cylinder was a fine device for holding a supply of charges ready to fire in true repeater fashion. As long as loose powder and ball were used, it was the simplest, safest, and probably the most obvious contrivance. But it was not the only way to store extra loads, and it had drawbacks that tempted inventors to try to perfect some other system. A cylinder with more than five or six shots tended to become bulky. A magazine that followed the line of the barrel or nestled within the stock would permit more loads and a smoother silhouette. Weight could also be reduced, and perhaps loading and firing could be speeded still further. Imaginative gunsmiths could see these possibilities and maybe others as well, and they set out to

228 *develop methods for holding reserve loads and feeding them into the chamber.*

No one knows when the first true magazine repeater was invented, or where, or by whom it was designed. As so often happens, early references are imprecise and it is frequently impossible to tell what sort of a repeating arm is mentioned. It is safe to assume, however, that such guns appeared relatively late, well after multiple barrels, Roman-candle loads, and the revolving cylinder had arrived on the scene. Such evidence as there is indicates that they probably began to appear early in the 1600's. Successful systems definitely had developed by 1640, and within the next twenty years they had spread throughout most of Western Europe and even to Moscow. Thus, the inveterate London diarist, Samuel Pepys, could write in his entry for July 3, 1662, that he had examined "a gun to discharge seven times, the best of all devices I ever saw, and very serviceable, and not a bawble; for it is much approved of, and many made...." And again on March 4, 1664, he wrote: "There were several people by trying a new-fashion gun brought my Lord this morning, to shoot off often, one after another, without trouble or danger, very pretty."

There is nothing in Pepys' comments to identify the repeaters he saw. Indeed, they could have been any of the earlier types. Nevertheless, the number of shots mentioned in the first entry and the date for the "new-fashion" gun in the second have led many students to assume that he referred to the two principal magazine repeaters of the era, the Kalthoff and the Lorenzoni. These were the first guns of their kind to achieve success and, since the actual inventors are unknown, each has been named after a famous family of gunsmiths associated with its early history.

The Kalthoffs were a German family from Solingen. They were a prolific brood and historians are uncertain as to how most of them were related. In about 1640 a number of them left home. Wilhelm went to France, Peter moved first to the Netherlands, then to Denmark. Mathias joined Peter in Copenhagen. Caspar went to England and his son, Caspar, Jr., moved on to Moscow. All of them made similar magazine repeating guns. Wilhelm was granted a monopoly for such arms in France in 1640, and Peter obtained a similar privilege from the States'-General of the Netherlands in 1641. It is not certain that a Kalthoff invented the repeating system the family used, although he well might have. It is at least probable, however, that it was invented in or near their native Solingen before they left home. Once established in their new locations, they taught the system to their apprentices. Soon there were a number of gunsmiths in England and on the Continent who could and did make such arms.

The Kalthoff repeater was a true magazine gun. In fact, it had two magazines, one for powder and one for balls. The earliest datable specimens which survive are two wheel-lock rifles made by Peter Kalthoff in Denmark in 1645 and 1646. In these arms the ball magazine is a cylindrical cavity in the stock under the barrel, while the powder magazine is hollowed out of the butt stock. A carrier large enough to hold one charge of powder plus a little more for priming is attached to the pivoted trigger guard. A single forward-and-back movement of this guard turns the breech chamber so that it receives a ball from the forward magazine, transports a charge of powder from the butt magazine and deposits it in the chamber, seats the completed load, turns the chamber back into position, primes the pan, and winds the wheel. This can all be done in one or two seconds, and the gun is ready to fire.

There were variations, of course. Only two of the wheel locks are known to survive. Most specimens made by the Kalthoffs and their contemporaries were flintlocks. The manner in which the breech chambers turned varied from maker to maker. Sometimes they moved laterally, sometimes vertically. Sometimes there was one chamber, sometimes three. The powder magazine might be in the butt stock or beneath the lock, and the number of charges in the magazines ran all the way from six or seven to thirty, if one can believe the verse on the barrel of one of Peter Kalthoff's wheel locks:

For defense and seriousness, for joy and nonsense
Will thirty shots be fired from me
Come, friend gun, and tell me freely
If any tube can be like me.

The Kalthoffs might well have been proud, for their guns were undoubtedly the first magazine repeaters ever to be adopted for military purposes. About a hundred flintlock rifles of their pattern were issued to picked marksmen of the Royal Foot Guards and are believed to have seen active service during the siege of Copenhagen in 1658, 1659, and again in the Scanian War of 1675-1679. It was almost two hundred years before another magazine rifle was carried into battle as an official weapon. No other gun could match the Kalthoff for the speed of its separately controlled shots, and no other multishot weapon was as safe. There was no direct communication between the powder magazine and the chamber, and thus no chance that a partially closed breech or a stray spark could explode the remaining charges.

With such advantages a gun could not help but attract attention. Examples spread throughout Europe wherever there were gunsmiths with sufficient skill and knowledge to make them, and patrons wealthy enough to pay the cost. Some forty specimens survive today, and at least nineteen gunsmiths are known to have made such arms in an area stretching from London on the west to Moscow on the east, and from Copenhagen south to Salzburg. There may well have been even more.

But the Kalthoff also had disadvantages which prevented it from becoming more popular and perhaps even a standard military arm for other countries. It was expensive and delicate. The careful fitting of the parts and the intricate system of gears, links, and springs re-

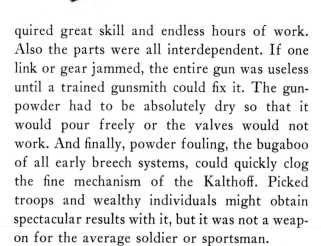

quired great skill and endless hours of work. Also the parts were all interdependent. If one link or gear jammed, the entire gun was useless until a trained gunsmith could fix it. The gunpowder had to be absolutely dry so that it would pour freely or the valves would not work. And finally, powder fouling, the bugaboo of all early breech systems, could quickly clog the fine mechanism of the Kalthoff. Picked troops and wealthy individuals might obtain spectacular results with it, but it was not a weapon for the average soldier or sportsman.

Much the same thing could be said for the Lorenzoni system. It had most of the advantages of the Kalthoff and most of its disadvantages as well. Once again there were two magazines in the stock, one for powder and one for ball. This time both were in the butt and there was a smaller magazine for priming powder attached to the lock itself. To load, the shooter held his gun with the barrel pointed up, seized

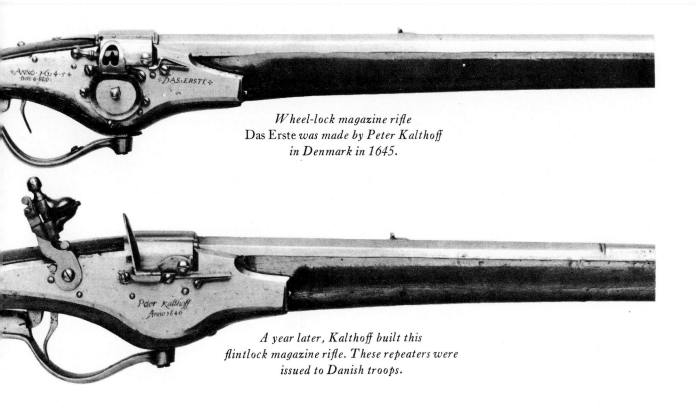

Wheel-lock magazine rifle
Das Erste *was made by Peter Kalthoff
in Denmark in 1645.*

*A year later, Kalthoff built this
flintlock magazine rifle. These repeaters were
issued to Danish troops.*

a lever on the left side of the gun, and pulled it back in an arc of 180 degrees. This rotated a cylindrical breechblock so that the two cavities it contained lined up with the openings of the magazines in the butt. Then the shooter pointed the muzzle down, filling the cavities with one ball and a charge of powder, and pushed the lever forward to its original position, thus carrying the ball and powder forward and dumping them into the chamber of the barrel. At the same time, the motion of the lever primed the pan and cocked the lock. It was a trifle slower than the Kalthoff, but still a remarkably fast and efficient action for its day. It was also a little simpler than the Kalthoff and, therefore, slightly less expensive to make, although it still cost infinitely more than the usual muzzle-loader.

The one area in which the Lorenzoni was definitely inferior to the Kalthoff was in safety. There was always the possibility of a direct connection between the powder magazine and the breech chamber by way of the rotating breechblock. If the block did not fit tightly or if the shooter did not lock it in the proper position when firing, flame might leak back and explode the powder in the butt. This could easily be fatal to the user—and such accidents did happen, as surviving specimens with shattered stocks bear witness.

The Lorenzoni also was developed during the first half of the Seventeenth Century. It was given its name because European students first became familiar with the mechanism in a gun made by Michel Lorenzoni of Florence, Italy, who worked during the mid-1600's. It is fairly certain, however, that the system was devised even earlier. Many Americans call this type of magazine repeater a Cookson because the first such gun to receive attention in this country bore the name of the English gunsmith John Cookson. It is probable that the system

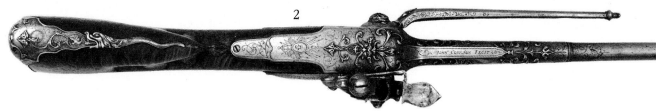

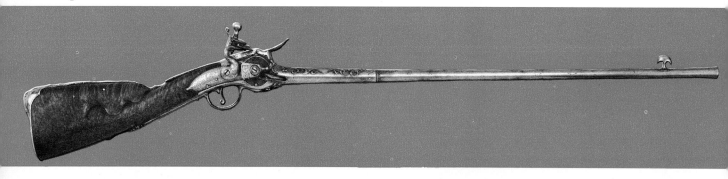

did develop in Italy or Central Europe and spread west from there. Abraham Hill patented it in London, March 3, 1664, and it is thought that this was the "new fashion" gun mentioned by Pepys in his diary the next day. Many other English gunsmiths also made guns with the Lorenzoni action during the next two or three decades, and interestingly enough H. W. Mortimer was still making repeating pistols of the same sort a century later.

The Lorenzoni system even found its way to America where records indicate that at least two New England gunsmiths actually manufactured such guns. The first reference is not absolute proof, but the implications seem clear. It is a description of a meeting with a group of local Indians in September, 1722. During the ceremonies the visiting aborigines were shown a weapon intended to impress them with the white man's power. This was a gun made by John Pim of Boston, a "curious piece of workmanship,—which though loaded but once, yet was discharged eleven times following, with bullets, in the space of two minutes each of which went through a double door at fifty yards' distance." It is not clear from this whether the bullets penetrated a double door at that distance or whether they merely passed through the opening formed by a double door.

There is no specific statement that this was a gun of the Lorenzoni principle, but it seems highly likely. The number of shots is too great for a gun with revolving barrels or cylinder, and the time interval is too long for a Roman-candle type. Thus, Mr. Pim must have been manufacturing a magazine repeater, and in that period it would likely have been a Lorenzoni.

The other reference to this system in America is more specific. Another gunsmith named John Cookson also lived in the Boston area. This was not the Cookson who had made magazine repeaters in London in the previous century, but he was probably a relative, possibly even a son. In any event he placed an advertisement in two issues of the Boston *Gazette* for April, 1756, which offered:

. . . a handy Gun of 9 Pound and a half weight; having a Place convenient to hold 9 Bullets, and Powder for 9 Charges and 9 Primings; the said gun will fire 9 Times distinctly, as quick, or as slow as you please, with one turn with the Handle of the said Gun, it doth charge the gun with powder and Bullet, and doth prime and shut the Pan, and cock the Gun. All these Motions are performed immediately at once, by one turn with the said Handle—Note, there is nothing put into the Muzzle of the Gun, as we charge other Guns.

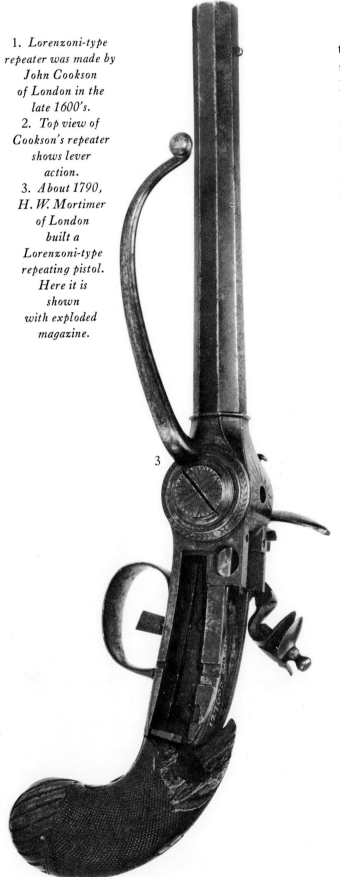

1. *Lorenzoni-type repeater was made by John Cookson of London in the late 1600's.*
2. *Top view of Cookson's repeater shows lever action.*
3. *About 1790, H. W. Mortimer of London built a Lorenzoni-type repeating pistol. Here it is shown with exploded magazine.*

This at least is an incontrovertible description of the Lorenzoni system, as well as evidence that there were highly skilled gunsmiths in New England at an early date.

The Kalthoff and Lorenzoni actions just described were probably the first and certainly the most popular of the early magazine repeaters. But there were many others. Another version, also attributed to the Lorenzoni family, boasted brass tubular magazines beneath the forestock. Simply releasing a lever and turning the forestock assembly a quarter turn to the right and back loaded, primed, and cocked the weapon. Guns of this type seem to have been made in several parts of Europe during the Eighteenth Century and apparently functioned well. And there were other systems, both flintlock and percussion, more notable for ingenuity than practicality.

As long as the powder and ball had to be loaded separately there was no hope for a simple and safe magazine repeater. Some means had to be found to package the ammunition and load it as a single unit before real progress could be made. The paper cartridges used in contemporary muzzle-loaders were too fragile. So were the combustible cartridges of the early breechloaders. The self-contained metallic cartridge was the key. Once it appeared the magazine repeater was assured success.

One gun, however, bridged the gap between the old ammunition and the new. From hesitant beginnings in the era of separate primed cartridges, it developed through the work of many skilled mechanics to become the Winchester rifle, undoubtedly the most popular single magazine arm in the world.

It all began with a mechanic who failed at almost everything except inventiveness. Walter Hunt was the archetype of all impractical geniuses. He had been born in upstate New York, but in 1826 he moved to Brooklyn and set himself up as a mechanic and inventor. There he devised literally hundreds of items in a wide variety of fields. Some of them were of far-

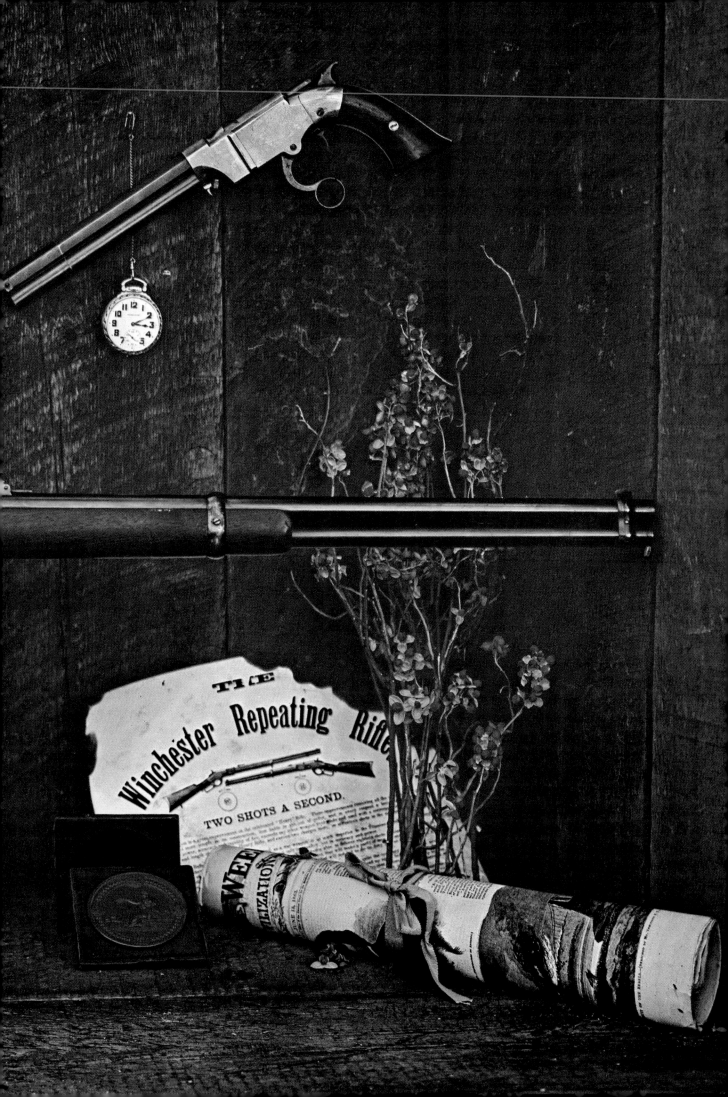

THE
Winchester Repeating Rifle

TWO SHOTS A SECOND.

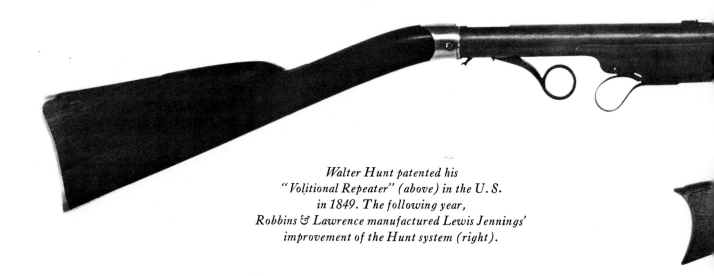

reaching significance, but he died a poor man in 1859. Among his developments were a flax-spinning machine, a heating stove, a spring trap, an iceboat, a nail-making machine, a fountain pen, a safety pin, and a sewing machine. The sewing machine was very similar to the one Elias Howe invented a few years later, but Hunt had not bothered to patent his device and so fame and fortune were Howe's instead. The safety pin was the direct antecedent of the form used today, and could also have brought Hunt a comfortable income, but the story goes that he designed it in order to pay a debt and sold all rights to it for $100.

It would have been astonishing if such a prolific inventor had not turned his hand to firearms and this he did, patenting both a new bullet and a gun to use it. The bullet came first, in 1848, and it was almost self-contained. It consisted of a cylindroconical projectile with its base hollowed out to hold the powder charge. This opening was then closed with a cork pierced with a small hole in the center to admit the flash from a separate primer.

Such a bullet was strong enough to permit

using it in a single tubular magazine with a follower spring to push it toward the chamber. This is exactly the type of rifle which Hunt designed and patented the next year. He called it a "Volitional Repeater," and it was in many ways a brilliant achievement, for it contained the basic principles of many later arms. The tubular magazine was lodged along the underside of the barrel where it remained on all Winchesters. He also developed a straight-drive firing pin activated by a spiral spring which was years ahead of its time. But his repeating mechanism was too delicate and complicated for practical use. It needed further refinement, and a number of highly competent gunsmiths followed each other in providing the necessary improvements.

Hunt, as usual, lacked the capital and business acumen to perfect his gun. Thus it passed from him to others. Almost as soon as he had obtained his patent, he assigned his rights to a New York machinist named George Arrowsmith. In Arrowsmith's shop a skilled mechanic named Lewis Jennings simplified Hunt's mechanism and obtained an additional patent before the end of the year. Then Arrowsmith in turn sold the Hunt and Jennings patents to Courtlandt Palmer. In 1850, Palmer contracted for the production of five thousand of these new arms by the firm of Robbins & Lawrence in

Windsor, Vermont. Here Horace Smith and Daniel B. Wesson entered the picture. Each refined the arm still further and took out additional patents. By 1854 a vastly improved weapon was ready for production, and Smith, Wesson, and Palmer formed a partnership to make it. A plant was established at Norwich, Connecticut, but within a year the partners decided to sell their interests to a group of New Haven and New York capitalists.

This new corporation represented men from many walks of life. Seven were clockmakers, three made carriages, two were bakers, two were grocers; others were from the shipping and mercantile world. In all there were forty investors. And one of them was a shirt manufacturer from New Haven by the name of Oliver F. Winchester. It has been said of Oliver Winchester that he probably knew less about firearms than any other manufacturer connected with the business. It has even been alleged that he never personally fired a gun. The first statement is undoubtedly true. The second seems unlikely. But neither has any real bearing on the story of the Winchester rifle. Whatever depth his knowledge of firearms may have lacked, Oliver Winchester was a skilled financier and his faith and perseverance brought the gun to its fullest development. His influence was felt almost from the start and his initial eighty

shares of stock gradually grew to a controlling interest in the company.

With imagination, the new corporation called itself the Volcanic Repeating Arms Company. It manufactured pistols and rifles of the pattern developed by Smith and Wesson and the ammunition for these arms as well. This ammunition differed somewhat from Hunt's original design in that the hollow at the base of the bullet was filled with a percussion compound instead of gunpowder. This compound provided both the priming and the propellent charge, and the ammunition was thus self-contained. It would go off when struck by the firing pin. But it was necessarily a weak charge and the bullets had little force. Daniel Wesson had been dissatisfied with these bullets and had patented a true center-fire cartridge in 1854. The new corporation had obtained rights to this patent, along with the other assets, when it bought out Smith, Wesson, and Palmer, but for some reason it never used the Wesson cartridge. The repeating mechanism worked well, however, and the New-York *Tribune* even asserted that,

The Volcanic pistol and rifle seem to be the very perfection of firearms, and must be favorites with the public when they are fully known. We understand that orders crowd in upon the Company from all quarters.

Unfortunately this was not quite the case. *237*

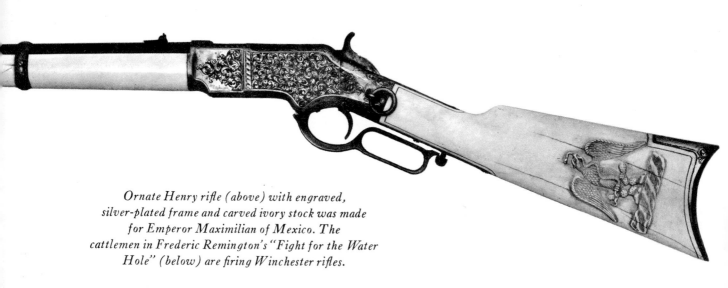

Ornate Henry rifle (above) with engraved,
silver-plated frame and carved ivory stock was made
for Emperor Maximilian of Mexico. The
cattlemen in Frederic Remington's "Fight for the Water
Hole" (below) are firing Winchester rifles.

Frederic Remin

The defects of the ammunition plus financial and managerial difficulties forced the company into bankruptcy early in 1857. Its assets were purchased on March 15 of that year by Oliver F. Winchester.

The shirt manufacturer was now in complete control. He organized a new stock company called the New Haven Arms Company and installed himself as president, holding a controlling eight hundred shares of stock valued at $25 a share. It is a tribute to the esteem in which he was held as a financier that he was able to persuade eleven of the men who had figuratively lost their shirts as stockholders in the Volcanic Arms Company to purchase shares in the new enterprise under his direction.

For his own part, Winchester devoted his efforts to financial matters and sales. He constantly sought new outlets, insisted that his arms be fair traded at list price, and advertised heavily. The testimonial from a satisfied customer was widely used in promotional work in that era and Winchester utilized it to the full. A circular of 1859 included this high praise from "among the numerous testimonials received":

Gent: — I consider the Volcanic Repeating pistol the ne plus ultra *of Repeating or Revolving Arms, and far superior in many respects to Colt's much extolled Revolver. I have fired, myself, over 200 shots from it without even wiping the barrel — this is an advantage which no other arm I know of possesses. I have had the pistol with me at sea for more than eighteen months, on a voyage around the world, and find that, with the most common care, it will keep free from rust far more so than Colt's. I find the Balls as good now as when I left New York. I have shown the pistol to my friends in San Francisco, Hong Kong, Manila, Canton, and Shanghai, and they were much pleased with it.*
C. F. W. Behm,
late of Clipper Ship Stag Hound

It was most convenient that someone should treat a pistol so roughly, carry it around in damp sea air, and then write a completely un-

solicited letter to compare it with the Colt and indicate that the new pistol had found favor even in remote parts of the world. Oliver Winchester had considerable talent.

The actual management of the New Haven plant was placed in the hands of Benjamin Tyler Henry. Here Winchester chose exceptionally well, for Henry was a skilled mechanic with a fine knowledge of breechloaders and their problems. He had even worked on a so-called "waterproof" repeater patented in 1839, and he was familiar with the Volcanic system from a previous association with Smith, Wesson, and Palmer. It was Henry who provided the mechanical ingenuity to bring the repeating arms to practical perfection and save the New Haven Company from following the Volcanic into bankruptcy.

Despite Winchester's activities and sales promotion, the firm was in dire straits. The ammunition did not perform satisfactorily and testimonials could not counter the voice of actual experience with the guns. Something had to be done. In 1858, Winchester set Henry the task of devising a cartridge that would be safe, self-contained, and powerful. In short order the young mechanic perfected a .44 rim-fire metal-cased cartridge and designed the alterations in the Volcanic arms so that it could be used. At the same time he modified the locking bolt and redesigned the firing pin so that it struck both sides of the cartridge rim at once and thus lessened the chance of a misfire.

The importance of Henry's contribution to the Winchester story can hardly be overestimated. The new gun and its ammunition were successful in every way. The New Haven Company was saved from certain failure and to all intents and purposes the Winchester rifle had been developed. For the time being, however, it was known as the Henry rifle and each cartridge was stamped with an "H" on its head in honor of the inventor.

Operating the new gun was simplicity itself. To load, the shooter compressed a long spiral spring in the tubular magazine beneath the barrel until he could swing the forward section to one side and drop fifteen cartridges into the opening. As the front section swung back into place, the spring bore against the column of cartridges and kept it under pressure. A simple forward-and-back movement of the trigger guard, in what is known today as the lever action, carried a cartridge from the magazine into the chamber and cocked the hammer. It was the work of a moment. Government tests revealed that a reasonably skilled man could fire one hundred and twenty rounds in three hundred and forty seconds—including loading time—or an average of one shot every 2.9 seconds. Experienced shooters often carried a cartridge ready in the chamber as well as the fifteen in the magazine, thus providing sixteen shots ready for instant use. And, indeed, the Henry is usually called a "sixteen-shooter" in early references. It could hit hard, too. Advertisements claimed a penetration of eight inches at one hundred yards, five inches at four hundred yards, and power to kill at a thousand yards.

The new repeater was ready for its debut early in 1862 and Oliver Winchester set out to

1

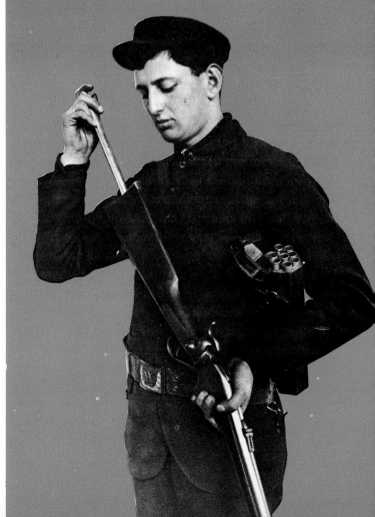

2

1. *Spencer carbine is the one found with John Wilkes Booth when he was killed in Garrett's barn, after having assassinated President Lincoln.*
2. *This War Department photograph from the 1870's shows a U. S. soldier employing the Blakeslee Quickloader to load his Spencer carbine.*
3. *Corporal Horatio Pratt carried the Spencer infantry rifle (above) during General Philip Sheridan's Shenandoah Valley Campaign of 1864 and 1865. Later, after the war, it was used as a presentation piece, and the silver plaque (below) was added to its stock. Sheridan greatly prized the extra firepower and quick-firing qualities of these Spencer repeaters.*

240

market it. Specially engraved models with silver plated frames were presented to Secretary of the Navy Gideon Welles, Secretary of War Simon Cameron, and others whose knowledge of the gun might be useful. Advertisements were printed and testimonials collected. The nation was at war and Winchester hoped for large government orders. In this he was disappointed. In the way stood the chief of Ordnance, Brigadier General James Wolfe Ripley, as staunch a conservative in the field of armament as ever admired the functional simplicity of a club. Ripley had been commandant of the

Springfield Armory when the rifled musket was developed and he was thoroughly devoted to that arm. He knew it would perform and he distrusted all the new inventions with possible, unknown problems. He worried that soldiers would waste ammunition if they could shoot so fast. He worried about the cost of this ammunition and about the weight of carrying it around and about the problems of supply. As a result of his opposition, the Federal government bought only some 1,731 Henrys, and these were issued primarily to the District of Columbia Cavalry and the 1st Maine Cavalry, which did

3

not see any real action until the Petersburg Campaign of 1864.

It was in the West that the Henry saw its principal military service and it came as the result of state and private purchases. Kentucky and Missouri were prime sales areas from the very beginning. There is a wild tale of the exploits of a loyal Kentuckian, Captain James M. Wilson, with a Henry rifle during the early years of the war. Winchester could never substantiate the story, but he was happy to use it as a testimonial and it soon found its way into serious books and papers with very happy effects on sales. According to the standard version of this thriller, Wilson was eating dinner with his family when seven guerrillas burst into the dining room and started firing wildly but without much result. Pleading with them to spare his family, Wilson persuaded the ruffians to take him outside to be shot. Once out of doors he dashed amidst another hail of poorly aimed bullets to an outbuilding.

Several shots passed through his hat, and more through his clothing, but none took effect upon his person. He thus reached his cover and seized his Henry rifle, turned upon his foes, and in five shots killed five of them; the other two sprung for their horses. As the sixth man threw his hand over the pommel of his saddle, the sixth shot took off four of his fingers; notwithstanding this he got into his saddle, but the seventh shot killed him; then starting out, Capt. Wilson killed the seventh man with the eighth shot.

The tale concludes with the remarks that in consequence of this feat the state of Kentucky armed Wilson's company with Henrys. Nowhere does it say what kind of guns the guerrillas had or why they seemed to be so inept in using them. True or not, Wilson's men did carry Henrys, and so did many other units who marched with Sherman to Atlanta and the sea.

Sales were so good, in fact, that the New Haven Arms Company found itself prosperous indeed. Stock values had increased almost eight times. The days of near bankruptcy were far behind and Oliver Winchester was ready to move ahead. The time had come to remove himself completely from the shirt business and devote his full attention to gunmaking. In 1866 he reorganized the corporation as the Winchester Repeating Arms Company, again with himself as president. A new version of the Henry, with improvements by Nelson King, was named the Winchester rifle, Model 1866. It was the first of a long and successful series. A dynasty had been thoroughly established and an almost legendary arm of the American West had come of age. The successful businessman even found time to serve one term as lieutenant governor of Connecticut in 1866 and 1867 and was addressed ever afterwards as "Governor Winchester" by his friends and employees.

The Henry had not been alone in the field of successful magazine repeating rifles, however. In fact, it was not even the first. That honor went to a seven-shot repeater invented by Christopher M. Spencer of Connecticut and patented March 6, 1860, seven months before the Henry. It was a fine gun, too, with a lever action that pumped cartridges from a tubular magazine in the butt stock into the chamber and then ejected them after they had been fired. It was not a self-cocking arm like the Henry. The hammer had to be pulled back by hand for each shot. And it held less than half as many shots. But it was simpler, sturdier, and cheaper —all very important features.

The Spencer story is one of the most fascinating in all American arms history. Both the man and the gun were equally interesting. Some writers have suggested that Christopher Spencer was the inspiration for Mark Twain's celebrated *Connecticut Yankee in King Arthur's Court*. Certainly he had all the attributes. Quitting school at the age of fourteen, he began work in the Cheney silk mills of his native Manchester. In order to vary his background he moved to Rochester, New York, to work in a toolbuilding and locomotive shop, then to the

Colt armory at Hartford, and finally back to the Cheney mills. Despite eleven-hour working days, he was back at his bench in the evenings, always building models or designing new gadgets or machines. He was still in his early twenties when he obtained his first important patent for an automatic silk-winding machine that brought great changes to the textile industry. Before he was thirty he was driving to work in his own steam-powered automobile, frightening horses until the town fathers asked him to keep his machine off the roads. This was in 1862, years before the internal combustion engine. His work in the field of drop forgings is credited with having advanced the accuracy and application of that technique more than the efforts of any other man. But his greatest invention was still to come: a screw-cutting machine with an automatic turret lathe, features of which are still used in all automatic lathes. Before his death in 1922, he had become interested in airplanes and greatly enjoyed flying in the adventuresome aircraft of the time. His whole life was devoted to a study of machines and his curiosity never faltered.

When the Civil War broke out, Spencer's new rifle was the first magazine repeater to be offered to the Federal government. The navy promptly tested the gun, liked it, and placed an order, but at army Ordnance, Spencer met the same cold reception from General Ripley as Oliver Winchester. Then help came from a higher authority. Abraham Lincoln fired the Spencer rifle personally and directed Ripley to place an order for the gun. This was in December, 1861. Production difficulties held up deliveries for another year while Ripley raised every possible obstruction and used technicalities to reduce the size of the contract. By spring of 1863, however, the Spencer began to make its presence felt in the field. At Hoover's Gap, Hanover, and Gettysburg it performed magnificently. More and more soldiers clamored for it and some regiments even used their own money to buy these fine new weapons.

Despite these outcries from the field, Ripley continued to delay. Strong measures were needed, and Spencer asked the President once again to witness a demonstration of his gun. Lincoln agreed. Receiving the inventor at the White House, he examined the weapon inside and out and asked Spencer to call the next day when they could "go out and see the thing shoot."

The following day was Tuesday, August 18, 1863. Promptly at 2:00 the President, with his son Robert, a naval aide, and Christopher Spencer, set out through the Washington heat for the Treasury Park to fire the gun. On the way, Lincoln sent Robert into the War Department building to ask Secretary Stanton to go with them to watch the tests. As they waited outside, Spencer broke his diffident silence to remark that it must be a great responsibility to govern such a vast country during a war. "It is a big chore with the kind of help I have," replied the President half seriously. In a few moments Robert returned with word that Stanton was too busy to go with them. "Well," said Lincoln, "they do pretty much as they have a mind to over there." And the four resumed their walk to the shooting area.

Arriving at the park, a pine board about six inches wide and three feet long was selected as a target. The naval aide made a roughly circular smudge at one end to serve as a bull's-eye, and set the board up against a tree. Spencer slipped seven cartridges into the magazine and handed the gun to Lincoln. The President paced off about forty yards, raised the rifle to his shoulder, and sighted it at the target. A moment later he lowered the gun and shouted to his companions to move the target. As soon as the board had been put in its new position, the President aimed and fired. The first shot struck about six inches below the smudge. The second hit it squarely, and the next five were all close.

"Now we will see the inventor try his luck!" remarked Lincoln, handing the rifle back to Spencer. The board was reversed and Spencer emptied the magazine, beating the President by 243

a small margin and eliciting the comment, "You are much younger than I am, have a better eye and steadier nerve." Returning to the White House the naval aide sawed off the end of the board at which the President had shot and gave it to Spencer as a souvenir. Spencer presented the rifle to Lincoln; and the next day they were both out shooting again.

Within two weeks there was a new chief of Ordnance, and the *New York Times* gleefully reported the retirement of "... the old fogy Ripley...who combatted all new ideas in the fabrication of firearms, artillery and projectiles." The new chief was Lincoln's genial friend and co-tester of new military devices, Colonel George D. Ramsay of the Washington Arsenal. There would be no more roadblocks for the Spencer or any other fine new weapons.

Much time had been lost. The war was in its third year, but now Spencers began to flow to the troops as fast as the factory in Boston could produce them. There were carbines with .52 caliber, twenty-two-inch barrels for cavalry and longer rifles for infantry. Over a hundred thousand Spencers were bought by the United States government, while state and private purchases may have raised the number actually in use to about two hundred thousand. Still it was not enough. "The demand for them is constant and for large quantities," wrote the new chief of Ordnance. "It seems as if no soldier who had seen them used could be satisfied with any

other." The Spencer had reached the heyday of its popularity.

Then came the decline. The war ended and the market contracted. The government bought a few more guns with a smaller caliber, but these were not enough to keep the factory operating. Refinements were added, including a cutoff that allowed the arm to be fired as a single-shot weapon while holding a full magazine of cartridges in reserve. Still the Spencer could not compete in the civilian market with the new Winchester Model 1866. Cowboys and sportsmen liked the smaller caliber and the higher velocities of the Winchester, and the greater number of shots also appealed to them. Soldiers had carried Blakeslee Quickloaders, a special box holding between ten and thirteen tubes of cartridges ready to pour into their Spencer magazines, but civilians didn't want to be bothered with such excess equipment. A sixteen-shot rifle and a belt full of cartridges were much more to their liking.

The Spencer Repeating Rifle Company could not continue. In 1869 all its assets were placed on the auction block and the company was dissolved. The Turkish government bought thirty thousand carbines at the sale, but the biggest buyer was Oliver Winchester whose rifle had won the western market and ruined Spencer. Now he had no rival. His production increased and became diversified with models for sportsmen, military arms for the United States, for

*Mauser bolt-action repeater of 1884 (left) was designed
with a tube magazine under the barrel. Above: Cartridge-clip Mannlicher
rifle of 1888. This clip—which first appeared in 1886—was
the final important improvement of black-powder arms.*

the Northwest Mounted Police, and for foreign governments throughout much of the world.

Lever-action repeaters with tubular magazines were a success. There was no doubt about it. Their performance on the battlefields of the Civil War and the western plains proved it to Americans and to a small number of European military observers. The slaughter of the attacking Russian armies by Turks armed with Winchesters at Plevna in 1877 brought the lesson home to the entire world. The tubular magazine had been standard from the days of the Kalthoff and the Lorenzoni. The European experts were willing to accept the fact that it worked well with metallic cartridges too, but they much preferred the bolt action to the lever for a repeating rifle. For one thing a bolt could be operated easier by a man lying prone.

Even before the end of the American Civil War, gun designers throughout Europe were busy with such designs. Frederick Vetterli of Switzerland studied the Henry and Winchester very carefully, and developed a bolt-action rifle with a tubular magazine under the barrel, a version of the Henry cartridge carrier, and a loading gate adopted from one of Nelson King's improvements for the 1866 Winchester. His gun was adopted in 1866 and production began the next year. In Austria, Ferdinand Früwirth designed a similar rifle which was adopted for the gendarmerie in 1869. In Germany, the great designer Peter Paul Mauser of Oberndorf

brought the bolt action to its true perfection for metallic-cartridge arms late in the 1860's. At first he concentrated on single-shot weapons, but finally he, too, developed a repeater with a tube magazine under the barrel which was adopted as the Model 1884. Even in America there were bolt-action repeaters with Spencer-like tube magazines in the stock. Two of them, the Hotchkiss and the Chaffee-Reese, were adopted as official arms for limited use.

But these arms were transitions only. A revolutionary new magazine was already in use before many of these arms were invented and it eliminated the weak springs, the space problem, and the danger of bullet distortion found in so many tube magazines. James P. Lee, a Scottish watchmaker who had obtained United States citizenship, designed a box magazine located directly below the bolt, and it was adopted for navy use in 1879. It was simple, cheap, and efficient and within ten years it had spread throughout the world.

There remained only one more step to bring the repeater to its full development—the loading clip. The idea of quick loading by means of a container of cartridges all ready to slip into a magazine had occurred to many men. This was one of the things Samuel Colt had had in mind when he provided extra cylinders for some of his Paterson revolvers, and the tubes of cartridges in the Quickloader for the Spencer were designed for the same purpose.

245

The new box magazine offered further possibilities, and Ferdinand Ritter von Mannlicher was quick to grasp them. An ardent Austrian patriot and a visionary in the field of weapons design, Mannlicher developed one hundred and fifty different models of repeating and automatic arms, including one bolt-action model in which the whole butt stock was honeycombed with tubular magazines. Many of Mannlicher's ideas, although sound, were years ahead of the technical capabilities of his time. Some have only recently become practical. Working independently of Lee, he also invented a box magazine in 1881. In 1882 and 1884 he improved the design, and then in 1885 he produced the cartridge clip. With this device a magazine load of cartridges could be fastened together in advance and loaded in a single motion. Almost all of the clips used today are variants of Mannlicher's design.

The magazine repeater had reached full development. The box magazine with its clip had joined the perfected tube. Lever and bolt actions had been applied successfully to both types, and a third system with a sliding lever, called a pump action, was becoming popular for sporting arms with tubular magazines. Future advances would come in other fields. Only minor improvements now remained to be devised for the manually operated repeater.

EPILOGUE

Perfection of the magazine repeater marked the end of an era. It had been some six hundred and fifty years since Friar Roger Bacon had concealed the formula for gunpowder in a code to protect the world from such dread knowledge. But the power that lay within the mixture of charcoal, sulphur, and saltpeter could not be suppressed, and soon men had invented guns to make this force work for them. Through six centuries they had constantly directed their efforts to perfecting these guns, gradually developing weapons that would shoot farther, faster, and surer. From the crude hand cannon and the clumsy matchlock, they had evolved the compact revolver and the smoothly efficient magazine rifle. Only the gunpowder itself had remained relatively unchanged.

Now even that must pass. New explosives made from nitrocellulose and nitroglycerin had been developed. The Mannlicher rifle Model 1886 was the last of the big-bore military rifles designed for black powder. That same year France adopted the new smokeless gunpowder and other nations soon followed her example. By 1900 it was almost universal for military weapons. Thereafter the new explosive would provide greater power without the huge clouds of smoke that had characterized warfare for so many years. The "smoke of battle" would become a poetic phrase without real meaning. Calibers would be reduced until they became less than half the size earlier generations had felt necessary. Yet the tiny bullets would do their job with even more efficiency. The force of the new smokeless powder would also be utilized within the guns themselves, making them either partially or fully automatic in operation. Oliver Winchester's "machine for throwing balls" would become a machine indeed. But this would be the story of a new and different force. Roger Bacon's era had ended. Even the smell of brimstone was gone.

German "Orgelgeschütz" of the 17th century.

SELECTED BIBLIOGRAPHY

Among the volumes consulted in the preparation of this book, the following works contain the most general and useful information for those who wish to pursue the subject further.

PERIODICALS

The American Arms Collector, *Towson, Maryland, 1957, 1958.*

The American Rifleman, *Washington, D. C., 1885——.*

Armes Anciennes, *Geneva, 1953-1959.*

Armi Antichi, Bolletino dell' Accademia di S. Marciano, *Turin, 1954——.*

The Gun Collector, *Madison, Wisconsin, 1946-1956.*

Journal of the Arms and Armour Society, *London, 1953——.*

Livrustkammaren, *Stockholm, 1937——.*

Svenska Vapenhistoriska Sällskapets Skrifter, *new series, Stockholm, 1951——.*

Vaabenhistoriske Aarbøger, *Copenhagen, 1934——.*

Zeitschrift für Historische Waffen- und Kostümkunde, *Dresden-Berlin, 1897-1944.*

BOOKS

ALM, JOSEF, **Eldhandvapen,** *2 vols., Militärlitteraturför eningens Förlag, Stockholm, 1933, 1934.*

Abridgements of the Patent Specifications Relating to Firearms & Other Weapons, Ammunition & Accoutrements from 1588-1858, *reprint editon, Holland Press, London, 1960.*

BAKER, EZEKIEL, **Remarks on Rifle Guns,** *eleventh edition, Joseph Mallett, London, 1835.*

BEHN, JACK, **".45-70" Rifles,** *Stackpole, Harrisburg, Pa., 1956.*

BLACKMORE, HOWARD L., **British Military Firearms,** *Herbert Jenkins, London, 1961.*

BLAIR, CLAUDE, **European Armour,** *Batsford, London, 1958.*

BOTTET, MAURICE, **Monographie de L'Arme a Feu Portative des Armées Françaises,** *Ernest Flammarian, Paris, n.d.*

BRUCE, ROBERT, **Lincoln and the Tools of War,** *Bobbs-Merrill, New York, 1956.*

DUCHARTE, PIERRE-LOUIS, **Historie des Armes de Chasse et de leurs Emplois,** *Crépin Leblond, Paris, 1955.*

ECKARDT, WERNER, & OTTO MORAWIETZ, **Die Handwaffen des brandenburgisch-preussisch-deutschen Heeres 1640-1945,** *Helmut Gerhardt Schultz, Hamburg, 1957.*

ERIKSEN, EGON, **Dänische Orgelespingolen mit Einheitspatronen,** *Tøjhusmuseet, Copenhagen, 1945.*

ESSENWEIN, A., **Quellen zur Geschichte der Feuerwaffen,** *F. A. Brockhaus, Leipzig, 1877.*

FULLER, CLAUD E., **The Breech-loader in the Service,** *Arms Reference Club of America, Topeka, Kans., 1933.*
The Rifled Musket, *Stackpole, Harrisburg, Pa., 1958.*

FULLER, J. F. C., **Armament and History,** *Scribner's, New York, 1945.*
A Military History of the Western World, *3 vols., Funk and Wagnalls, New York, 1954-1956.*

GEORGE, JOHN N., **English Guns and Rifles,** *Small-Arms Technical Publishing Co., Plantersville, S. C., 1947.*
English Pistols and Revolvers, *Small-Arms Technical Publishing Co., Plantersville, S. C., 1938.*

GLUCKMAN, ARCADI, **United States Martial Pistols and Revolvers,** *Otto Ulbrich, Buffalo, 1939.*
United States Muskets, Rifles and Carbines, *Otto Ulbrich, Buffalo, 1948.*

GLUCKMAN, ARCADI, & L. D. SATTERLEE,
American Gun Makers, *revised edition,*
Stackpole, Harrisburg, Pa., 1953.

GRANT, JAMES J., **More Single-Shot Rifles,** *William Morrow,*
New York, 1959.
Single-Shot Rifles, *William Morrow, New York, 1947.*

GUTTMANN, OSCAR, **Monumenta Pulveris Pyrii,**
privately printed, London, 1906.

HANSON, CHARLES E., JR., **The Northwest Gun,**
Nebraska State Historical Society, Lincoln, 1955.
The Plains Rifle, *Stackpole, Harrisburg, Pa., 1960.*

HANGER, GEORGE, **To All Sportsmen, Farmers and Gamekeepers,**
J. J. Stockdale, London, 1814.

HARPER, CHARLES G., **Half-Hours with the Highwaymen,**
2 vols., Chapman and Hall, London, 1908.

HATCH, ALDEN, **Remington Arms,** *Rinehart & Company,*
New York, 1956.

HAWKER, COL. PETER, **Colonel Hawker's Shooting Diaries,**
edited by Eric Parker, Philip Allan, London, 1931.
**Instructions to Young Sportsmen in all that Relates
to Guns and Shooting,** *edited by Eric Parker, Herbert Jenkins,*
London, 1922.

HELD, ROBERT, **The Age of Firearms,** *Harper, New York, 1957.*

HICKS, JAMES E., **Notes on French Ordnance,** *privately printed,*
Mt. Vernon, N. Y., 1938.
Notes on United States Ordnance, *2 vols.,*
privately printed, Mt. Vernon, N. Y., 1940.

HIME, HENRY W. L., **The Origin of Artillery,** *Longmans, Green,*
London, 1915.

HOFF, ARNE, **Aeldre Dansk Bøssemageri,** *2 vols., Tøjhusmuseet,*
Copenhagen, 1951.
The Rasmussen Revolving Guns, *Tøjhusmuseet,*
Copenhagen, 1946.

JACKSON, HERBERT J., & CHARLES E. WHITELAW,
**European Hand Firearms of the Sixteenth, Seventeenth and
Eighteenth Centuries,** *Martin Hopkinson, London, 1923.*

KARR, CHARLES LEE, JR., & CAROLL ROBBINS KARR,
Remington Handguns, *Stackpole, Harrisburg, Pa., 1956.*

KAUFFMAN, HENRY J., **The Pennsylvania-Kentucky Rifle,**
Stackpole, Harrisburg, Pa., 1960.

KINDIG, JOE, JR., **Thoughts on the Kentucky Rifle in its
Golden Age,** *George N. Hyatt, Wilmington, Del., 1960.*

LAKING, SIR GUY F., **A Record of European Armour and Arms
Through Seven Centuries,** *5 vols.,*
G. Bell and Sons, London, 1920-1922.

LENK, TORSTEN, **Flintlåset, dess Uppkomst och Utveckling,**
Nordisk Rotogravyr, Stockholm, 1939.

LEWIS, BERKELEY R., **Small Arms and Ammunition in the
United States Service,** *Smithsonian Institution,*
Washington, D. C., 1956.

LOGAN, HERSCHEL, **Cartridges,** *Standard Publications,*
Huntington, W. Va., 1948.
Underhammer Guns, *Stackpole, Harrisburg, Pa., 1960.*

MARGERAND, J., **Armement et Equipement de l'Infanterie
Française,** *Les Éditions Militaires Illustrées, Paris, 1945.*

MORDECAI, ALFRED, **Military Commission to Europe in 1855
and 1856, Report of Major Alfred Mordecai of the Ordnance
Department,** *Washington, D. C., 1860.*

NAPOLEON, LOUIS, & COL. M. FAVÉ, **Études sur le Passé et
l'Avenir de l'Artillerie,** *6 vols.,*
Librairie Militaire, Paris, 1846-1871.

NEAL, W. KEITH, **Spanish Guns and Pistols,**
G. Bell and Sons, London, 1955.

NUTTER, WALDO E., **Manhattan Firearms,** *Stackpole, Harrisburg,*
Pa., 1958.

OAKESHOTT, R. EWART, **The Archaeology of Weapons,**
Lutterworth Press, London, 1960.

OMAN, SIR CHARLES, **A History of the Art of War, the
Middle Ages,** *Methuen, London, 1905.*
A History of the Art of War in the Sixteenth Century,
Methuen, London, 1937.

PARSONS, JOHN E., **The First Winchester,** *William Morrow,*
New York, 1955.
Henry Deringer's Pocket Pistol, *William Morrow,*
New York, 1952.
The Peacemaker and its Rivals, *William Morrow,*
New York, 1950.
Smith & Wesson Revolvers, *William Morrow,*
New York, 1957.

PARSONS, JOHN E. & JOHN S. DU MONT, **Firearms in The
Custer Battle,** *Stackpole, Harrisburg, 1953.*

PARTINGTON, J. R., **A History of Greek Fire and Gunpowder,**
W. Heffer & Sons, Cambridge, 1960.

PETERSON, HAROLD L., **Arms and Armor in Colonial America,**
Stackpole, Harrisburg, Pa., 1956.

REID, MAJ. GEN. SIR ALEXANDER J. R., **The Reverend
Alexander John Forsyth,** *Aberdeen University Press,*
Aberdeen, Scotland, 1955.

REYNOLDS, MAJ. E. G. B., **The Lee-Enfield Rifle,**
Herbert Jenkins, London, 1960.

ROBERTS, NED H., **The Muzzle-Loading Cap Lock Rifle,**
revised edition, Stackpole, Harrisburg, Pa., 1952.

ROHAN, JACK, **Yankee Arms Maker,** *Harper, revised edition, 1948.*

RUSSELL, CARL P., **Guns on the Early Frontiers,**
University of California Press, Los Angeles, 1957.

SABINE, LORENZO, **Notes on Duels and Duelling,**
Crosby, Nichols, Boston, 1855.

SCOFFERN, J., **Projectile Weapons of War and Explosive
Compounds,** *Longman, Brown, Green, and Longmans, London, 1858.*

SERVEN, JAMES E., **Colt Firearms,** *published by the author,*
Santa Ana, California, 1954.

SMITH, W. H. B., & JOSEPH E. SMITH, **Small Arms of the World,**
revised edition, Stackpole, Harrisburg, Pa., 1960.

SMITH, WINSTON O., **The Sharps Rifle,** *William Morrow,*
New York, 1943.

STEINMETZ, ANDREW, **The Romance of Duelling,** *2 vols.,*
Chapman and Hall, London, 1868.

STØCKEL, JOHAN F., **Haandskydevaabens Bedømmelse,**
2 vols., Tøjhusmuseet, Copenhagen, 1938-1943.

STONE, GEORGE CAMERON, **A Glossary of the Construction,
Decoration and Use of Arms and Armor,**
Southworth Press, Portland, Me., 1934.

THIERBACH, MORRITZ, **Die Geschichtliche Entwickelung der
Handfeuerwaffen,** *Carl Hockner, Dresden, 1888.*

WILLIAMSON, HAROLD F., **Winchester, the Gun that
Won the West,** *Combat Forces Press, Washington, 1952.*

WILSON, R. LARRY, **Samuel Colt Presents,**
Wadsworth Atheneum, Hartford, 1961.

WINANT, LEWIS, **Early Percussion Firearms,** *William Morrow,*
New York, 1959.
Firearms Curiosa, *Greenberg, New York, 1955.*
Pepperbox Firearms, *Greenberg, New York, 1952.*

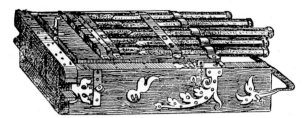

Ribauldequin used during the 15th century.

INDEX

Italic numbers refer to illustrations.